CHEAT
TO
WIN

THE HONEST WAY TO BREAK ALL
THE DISHONEST RULES IN BUSINESS.

Robert W. MacDonald

Paradon Publishing
Minneapolis, Minnesota

Paradon Publishing Company
3110 Blaisdell Ave. S.
Suite 1802
Minnneapolis, MN 55408-3100

Library of Congress Catalog Number: 2005924506

Printed in the United States of America

Attention: Business and Nonprofit Organizations:

Cheat to Win is available at quantity discounts with bulk purchases by businesses, educational, and nonprofits uses. For information write to: Special Sales, Paradon Publishing, or visit us online at www.paradonpublishing.com.

This book is dedicated

To the Owners . . . each and every one . . .

Also by Robert W. MacDonald

Control Your Future: A Candid Guide to Successful
    Life Insurance Selling

Contents

*Editor's Note

Bookstore shelves these days are laden with books that are ostensibly written by the author whose name is bannered across the dust jacket but qualified by that ubiquitous addendum, "With James Jones" or some other totally unknown writer.

To my way of thinking, that sets off an immediate alarm of cautionary acceptance. And you know why: A rich and successful businessman (or movie star) on a runaway ego trip hires a "ghostwriter" to cobble together a readable yarn about his exploits and how his revolutionary acumen is going to change the way the world thinks and business operates.

The usual result, however, is a half-baked treatise that neither entertains nor enlightens but merely fills the pages allotted to this self-gratifying exercise in literary life-extension.

I, for one, refuse to participate in this kind of deception. Bob MacDonald was willing to give me that coveted second billing, but I turned it down—for simplest of reasons. I didn't ghostwrite this book—Bob MacDonald wrote it. And, "Without" Charles Wetherall is my way of telling you that.

Keep in mind that this is the CEO who has, in the opinion of his business contemporaries, brought "thinking outside the box" to a world-class level. Bob is acknowledged to be one of the true visionaries and forward thinkers in the financial services industry, which is notorious for being hidebound. And if I had written this book, I would have proclaimed that frequently and loudly. That's what ghostwriters do, isn't it? And even great ghostwriters would salivate at the prospect of touting a zany, madcap chief executive who turned the insurance industry on its ear and built—from scratch, zero, nada—a major life insurance company that he sold a dozen years later for $540 million.

Or maybe I would have let the business press trumpet his unique, contrarian management style that has caused many leaders to swear by this management philosophy and style and others to just swear. For example, just listen:

"Bob MacDonald has never been afraid to make waves in an industry justifiably famous, infamous really, for bureaucratic inertia, painful cost-cutting and massive layoffs."

Another writes, "One of the most successful and hated (by competitors) men in the insurance business . . . He's a mover and a shaker" (a bromide MacDonald despises).

The *New York Times* says, "Seldom does a company president acknowledge that his old products are obsolete and expensive. Yet that's exactly what MacDonald did."

The *Wall Street Journal* boasts that MacDonald is "Long the self-styled bad boy of the insurance business" who helped lead the industry rebellion against whole-life insurance and different rates for men and women.

One business publication claimed, "Bob MacDonald put the 'life back into life insurance because he had a great slingshot; his was the first insurance company that rewarded people for living, not dying."

In short, I could have cleaved together a book merely by collecting the accolades that his pioneering management style has produced. But I didn't because Bob would have never let me do so.

But if a well-placed sense of modesty is one of Bob's key attributes, then humor, even outrageous pranksmanship, has to be another. And he probably wouldn't let me write about that, either. You need a true example?

Here is the chairman and CEO of a major national life insurance company who left voice-mail greetings that were so off the wall that scores of people would call his number each week, just to hear of his latest exploits, often tied to world affairs. If the Dream Team was getting ready for the Olympics, MacDonald was out of the office practicing with them. Or he might be meeting with the Olympic Pygmy Sumo Wrestling team sponsored by LifeUSA. If the Pope was visiting America, MacDonald was out skiing with him in Colorado. Think these are outrageous and unbelievable? They're not.

If you know Bob MacDonald, *nothing* surprises you. The *Minneapolis StarTribune* was ready to run a story about MacDonald negotiating presidential debates between Bush and Clinton, before being informed that Bob wasn't really doing that. So many people believed his voice mail messages that company receptionists were driven dizzy trying to run interference for amazed callers who were sucked into his craziness. The ultimate voice-mail put-on might have been at the time of Richard Nixon's funeral, when MacDonald left a message saying he was out of the office to deliver Nixon's eulogy. It was so authentic that receptionists wound up trying to pacify a U.S. congressman who called the company to see if he could wheedle MacDonald into getting him an invitation to the funeral. This is Bob MacDonald.

Now, I ask you, who needs a ghostwriter when your author is this zany? An author who shows up at a corporate meeting in a bumblebee suit, or answers his telephone calls on a Mickey Mouse phone? Or challenges visitors to play him on pinball machines in his office? See what I mean?

And by the way, let me add a word of warning to readers. Bob loves to pull your leg. As you read his book, don't say I didn't warn you. He's the guy who, after all, delivered a speech before a distinguished group of German business executives, and openly decried the 1941 bombing of Pearl Harbor by the *Germans*. His audience, of course, was aghast. Until they realized that this is vintage Bob MacDonald. So *achtung!* Read carefully.

It would be a grave error, however, to mistake Bob's lighthearted approach to business with any lack of seriousness about his subject. He is deadly earnest about helping others succeed. And this seminal book, that he has so terrifically written (yes, Bob wrote every sentence, every paragraph, every chapter), will prove it.

So what did I do if I didn't "with" his book? Well, I sat and listened to his powerful strategies. I frequently cajoled (Bob is a busy man). I fiddled with such editing as punctuation and grammar as I was permitted. On page 133, for example, it was I who added that word, *schadenfreude,* to Bob's otherwise excellent description. And yes, I moved a few sentences around. But I didn't write it. And I cede any claim to having done so. More than anything, I *learned*.

If you're anything like me, by the time you reach the first or second chapter, you'll discover that his techniques have a way of seeping into your thinking. You'll undoubtedly begin asking yourself, as I did, "How would Bob MacDonald handle this situation?"

And when he talks about key concepts such a "parallel interests" or "reminiscing about the future" you're likely to be stunned, as I was, to find that these principles are so simple, yet powerfully effective. Perhaps you, too, will admonish yourself for conducting your business life like a contestant on TV's *Survivor,* where your universe seems peopled by a chorus of adversaries to be crushed as you selfishly claw your way to the million dollars. I began to think, as you will, of my compatriots as *equals,* partners in a life's work where *everybody* can win. That's the first step in learning how to Cheat to Win.

By the end of this work, you'll be able to fully understand the world from the unique perspective of Bob MacDonald. And, if you choose, you can put many of these precepts to work in your life, whether you're working in the mailroom or that big office in the corner.

Well, that's why you'll see no "With Charles Wetherall" on this book. Bob shares a practical, yet extraordinary business perspective that resonates all the more brilliantly when hack writers like me get out of the way and let the master tell his own compelling story. Great things happen when you don't care who gets the credit. Bob MacDonald taught me that.

Enjoy!

Charles F. Wetherall

On a Personal Note . . .

There is a saying in football that could just as easily apply to business: "When the team wins the quarterback gets too much credit, and when the team loses the quarterback gets too much blame." During my business career I was fortunate enough to quarterback a number of winning teams. And for that, I received much more credit than I deserved. (Not more than my ego wanted, just more than should have come my way.)

This is especially true as it related to LifeUSA. Observers would often comment to me, "It is amazing what you did to build LifeUSA into such a successful company." When complimented, my response was always the same—and I meant it—I could not justifiably claim credit for the success of LifeUSA. I was not responsible for building LifeUSA; but rather, the thousands of people who joined with me deserve the credit for the success of LifeUSA. My only claim to fame (which is proudly accepted) was that LifeUSA would not have come into existence if it had not been for me. What I did was create the opportunity for others to be successful. Fortunately for me, they took the bait and made it happen. For their work I get too much credit, but I know the truth—they were the real heroes of the story.

Reading this book in abstract could give the reader the idea that the concepts and accomplishments mentioned are the sole possession of the author. Nothing could be farther from the truth, and I know that. This book was written, not because of what I did, but because of what others did. In reality, what we did *together*.

This book is not about Bob MacDonald, LifeUSA, or even the people of LifeUSA. Instead, this book is about sharing with you— for your use—the ideas and concepts discovered and used by the people of LifeUSA who worked in parallel to develop successful careers, a corporate culture that offered opportunity for all, and a philosophy that cheats on old rules and makes winning a way of life. To avoid slowing the reader down (any more than my writing style will do), and to make sure the focus is on the ideas rather than the people (although one could easily argue for the reverse), the names of individuals involved have been kept to a minimum. This is not out of disrespect for their efforts and contributions, but out of respect for the reader.

However, it would be cheating on my part to produce this book and not mention, at least once, some of the talented and wonderful people who were instrumental in my success. Unfortunately, there are many more who could and should be listed. It is just not possible in this format. You know who you are, but more important, I know who you are and will be forever grateful. Those listed below understand that they represent the many thousands more who deserve as much credit as any.

But here goes ... Thanks to ... Dan Rourke, Don Urban, Joe Carlson, Peyton Huffman, Joanne Halek, Ralph Strangis, Ken Dahlberg, Kate Bartlett, Bruce Parker, Mark Zesbaugh, Maggie Hughes, Denise Blizil, Sue Smith, Bob Miller, Roger McCarty, Joe Lehman, Dave Sunderland, Ann Yaggie, Steve Kerns, Linda Burm, Robin Aeshilman, Leo Anderson, Pam Inniger, Hugh Alexander, Lisa Diers-Arneson, Dan Schaefer, Jason Brandt, Neil McKay, Chuck Kavitsky, Dennis Brown, Tom Wade, Jim Brown, Pat Allen, Rosie Wineland, Lisa Carlson, Pam Smith, Deb (Cher) Wesenberg, Ed Omert, Ron Bradley, Ted Charles, Jan Charles, L. J. Fredrickson, Joe Burke, Harold Singh, Carolyn Cosgrove, Mike Eitel, Dick Griffith, Barb Ward, Tim Hansen, Dean Slyter, Ray Brown, Stan Katlin, Tom Kestler, Vickie Fiske, Shari Friedrichsen, Tracy Gardner, Gabby Matzdorff, Jeff Girod, Lois Jeronimus, Ann Kagel, Tammy Knoblauch, Julie Letner, John Amann, Brenda K. Berkenes, Ron Berger, Bill Lance, Bill Rowett, Wayne Silfies, Scott Wheeler, Carey Gorham, Annie Funke, Ray Hurd, Lane Kurle, Sue Petty, Phil Rosenbaum, Dave Sandberg, Bernie Berger, Carie Thiele ... Thanks to all of you and those you represent for making cheating on the rules to be better so much fun.

Of course, I can't end this personal retrospective without mentioning one other person. Brenda Duenwald (Brenda D) worked at ITT Life and then became "Owner Number 9" at LifeUSA. Over the years, "Brenda D" willingly took on any job that needed to be done to make the company better. She epitomized the spirit, commitment, hard work, and dedication that talented people will bring to an effort when offered the opportunity to own the vision and share in the value. Then, after over twenty years of working with me, in 2001 Brenda made the ultimate sacrifice by becoming "Brenda Mac." For me, she was the real prize ...

Thoughts of the Author

YOU CAN'T DO THAT...

How many times over the course of your life have you heard that confining directive? I am willing to bet quite a few times, because that's not unusual. The customary mantra uttered any time someone tries to do something a little different and out of the norm is ...*you can't do that!*

All of us have been told this at one time or another.

As I've worked on writing this book, certainly the most frustrating experience has been to hear that decree over and over again—simply because of the title *Cheat to Win*. As the concept of the book is explained, most people show interest, excitement, and even enthusiasm for the project. However, as soon as the title of the book—*Cheat To Win*—is mentioned, the reaction was always the same—there would be a pause ... a smirk ... a chuckle ... and then, "That's really a great title for the book, *but you can't do that!*"

This response has been virtually universal—from friends, associates, publishers, and writers—from everyone! And the reaction continued right up to the time this book was finally completed for publishing. (It won't surprise me to find a number of bookstores that are unwilling to carry the book simply because of the title.) During the process of offering the book for distribution, a number of major publishers expressed interest in publishing the book, but shied away from the title. By way of example, I received the following e-mail from the editorial director of McGraw-Hill, "While I am not personally against the title, and do understand the ironic and wry use of 'cheat,' I know you will understand that McGraw-Hill as the world's leading educational publisher … cannot publish a book called 'Cheat To Win.' McGraw-Hill is very protective of what their brand stands for around the world, and doesn't like to be involved in controversy!"

They were not alone. John Wiley and Sons, the century-old national publishing firm, was enthusiastic about publishing the book. So much so that a formal contract was actually tendered, signed, sealed, and delivered—including a $25,000 advance. Yet, a week after the contract was signed, the following e-mail was received from the editor at Wiley: "Bob, I'm very perturbed—the general manager of my group has nixed your book title/subtitle—refusing to publish any book with the word 'cheat' in the title or subtitle. This hasn't happened to me since I've been here and it's very troubling to me." In a subsequent e-mail he wrote, "Bob I know this is disappointing to you. I know how I feel. I think if we can move off the 'cheat' everything will be fine—we have a strong author, great content and I'm behind it."

You know what? I appreciate the comments and understand where everyone is coming from regarding the title, but the reaction received—simply to the title of the book—is exactly why I pressed forward to write it and retain the title. (Besides, there is a very special secret coded message from Commander MacCody hidden in the title of the book. The publishers could not figure out the code, but if you drink your Ovaltine and read all the way to the end of the book you may be able to decode the message. Here is a hint—CTW)

This book does not encourage people to be dishonest. The thesis of the book, rather, argues that the only way to be honest with yourself and others is to go against the dishonest rules that are imposed on us by others. To me the hypocrisy is not that people disagree with what is written in the book—they *agree* the rules should be cheated on—it's just that they are controlled by the "You can't do that" rule. It boggles my mind that people would even think that you would write a book that actually encourages people to "cook the books" and do something blatantly unethical. It just shows how closed and limited some people's thinking can be! It also demonstrates why a book like this is needed.

If the comments offered had been for the right reasons—such as suggesting that the title was not "punchy enough," or did not adequately describe the book and convey the ideas espoused—and had suggested a better title, I would have been happy to consider a change. (Although several compromises were offered to Wiley.) But it would be wrong to cave in and change the title simply because of "what other people might think," or because it is too "controversial" and "out of the norm." As you will discover, that is exactly the point I will try to make in the book.

To have such an attitude is like saying, "Shame that we should ever be involved in any type of controversy!" Yet anyone worth their pepper (salt is not good for you) who has ever made a difference in this world has been involved in some type of controversy in order to make a difference. I am of the firm belief that most of us fail to achieve our dreams and desires—not because of lack of ability or opportunity—but because we fall prey to the rules and expectations of others, who discourage, inhibit, and hamper our chance to be a real winner. This book was written to expose the hypocrisy of everyday accepted rules and traditions that serve only "to keep us in our place."

Some have told me that there are those who will be offended and will not read *Cheat to Win* simply because the title will scare them away. Maybe so, but if that is the case then the book would do those people no good anyway. This book is not for those who are happy "playing along to get along." No, this book is for those who want to blaze a new path, not be stuck to it.

If I had listened every time someone told me what I could not do in life – rising from college dropout to president of a company to forming my own company, right up to the title of this book—then none of this would have happened and I would be just like the millions of others wading through life just wishing for something better.

If you choose this book precisely because of the title—thanks and congratulations—you are exactly the type of person this book was intended for.

Cheat to Win is a book about *winning* the honest way and not being *cheated* out of the opportunity to live our lives as we desire. The premise of *Cheat to Win* is simple: You can earn rapid success in the business world by breaking—rather than following—the antiquated rules of the establishment. Successful leaders of the past and present are those who have identified bad rules, cheated on them, offered creative alternatives, and won. *Cheat to Win* will help you take your place in that special group of honest and successful cheaters. The ideas in this book are aimed at those who want to be in control of making their own futures, achieve serious success, and enjoy the rewards it brings.

What separates the winners from the losers in life—the leaders from the followers—is the willingness to question, challenge, and—under the right conditions—violate the rule that says, *You can't do that . . .*

As you read this book, you will discover that when I refer to cheating, I am not talking about doing something immoral, deceitful, dishonest or even fattening. Quite the contrary: you will find that I am writing about honesty in its purest form.

This book will chronicle many of the rules I cheated on in a battle to overcome a poor start to my career and all the rules (reasons) why I could not be successful. Lacking the opportunity and advantages that many of my peers possessed (through no fault other than my own), I had to create my own rules and cheat on those rules that were only designed to inhibit my prospect for success. My hope is that as you read this book, you will learn, as I did, to use the philosophy of *Cheat to Win* to take control of your life and achieve your personal aspirations.

On the pages within, I try to make the point that no matter what your background is, no matter who you know or don't know, your life does not have to be controlled by others and the myriad stupid rules they thrust upon you. To accomplish this objective, you will read of specific, real-life examples of successful "cheating" on the expectations and limitations imposed on us by others. By recognizing this state of affairs, you will finally be in a position to make your life what you want it to be—on your own terms. The honest truth is that cheating on some of the rules imposed on us is the only honest way to live.

I honestly believe that if the philosophies espoused in *Cheat to Win* that deal with personal actions, management style, and corporate culture had been firmly in place, then the illegal and immoral transgressions of Enron, WorldCom, Arthur Andersen. And their cadre of other nefarious companies would never have occurred.

There exists in the world today a hypocrisy of double-speak regarding how we should and should not lead our lives and what we can and cannot do. The result is an unplanned yet powerful "conspiracy of rules" that controls our potential and limits our freedom. This book seeks to debunk these rule-myths by deflating the pretense and translating the double-speak so that you have the power to discover a clear, clean, and honest path to success.

Cheat to Win is not anti-business—it is *pro-individual*. It's a no-frills, down-to-earth approach to a successful, modern-day "success" evangelism, offered by an average person who has demonstrated and gained an advantage in the business world because of a willingness to go against the rules that are either outdated or in place for the wrong reasons.

Cheat to Win will prove that it is not only possible for the individual to survive, but to thrive. The ideas in this book will not only help you rise faster and achieve more, they'll also help you to be a better manager. So if you are not a crowd-follower, if you're often frustrated by the system and want to build a successful life, career, or business, at your own speed on your own terms, then you will benefit from reading *Cheat to Win*.

My hope is that the ideas and philosophies expressed in this book will resonate with a number of groups. Specifically, this book will offer some fundamental ideas that will allow you—whatever your station in corporate or business life—to be identified as "high potential" and advance rapidly in your career. It can give fresh insights as you tread through the bewildering and often inane array of office rules and politics.

If you are one who really seeks to control your future by becoming an entrepreneurial business leader, then *Cheat to Win* will help you identify the rules that block the survival and success of your business and show you a way to turn them to your advantage.

For those in positions of leadership (or when you get there), *Cheat to Win* offers thoughts on modern corporate culture and management. The calendar may say we are in the twenty-first century, but many management styles still seem to live in the nineteenth century. *Cheat to Win* talks about breaking the rules of antiquated management styles and moving from conflicting to parallel corporate cultures.

As much as I may like to, the one thing I can't promise you is that reading this book will guarantee your success. Unlike many other "business success" books, you will not find any magical "Ten Steps to Wealth and Success" outlined here. Nor will you find an attempt to outline a measured recipe for success, but you will find the ingredients of success that will allow you to concoct your own tasty recipe for success.

This book is neither a magic pill nor a silver bullet. In reality, the way of life espoused in this book is quite simple, basic, and fundamental—some would even say mundane. However, I do promise you that it will provide proven, winning principles that have worked for me and others; all you have to do is provide the manpower. This book is like a popular diet; it's not the *diet plan* that makes you thin, it's the *application* of the plan that triggers weight loss. In the same way, reading *Cheat to Win* will not assure your success, but it will identify what it takes to be successful.

My promise to you is simple: Apply the concepts of *Cheat to Win* to your own life and you will create an extraordinary opportunity to achieve your aspirations—and do it in the most honest way possible. The publishers may have been afraid to publish this book, but I thank you for not being afraid to read it. The bottom line is ... *you can do it!!*

1

A Natural-Born Cheater

Looking back, I think I was born to cheat.

Not even **Nostradamus** could have predicted the future of Bob MacDonald in the summer of '65. As a 22-year-old college student at Loyola University in Los Angeles, I was enjoying the California sun (and I mean *enjoying*) when the light at the end of my academic tunnel grew dim, then dark. To the surprise of no one, my scholastic career at Loyola came to an abrupt end. No, not with a presentation of a sheepskin and a glorious walk down the aisle with "Pomp and Circumstance" echoing in my ears; instead, I was presented with a letter from the Dean's office asserting that I had no future at his college. The stiffly worded missive further suggested I had no future on anyone else's campus, either.

I can hardly describe my despondency as close friends trooped off to graduate school or mounted the first rung of their career ladders, while I remained with no degree, no money, no job, and no decent prospects. In fact, the only unsolicited job offer that came my way was courtesy of the federal government. Eight thousand miles away, our country was fighting a land war in Asia, and they were using real bullets. While I may not have been up to Loyola's standards, the army seemed to feel that I was good enough to be shot at. So, while my friends moved on to better things, I was in serious danger of becoming a professional blood donor. I needed a job and was desperate to pick up anything, other than a rifle.

Fortunately, I received two job offers—one to sell caskets, the other life insurance door-to-door. Maybe I should have thought about doing both, and I really could have made a killing. However, I picked the insurance business, despite the fact that, other than selling caskets, I cannot think of any occupation that leaves the general public with a cold and clammy feeling quite like selling life insurance. Of course, it could have been worse. When it comes to the ranking of jobs, life insurance is not quite at the bottom of the list. Actually, it ranks just below U.S. congressman and just above purveyors of mail-order aphrodisiacs.

At the time, my entire view of the life insurance sales career amounted to what I had seen in the 1960 Billy Wilder movie, *The Apartment*. C. C. Baxter, the main character played by Jack Lemmon, worked for the mythical "Consolidated Life of New York" on the nineteenth floor, Ordinary Policy Department, Premium Accounting Division, Section W, desk number 861. Any enthusiasm I might have had for my entrée into my new career field was tempered by the movie's representation of Consolidated Life, with its "acres of gray steel desks, gray steel filing cabinets, gray suits and gray faces under indirect light."

Yet here I am, forty years later, retired (at least as much as I want to be) and enjoying the fruits of a prolifically successful career, which has taken me on an exciting, fulfilling, and yes, lucrative path that no one forty years ago could have predicted—certainly no one in Loyola's Dean's office.

During my four-decade-long career, I rose to be the leader of the very same companies that, in the beginning, would not have given me the time of day. In fact, my rise through the ranks was so rapid that I spent more than half my career as a CEO of large national companies. I tell you this not to impress you, but to impress upon you my guiding belief: anyone, really, *anyone* can make it to the top.

My humble career began as a neophyte life insurance agent for one of the oldest and most respected companies in the industry, New England Mutual Life. New England offered me a draw against commissions of a not-so-impressive sum of $100 per week. I ended my career selling LifeUSA, the insurance company I founded and grew with the help of hundreds of talented people, to Allianz AG, the multinational financial giant, for a value of $540 million. By that time, New England Mutual had failed and was absorbed by Metropolitan Life, its charter dissolved. At the beginning of my career, you could have drawn some long odds in Vegas if you wanted to wager that New England Life would fail in the business before I would.

But life is about more than quantified wealth. During my career I was fortunate to have the opportunity to create, build, manage, merge, and turn around companies, while at the same time creating thousands of jobs and rich opportunities for others to achieve dreams they never thought possible.

Twice in my career I was named Entrepreneur of the Year in Minnesota. The guy whose most attractive career prospect was selling caskets door-to-door, today serves on corporate boards, functions as a media resource for corporate governance, and contributes articles to nationally renowned publications on corporate management. Not many would have imagined the guy who couldn't even get in the corporate door now traveling the world to meet with international companies knocking on his door for advice.

How do you account for this dramatic reversal of fortune? It's simple—I cheated!

Being Different Seemed Normal

For some reason, I've always had a difficult time accepting rules simply because they were rules. That might explain why my parents sent me to a military school for my primary education. My secondary education consisted of several years of schooling by the mild-mannered, self-effacing Jesuits. (In case you are unfamiliar with the Jesuits, they are a religious order who were once part of the Catholic Church, but broke away after discovering they were better than all the others.) My parents thought the combination of the existential Jesuits and the required conformity of military school would shape me up. Happily, each had just the opposite of the intended purpose.

Instead of teaching me the wisdom of toeing the line, these experiences offered an ample store of ostensibly asinine rules against which I could and did rebel. By the time I was a teenager, my disrespect for the rules was, well, irreversible.

During my high school years, I was in detention so often that the good fathers at L.A.'s Loyola High finally decided to count it as a credit toward graduation. The school was so anxious to break me of my rebellious attitude that it actually suspended me from the varsity team for most of my junior and senior years. And I'm not referring to the football team—I was actually suspended from the varsity debate team. I may have been the only person ever suspended from a debate team.

I spent so much time challenging the precepts and beliefs of my Jesuit teachers that finally the vice principal of the school offered to give me a "C" in religion if I would simply agree not to attend any further religious classes. Since this would significantly raise my GPA, I was quick to accept.

Although I was born in New York, my family moved to California in 1946, when I was three years old. We were, I think, your average middle-class family. My father had been a mortician before the war but became an X-ray technician when he developed an allergic reaction to embalming chemicals. My mother also worked in the medical field as a nurse and medical secretary.

I grew up in a family of health care specialists, but my interests were anything but medicine. While other kids had jobs like delivering newspapers and stocking drug store shelves, my first job was, of all things, giving speeches. And I was a junior in high school, no less.

This escapade started because, as punishment for some silly infraction, my English teacher required me to enter a citywide essay contest sponsored by the old *Los Angeles Examiner*. You know, write 500 words on the meaning of the Bill of Rights. You get the picture.

Much to the chagrin of my teacher, I won. And in addition to a suitably framed certificate, I got to attend an awards banquet at the old Ambassador Hotel in Coconut Grove, the same hotel where Robert Kennedy was assassinated in 1968. I had a terrific time rubbing shoulders with L.A. Mayor Norris Poulson and other local dignitaries.

At the tender age of seventeen, I was pretty happy with myself when one of the contest sponsors, a guy named Joe Crail, came up to me after the affair and offered me a job at his company, L.A.'s Coast Federal Savings & Loan. Crail was a member of a wealthy California family. His brother was a congressman, and the family had close ties with a group of conservative politicians that included Richard Nixon, Walter Knott, of Knott's Berry Farm fame, and Ronald Reagan.

The summer between my junior and senior years in high school, Crail gave me a job writing speeches about free enterprise, the glories of capitalism, and similar patriotic themes. I delivered these presentations to rotary clubs, churches, veterans' groups—basically any organization that would have me. This was a fun job, and I kept delivering the speeches through my senior year in high school and into college. What made it really fun for me was that I was getting paid good money just to talk. Most of my friends at the time had jobs paying just $1.50 per hour. When I started out, Crail paid me $50 a speech and gas mileage, plus a buck for everybody in the audience. If there were 150 or 200 people in the audience, I got over $200. That was big money in those days for a kid barely old enough to shave.

Cheater Senior Grade

My attraction to the contrarian lifestyle blossomed in 1960, when the Democrats held their national convention in Los Angeles. In those days, every weirdo in the country migrated to L.A., which hardly seemed like a real city. There was no downtown, no major hotel, and no form of mass transit. The closest thing to a large meeting facility was the freeway system. Distances between points were so vast that L.A. cab drivers were the first Californians to have Japanese gardeners.

Since the delegates had to be housed in hotels all over the city, members of the Loyola High debate team were asked to schlep the delegates around. One of the student drivers hired to chauffeur the dignitaries around was my debate partner Bob Shrum, who has gone on to be a driving strategist for the Democratic National Party. As the token Republican and incorrigible rule-breaker on the team, however, I wasn't even asked. Even if I had been allowed to play chauffeur, I knew it would be much more fun to be a delegate than to drive one around. Of course, the rules say a seventeen-year-old kid can't be a delegate to a political convention. But like I said, to me breaking the rules just seemed to be something fun to do.

With no adequate convention hall in town, the Democrats staked out the Biltmore Hotel as their headquarters. Previously, the Biltmore's main function was to serve as a launching site for the pigeons to bomb the weirdos across the street in Pershing Square. The lobby was about the size of a good two-car garage. The Democrats set up two registration tables. On the first were several big black books listing all the states and delegates. After party workers checked the delegates' name and state against the list in their books, they were sent to the next table for their official badge.

After watching this confused process for a while, I saw my opening. I simply skipped the first table with the black books and proceeded to the real gatekeepers: the badge line. In my official black debate suit, I figured I looked twenty-five, but it didn't matter. The harried ladies making up the badges hardly had time to look up. When it was my turn in line, I calmly stated, "Bob MacDonald from New York."

"Is that m-c or m-a-c?" someone asked.

I was so nervous that I mumbled, "Oh, I don't care."

The lady glanced at me and said, "Mr. MacDonald, we have to get this right because this is your official registration badge."

"Ok," I said. "M-A-C."

With that, I was off to a week of what only a debate nerd could consider fun. I mingled with delegates, stood next to John F. Kennedy on stage as he greeted delegates, got kowtowed to by Lyndon Johnson, and was ushered into a quiet room where none other than Bobby Kennedy gave the seventeen-year-old "delegate" from New York a PT-109 tie clip.

In another smoke-filled room, I was schmoozed by campaign workers about how I thought the New York delegation would vote.

"Can we count on your vote?" they begged.

The party might have gone on forever, but a suspicious newspaper reporter finally did a little checking and discovered my fraud. His discovery, however, hardly cured me of cheating. Far from it, because in the next day's *Herald-Examiner* there was a profile and picture of "the delegate who wasn't." I was hooked.

This was an exhilarating experience for me, and I was determined to relive it later in the presidential campaign of 1960 when John F. Kennedy was the featured speaker at a rally at the Shrine Auditorium in Los Angeles (where the Academy Awards shows used to be held). Bob Shrum and I, along with another friend named John Torelli, decided we would go to the rally. However, we had a slight difference of opinion. Whereas they wanted to attend the rally, I wanted to be *in* the rally.

With Bob and John seeking to lay claim to some good seats and me wanting to case the place for some fun, we decided to arrive a couple of hours before the meeting was scheduled to start. Those setting up the auditorium paid little attention to three young guys dressed in undertaker suits walking around and trying to look busy, a talent that later proved to be of immeasurable value to me in the army.

The stage had a main podium, and workers were busy setting up a block of folding chairs directly to the left of it. According to procedure, you were expected to come to the meeting, get in line, get your seat, wait, hear the speaker, applaud, and then leave. We were already breaking the rules by being behind stage, and my friends were getting a little nervous. I knew it would be more of a romp to be on stage than to be one of over 4,000 idle souls sitting in the audience. Shrum was scared to death we would be caught. One thing you can't be when you're breaking a rule is nervous—at least, you can't show it.

I remember saying to Bob, "So what if they catch us? Are they going to shoot us? I can see the headlines now, 'High school students apprehended at Kennedy rally—executed.'" But he would not be convinced. He was so nervous that one of the workmen came up to him and said, "Sir, in case you didn't know, the men's room is back over there on the left." That did it—Shrum and Torelli went to stand in line with the other good rule-followers.

The rally started with a band and a few short warm-up speeches. Then, the reason for all the chairs on stage became apparent. Local Democratic candidates for congress, the legislature, and other posts would be introduced to the crowd and then sit on the stage to bask in the aura of the presidential candidate. About halfway through the introductions, someone who was supposed to be there was not. At the second calling of his name, out I walked with my briefcase and took the chair closest to center stage.

Minutes later, the crowd went wild as Kennedy walked out onto the stage. He paused to shake hands with those of us on the stage and then went to the podium. For about fifteen minutes, Kennedy gave his standard speech, encouraging his supporters to continue their hard work. Sitting about five feet from him was a young high school student holding a briefcase full of Nixon bumperstickers.

As soon as the speech was finished, a group of men surrounded Kennedy and formed a bubble that floated through the crowd. Being so close to the candidate, I found myself inside the security bubble. The security people, arms interlocked, prevented people from getting in or out of the small circle. This little group moved along and out the door to the limousine waiting on Jefferson Boulevard.

Around the waiting car was the same type of security bubble, only larger. Outside the bubble was a massive pushing crowd. Inside, everything was calm and almost quiet, like the eye of a hurricane. The small cordon around Kennedy transferred responsibility to the unit around the car, and I suddenly found myself standing next to the car as Kennedy disappeared into it. I suppose I could have followed him into the car, but you have to know which rules to break and when to stop.

The security people were busy looking out at the crowd. The crowd was busy looking at Kennedy. No one saw me walk around to the back of the car, open my briefcase, and slap a Nixon sticker onto the back of the car. A few days later a newspaper columnist wondered why Kennedy had been driving around Los Angeles with a Nixon bumper sticker prominently displayed on his car.

Looking back, what seemed to be adolescent pranks at the time were really defining experiences for me. I learned that sometimes cheating could be fun—and rewarding! From then on, I knew I would always be a cheater.

Gaining Experience from Youthful Pranks

I didn't recognize it at the time, but the experience at the Democratic convention, the presidential rally, along with a number of other "incidents" I won't mention, taught me the benefits of doing the unexpected. Military leaders have known for centuries that the way to win the big battles is to do the unexpected. Remember, conventional wisdom held that Hannibal could not cross the Alps with his army in the winter. Did anyone expect him to use elephants? Successful military leaders know that doing the unexpected requires creativity and boldness.

The Lesson I Learned

My experiences as a teenager taught me a lot about cheating to win in life and in business. At a very young age, I learned there was fun to be had and much to gain from challenging the traditions and the expectations of those who established the rules and those who blindly followed them.

Tradition is fine. I'm all for it. If one wants to be successful, however, it is essential to recognize that traditions and rules are things to build on and use—not hide behind. Followers cite tradition—winners challenge everything. It is interesting to note that many traditions are founded upon instances of rule-breaking.

Today's traditions started when someone found a new and effective way to do something different. Our personal or business heroes today were winners for one reason—they innovated. They looked for better ways to do something. Past winners resisted the onerous pressure to accept things as they were. We'd still be washing carbon smudges off our hands if Chester Carlson, an arthritic patent attorney, hadn't grown tired of making multiple copies of the endless stream of documents he had to file with the patent office. What did he do? He invented Xerography, a copying process that utilizes electrostatic energy. It took him many years to find an investor interested in his invention, but he finally found one in the Haloid Company, later known as Xerox Corporation.

And the Moral of the Story Is . . .

It is simple, fun, and rewarding to cheat on established rules and customs that have outlived their purpose. Why? Because most people follow the rules and assume that others do the same. And the good news is that these tired rules and customs are everywhere you look, and new ones are being formed every day.

Cheating to win begins with one simple question—"Why?" The fundamental act of questioning is the cheater's tool of the trade. Sure we've always done it that way, but why? Isn't there a better way? What if we did it *this* way? A successful cheater habitually questions and challenges the rules others want us to follow. It's what carried me from my prankish youth to the top of the life insurance business. You can use the same practice to carry you to the top or, as in Hannibal's case, over any mountain you seek to climb.

2

I Can See Clearly Now
That The Rules Are Gone

*Cheating is not the only way to win, but,
when you cheat honestly, it's the best way.*

Cheat to win? You've got to be crazy. We all know that to get along we have to go along. Keep your yap shut, do as you're told. Above all, *follow the rules.* The rules, as everyone knows, keep us out of trouble. Rules promote consistency and organization.

"You can't do that . . ."

"You can't say that . . ."

"That's not the way it's supposed to be done . . ."

"Well, we've always done it this way . . ."

"The rules are here for a reason . . ."

Rules are especially prolific in the business world. We are given rules for writing our resume, for applying for a job, and still other rules for how to conduct ourselves in an employment interview. We're given more rules about what to say and do when we're hired and for treading through the often bewildering array of office politics.

We are told how to "dress for success." We are inundated with strategies and tactics for getting promoted, winning raises, and advancing our careers. There are rules for practically everything.

Rules are the gospels of the business world and they are perpetuated by a plethora of business books and newspapers that proclaim that "following the rules" is the proven path to the American dream. The *Wall Street Journal* is arguably the diary of the rule-keepers, and a multitude of business books reinforces the drumbeat of rules. With few notable exceptions, business books and newspapers offer the promise of success for those who learn to obey what the writer perceives as the "special rules" of the business game. That's all they really offer—rules, and more rules.

Rules and Their Reasons

The rules, of course, are ostensibly formulated to help us succeed, to keep us out of trouble, to achieve happiness, the coveted six-figure salary, and a BMW in the corporate parking lot. But there's a problem with some of these rules and the books that chronicle them. The bitter truth is that most of the rules we confront are instituted not to help us succeed, but rather to control us, to limit us, and to keep us from assuming command of our destinies. The deluge of business books on the shelves simply catalogs the rules established by others to control your future.

Don't get me wrong; I am not against all rules. For example, at least nine of the Ten Commandments are good rules. So is "keep to the right" and "women and children first." They should be obeyed. But there are other rules such as, "You can't sail west or you will fall off the edge of the world!"; or "Do not remove this tag under penalty of law." Rules like these are, for lack of a better description, stupid. They should be broken. And this book is dedicated to teaching you how to identify which rules are foolish and how to effectively break them to achieve a more successful future.

As the previous chapter readily suggests, I was a cheater from the beginning. Yes, I was a bit more rebellious than most and given to prankish escapades and youthful tomfoolery. But I think what really separated me from the flock, then and now, was that my basic cheating instincts were not hammered out of me by a callous and unthinking upbringing.

34

I happen to think that most of us are natural born rule-breakers, but the great majority has this attitude wrung out of them. I was fortunate. My parents, teachers, college professors, military drill instructors, business superiors, and associates were simply unable to quell the rule-breaking, take-a-chance attitude from my soul. Somehow, I mustered through all of the brainwashing relatively unscathed. Others are not nearly so fortunate.

When someone questions the assumptions of those around them, they are typically rebuffed and threatened with exclusion and isolation. This is the point at which most succumb to the pressure and settle into comfortable acceptance. The will to preserve the status quo is a force, like gravity. You may not be able to see it, but it is just as real and at least as powerful. And so the rules proliferate, and the lemmings blindly follow each other into the sea.

The Philosophy of Cheating

It's important now that we make a distinction. There are two types of cheating. There is the bad cheating, which I call "cheating to lose." And, there is good cheating. I call that "cheating to win."

"Bad cheating" is immoral, unethical, dishonest, and often illegal. And you know what I'm talking about. We've seen a lot of it in recent years. How can anyone compete with Dennis Kozlowski, CEO of Tyco International, for sheer profligacy and conspicuously vulgar consumption? We've all heard the stories now of the infamous $15,000 umbrella stand, the $6,000 shower curtain, the ice sculpture of Michelangelo's David urinating vodka — all paid for with company funds. Kozlowski and his Tyco cohorts allegedly plundered $600 million from corporate accounts and skimmed company profits to buy themselves swanky apartments and vacation homes, festooning them with fine art and expensive baubles.

But Kozlowski is just the tip of a terribly brackish iceberg. We've also got Enron and WorldCom and Adelphia. You remember Adelphia, the big cable television network founded by John Rigas and two of his sons, who were convicted of concealing $2.3 billion in loans and looting to the tune of $100 million, all the while lying to shareholders and the government about its finances. Toss in a little Martha Stewart, some Leona Helmsley, a pinch of Halliburton, and many others like them, and what have you got? An encyclopedia of "bad cheating" to instruct us how *not* to govern ourselves.

Anyone who engages in that kind of cheating is "cheating to lose"—not because the Bible says so, not because the offense is codified in law, or because it evokes pangs of conscience, but for the most pragmatic reason of all: *bad cheating doesn't work*. An individual may derive some short-term benefit, but beware! The long-term consequences can be awful. Just ask Martha.

The philosophy of cheating to win espoused in this book, on the other hand, is highly moral, fundamentally ethical, and the most honest way to live your life and interact with others. This kind of cheating breaks rules that are inane, ineffectual, and counterproductive, rules that exist only because they have been entrenched by the imposing twin pillars of "custom" and "tradition." Look for these types of rules. They are trail markers on your journey to unprecedented personal success.

Just Faces in the Crowd

It's sometimes difficult to identify those with a true proclivity for rule-breaking behavior, but one doesn't have to look far to find conformists who are happy to play the game of life "inside the box." Breaking the rules means thinking outside the box, not being satisfied with the way things are, questioning the status quo. Conformists assume the best is behind us. Charles H. Duell, for example, director of the U.S. Patent Office, proclaimed in 1899, "Everything that can be invented has been invented."

Conformists characteristically find it difficult to recognize the value of an idea. To them, sometimes an idea is a thing to be feared. They accept rules as if they were answers and rarely invest the effort or take the risk needed to ponder an alternative. Their life is governed by a meticulously assembled script of answers to questions they never bothered to ask themselves.

Some label them as conservatives; I call them wusses. Their conformity spreads like a cancer, thwarting the will of would-be rule-breakers. They are society's wet blankets, the first in line to proclaim your idea "won't work" or that it's just "too risky." Committed wusses are totally oblivious to the potential for better. They are like the people who kept their black and white TV for decades because it worked perfectly well for them.

The Rule-Breakers Are Different

The first sign of a good cheater is relentless curiosity. The cheater is constantly asking questions and challenging the way things are done. Good cheaters take exception to established procedures and mores.

Rule-breakers often exhibit other attributes as well:

- The willingness to adopt new perspectives whenever possible
- The openness to try new things and to do old things differently
- The compelling drive to act on ideas to test their true value
- The eagerness to listen to others and profit from their input, regardless of who gets credit
- Respect for and support of others when they propose new courses of action

Rule-breaking behavior requires an openness and willingness to look at the world in new ways. Rule-breakers know that new ideas need nurturing and support. But they know that thinking about a new idea is not enough. The true value of a good idea resides in its implementation. As management expert Peter Drucker said, "Ideas are cheap and abundant. What is of value is the effective placement of these ideas into situations that develop into action."

On the surface, rule-breaking doesn't require any special skills. You don't have to have an MBA from an Ivy League university. In fact, you don't need a degree at all. But if it's so easy to be a cheater, and the potential for reward is so great, why, then, doesn't everybody do it?

The Will to Cheat Is Hammered Out of Us

When we're young, we're much more apt to be cheaters. Children commonly exhibit the cheater's inclination to question why things are done the way they are. It's natural. As soon as babies can talk, they ask, "Why?" It's often irritating for parents because they don't always have the answers. So the response is "Because." Or, if the kid persists, "That's the way it is. Go watch TV."

Schools only exacerbate the problem. The educational system is founded upon the pedagogy of answering questions, not asking them. Students are rewarded for the proper rote playback of answers, not their ability to question the reasons for the answers or, sometimes more important, the assumptions behind the questions. The pressure to "go along with the crowd" is overwhelming for anyone, particularly kids in their formative years. Not surprisingly, most buckle under the pressure. A child is forced to see things the way their peer group does, dress as they do, talk as they do, and worse, *think and act* as they do. Pretty soon, a child's willingness to question and break rules is exorcised as if it were a troublesome evil spirit.

Rule-Breakers on the Fringes

We have to recognize that daring to think and do things differently exposes us to risks as well as rewards. But you know what? Even though you may risk the ridicule and tsk-tsk of your friends, teachers, parents, business associates, boss, and an endless string of others; even though there is a risk that you'll come up with a dumb idea for which you'll be chastised; even though some may perceive you as a show-off or know-it-all; even though all of this may be true, when you finally succeed by doing things differently, the reward and personal satisfaction is so much better than the punishment, it's not even a contest.

The only reason the downside exposure exists is simply to control you: to intimidate you so that you'll be unwilling to be a rule-breaker and a creative thinker. The result? Many potential rule-breakers are afraid to engage in behavior that could potentially make waves. Instead, they lay low and avoid the possibility of future embarrassment and pain. The bottom line is that, even though we start out in life as rule-breakers and cheaters, most of us become timid feeders in a sea of conformity before we ever get our first job out of college.

Fortunately, even if one is not a born cheater, cheating can be an acquired talent, a talent well worth learning and practicing. To develop and nurture this talent for ourselves, we have to overcome the way our psyche has been bullied for so long in an effort to get us to stop asking questions. To achieve real success in our life and career, it is essential to recondition ourselves to challenge convention. I know that this is easy for me to say. I've made my millions, and I have little to lose now by rocking the boat. But I insist that you can do it too.

History Is Rife with Cheaters

Keep in mind that if it weren't for cheaters, we'd probably still be dragging our knuckles across the African savanna, without the chutzpah to rub two sticks together. Sometimes we forget how deeply ingrained cheating is in our national heritage. We are, in fact, a nation of cheaters, going all the way back to Columbus's willingness to ignore the conventional wisdom that his voyage was too far and too dangerous to produce anything more certain than death. As historian Gianni Granzotto has written, "What saved Columbus was not geography but his courage, the very same that we encounter in his refusal to conform to that which everyone believed to be true." This is the portrait of a great cheater.

Whether by land or by sea, only by cheating convention can we extend the borders of our world and the reach of our capabilities. Far too many of us become simpleminded yes-men. We agree with everything that is said; we support, without critical evaluation, every opinion or proposal. And so instead of *questioning* rules, we end up being *controlled* by them. The best cheaters are always asking "Why?"—or, as with Columbus, "Why not?"

Start Your Renaissance

To suggest that I have any kind of monopoly on rule-breaking is to belie what this book is all about. We *all* can cheat to win. You've just got to give rule-breaking a chance. Start by simply getting in the habit of following your natural curiosity. Consider, for example, a scene we've all experienced: You've just listened to a speech or a presentation by an authority on some subject. "Are there any questions?" the speaker asks. You, and many more people in the room, have plenty of questions. But no one wants to raise their hand for fear of looking stupid. Finally, one person exercises his curiosity. Far from laughing hysterically at his question, everyone is relieved. More questions follow. The ice has been broken.

If this example seems simple, it's because it is. And you'd be amazed as just how simple it is to get into the habit of being the first one to raise a hand. Leadership and success are built upon such simple habits.

If that's still too difficult, begin by simply asking yourself questions. Look for the answers privately. Seek them under cover of darkness. Remember, the questioning doesn't always have to be verbal. Many times it's to the cheater's advantage that others not know what he is questioning. The important thing is to get into the habit of questioning convention. It's only a matter of time before such an attitude leads to innovation, and innovation to success.

Most people don't want us to ask new questions because they may be forced to deal with new answers, answers that threaten the tempting comfort of the status quo. Acceptance of the status quo may allow us to get along, but it sure doesn't help us get ahead. As Daniel Boorstin wrote in *The Discoverers,* "The great obstacle to discovering the shape of the earth, the continents, and the ocean was not ignorance but the illusion of knowledge."

And the Moral of the Story Is . . .

When looking for cheaters, look for those who do the unexpected. Douglas "Wrong Way" Corrigan did the unexpected and achieved fame. Scheduled to take off from Brooklyn, Corrigan filed a flight plan that would take him to California. Just over twenty-eight hours later, he arrived in Ireland. Much to the chagrin of the aviation authorities who originally rejected his request for a trans-Atlantic flight, Corrigan claimed his compass must have malfunctioned. By doing things the "wrong way," Corrigan became a national folk hero.

How many times have we read of war battles where the losing side was overrun because the winner did the unexpected? From Hannibal to MacArthur, successful military leaders rejected the accepted rules of battle and did what couldn't or shouldn't be done.

One thing is certain about rule-breakers: they like doing things *differently.* They resist going along with the crowd. Cruising along with the flow of things just isn't their lifestyle. They continually ask why things are the way they are—why they aren't different. Why they're not *better.*

With almost relentless enthusiasm, they are curious about their surroundings and anxious to experience something new. Rule-breakers set their minds to roam on hitherto unexplored mental and physical frontiers. They chart new courses to create new solutions to problems old and new, silly and significant. They find emptiness in the routine, the repetitious, the boring. They delight in fresh currents of thought, fanciful new ways of thinking, and innovative ways of perceiving the reality that surrounds us all. They marvel in the thought that their creative energies, their rule-breaking élan, come from within, that they can change the rules to reshape our reality.

I don't think anyone has expressed the cheater's ideology better than Harry Gray, the CEO of United Technologies in the 1980s, in the following full-page newspaper ad, a manifesto for cheaters everywhere.

Will The Real You Please Stand Up?

Submit to pressure from peers and you move down to their level. Speak up for your own beliefs and you invite them up to your level. If you move with the crowd, you'll get no further than the crowd. When 40 million people believe in a dumb idea, it's still a dumb idea. Simply swimming with the tide leaves you nowhere. So if you believe in something that's good, honest and bright—stand up for it. Maybe your peers will get smart and drift your way.

Reprinted through courtesy of Harry J. Gray, Harry Gray Associates

3

Your Whole Life Is a Mistake . . .

*The ability to cheat to win begins only after
you become totally honest with yourself and
your environment.*

It was March of 1980. I had just turned thirty-seven years old
and was the newly elected president and CEO of ITT Life of
Minneapolis. Since my personal goal had long been to become
an insurance company CEO, I considered this to be my crowning
achievement. I could now be in the "god club," just like all the
other CEOs. I felt I had made it. At the time, I was just happy to be
part of the club. Cheating was the farthest thing from my mind.

But little did I know that I was on the threshold of a trial by
baptism, soon to be both loved and hated for what I was about to
do. I would wind up turning the insurance industry on its ear, inciting
fear and downright loathing from other insurance companies, large
and small, and, before it was all over, building a mega-billion-dollar
business from the ground up.

But something else was going to happen that was even more
important. I was about to turn a corner in my life. Most people live
life as it comes, as it is dealt. We respond to life's challenges with our

God-given intellect, whatever schooling we're lucky enough to get, plus the savvy we pick up in life's school of hard knocks. We all have a talent, but sometimes it takes a single, life-altering event to help us understand and focus on what we can do to be better.

And that's how it was for me. I learned from experiences during my youth and early career that it was okay not to be normal; that just because everyone did something, it did not necessarily mean it was the right way to do it. This inclination to be different manifested itself in numerous youthful pranks, but had never been applied in an organized, cohesive fashion. My actions came more from instinct than plan. Then I joined ITT Life. This life-altering experience transformed what had been a loosely organized management strategy into an interrelated, dedicated program founded upon the principles of what would become the cheat-to-win philosophy.

And, by the end of this chapter, you'll know enough about this disarmingly simple strategy that you may wish to put it to work in your life, regardless of the business you're in. My business happens to be life insurance, but it can work for anyone in any field.

CEO for Dummies

When the hullabaloo died down and the honeymoon faded away, the panic set in. Now what? What the hell was I supposed to do? Where would I go? How would I build this company? I missed graduate school; hell, I missed college, and no one ever taught me how to be a CEO. Worse, I didn't drink or play golf, so I already had two strikes against me.

Besides, it wasn't like I had been elected president of Prudential or something. This was ITT Life. I didn't learn until later that the ITT in this case stood for "It's Totally Terrible." Nor did I have to win out over a slew of rivals vying to be elected president because of ITT Life's raging success. The only reason the executives of Hartford Insurance, the direct parent of ITT Life, were willing to shoulder the additional risk of elevating the young and inexperienced Bob MacDonald was because the company was a small and relatively insignificant piece of their massive empire.

My Challenging Inheritance

To say that ITT Life was part of the backwater of the insurance industry would be kind, perhaps overly so. The company made most of its paltry income by writing insurance policies considered by the industry to be second-rate and on the fringe of respectability. For example, when you upgraded to that new, used doublewide trailer in the middle of rural Wisconsin, ITT Life would be there to write credit insurance on your loan at the dairy credit union. They'd also write a lot of those so-called "nursing home policies." These policies were designed to pay for the cost of nursing home care, provided that you were not presently in a nursing home and that your present life expectancy was about the same as an ice cube in a microwave. The company also offered those specialized cancer policies that were so restrictive they might only pay out if you happened to contract cancer on a Thursday afternoon while you were living on the second floor of a cave in northeastern Montana.

To a large extent, an insurance company's success rests upon its distribution channel—the insurance agents who sell its products. I don't want to suggest that ITT Life's distribution system left something to be desired, but the leading production source was a group of individuals who set national sales records selling sewing machines to people in rural Florida who did not have electricity in their homes.

Got the picture? My dream job was slowly becoming a nightmare. My charge from The Hartford was simple enough, however: turn this salvage scow around and make it a real insurance company. I was to construct a company that would not only be profitable, but respectable as well—sort of like an *Extreme Makeover* for corporations.

I didn't have any experience as a company quarterback, but I had been studying the game plan for years. The only business I knew was life insurance. During the fifteen years leading up to this point, I had worked my way from neophyte agent out on the street selling policies, to a variety of management, marketing and administrative assignments. With tutelage from some of the leading companies in the industry, like New England Mutual and State Mutual, I had a good idea of the industry's standard business model. The problem was that ITT Life did not fit very well into that business model. It wasn't even close.

Money, Money, Money Everywhere

No business is better than the money business because it's so simple. The money business—insurance, banking, and investments—is good because you give us your money, and we promise to give it back when you need it or want it back—maybe. In the meantime, we get to play with your money. The money business has no inventory, manufacturing, or transportation problems. It's all about money on money. Being in the money business in America is especially nice because there is so much money to be had.

For most of the twentieth century, the life insurance industry and its member companies were the dominant institutions in the money business. The widest margins, highest profits, and largest buildings all belonged to the insurance companies. The insurance companies were happy with the world as it was and were determined to maintain the status quo.

The size and success of the life insurance industry caused its leaders to be leery of two things—competition and scrutiny. The insurance industry panjandrums worked very assiduously and effectively to keep the evils of competition and the heat of scrutiny at bay. Believe it or not, at the time, both state and federal law prohibited banks and investment firms from competing in the life insurance industry. Federal tax laws favored life insurance over other financial products because the products were deemed a "social good." How could anyone scrutinize an industry that was selling a product like life insurance? The industry wanted you to believe that questioning the life insurance industry was akin to challenging Mother Teresa simply because she didn't keep good records.

On another front, in 2004 Eliot Spitzer, the attorney general of New York began investigating the insurance industry. The Spitzer investigation was a fairly unique experience for the insurance industry.

He uncovered many abuses that had been kept under the blanket for decades. The December 31, 2004 issue of *SCHIFF'S Insurance Observer* reported, "Eliot Spitzer's investigation into the insurance business is the biggest thing to hit the industry since ... well, since forever. Never before has the industry been scrutinized so closely by the general-interest media. Do the insurance industry's shenanigans deserve so much attention? Yes. Is the stuff Spitzer is known to be investigating the sleaziest stuff that's ever gone on in the insurance business? No."

Yet, the money business was far too lucrative for the industry to rely on mere federal law and social mores to protect their dominant position in the financial services industry. So the industry had become very adept at designing esoteric products, abstruse accounting systems, and exotic legal structures to camouflage it from the outside scrutiny of consumers and government bureaucrats.

Even though it was obvious to anyone that only a few large, clubby companies dominated the industry, the basic operating rule was to exude the appearance of being highly competitive. However, there was a twist as to how the mucky-mucks of the insurance industry defined "competition." To their way of thinking, competition meant competing *with* all the brother companies *against* other financial services sectors was fine, but never *ever* compete against your brethren. There were over 2,000 companies in the industry, giving outsiders the impression of a fiercely competitive marketplace. But if all the companies sold the same product, for virtually the same price—which they did—just who were we kidding here about competition? There was about as much product differentiation as a quart of milk purchased from the neighborhood 7-Eleven versus Qwicki-Mart. The unspoken code was that if all of the companies stuck together, while giving the impression of fierce competition, consumers would be pacified, outside competition intimidated, and regulators kept at bay.

Not only were the companies offering similar products, they did it in a shameless way by cozying up to state insurance regulators to ensure that state laws codified homogenous product designs and inhibited the development of new products. Sure, insurance agents were in fierce competition among themselves, but the companies avoided competition with each other because they believed there would always be enough business to go around.

At the start of industry meetings, just after the prayers for the death of banks and the failure of investment firms, we would all rise, place our hands on our wallets, and sing the industry anthem "Don't Rock the Boat Baby" (to the tune of "Rock-A-Billy Baby"). At the conclusion of each meeting, we would again rise up as one, join hands, and, swaying together like a southern Baptist choir, sing "We All Gots to Go Along to Get Along" (to the tune of *He's Got the Whole World In His Hands*).[1] It was beautiful, inspirational, and quite succinctly summed up the collective attitude of the life insurance industry regarding operating strategy and competition.

A Proud Partner in Progress

It's not that the life insurance industry has not played a valuable role in the economic development of America; it has. As the economy shifted from an agrarian, barter-based structure to an urban cash system, life insurance companies accommodated a pressing economic need of the time—protection against the economic cost of the family breadwinner dying unexpectedly. We forget today that at the opening of the twentieth century, the life expectancy of the average male in America was forty-two years. For most of that century, the risk of a family suffering financial hardship at the death of the breadwinner was very real and the consequences quite severe.

The life insurance industry correctly identified this problem and developed products that offered a solution—a perfect marketing and social quid pro quo. For their effort, the life insurance industry was rewarded with consumer trust, steadily increasing sales, growing profits, and the accumulation of vast amounts of wealth. In short, the life insurance industry earned its leading role in the American economic fabric.

The problem was not that the insurance industry earned this status; the problem was the way it reacted once it did. The life

---

[1] Editor's note: I told him he couldn't say that. He said it anyway.

insurance industry behaved the same way most entities do when they perceive themselves as invulnerable—they become soft, lazy, complacent, and then, utterly arrogant about their status. The industry shifted from an achievement to an entitlement mentality. It's an old story. In *The Reckoning*, a book about the decline of the auto industry in Detroit, David Halberstam argues that General Motors became so arrogant with its success that it was unable to continue to do the things that made it successful—and was self-deluded about the threat posed by emerging competition from Japan. It could be argued that IBM, the "Big Blue," nearly failed and went out of business because it had been so successful that its culture assumed it had a right to always be successful. Need we mention the Roman Empire?

Absolute Power Corrupts Absolutely

The life insurance industry and its leaders were no better and no worse than these examples. The insurance industry deserved the success it had achieved, but then it became fat, happy, and, above all, dumb.

Like a leader who has been in power for too long, the industry felt it knew all the answers. Instead of being an industry that listened and responded to the needs of the consumer, it thought it could tell consumers what they wanted. The success of the life insurance industry intoxicated its leaders with the illusion of invincibility. In such a climate, any change was perceived as a threat.

This attitude fostered a calcification of ideas that caused the industry to fall into the fatal pattern of listening only to its own voices and drowning out the sound of shifting consumer needs and tastes. The industry blindly assumed the right to sell the products it wanted to sell (just like GM felt it had a right to sell oversized cars), rather than the products that consumers needed.

Enter: Bob "I Should Have Known Better" MacDonald

As the new president and CEO of ITT Life I stepped right into the middle of this bedlam. Of course, my initial inclination was to get on board and play the game just like everyone else. It would have been an accepted, natural, and easy approach just to play by the industry rules.

The rules were simple: Since there was enough of the insurance pie for everyone, the market could be divided up based largely on seniority and size, so long as everyone was willing to sit at the table and wait their turn. In short, it was a classic story of "going along to get along." Play by the rules, wait your turn, support the status quo, compete *with* the other companies, not against them, parrot the party line . . . then there are enough pieces of the pie for everyone. That is, so long as someone does not upset the cart. Then there could be penalties. If you became Oliver-like and asked for more, you could be banished from the table altogether.

We Wanted a Bigger Bowl

But there was a problem. I knew that if we played by the rules, ITT Life might survive and be accepted as a junior member of the club, but we would never be invited to join the inner sanctum. If ITT Life played by the rules of the industry, we'd get some of the business, but only the crumbs from the table of the big boys. That wasn't enough.

What got under my skin the most was the way the rules were set up in the industry. Like victims of the school bully, those of us running smaller companies were told that we could play in the schoolyard, so long as we played by the rules of the bully and didn't rock the industry boat. The more I assessed the situation, the more troubled I became.

Is This America or Armenia?

Was I missing something? Hey, I was just an inexperienced new kid on the block, but I thought the whole idea of free market capitalism was fair but ferocious competition. My understanding was that the way to gain a market share was to offer a better product, not divvy it up like boiled potatoes at an Irish wedding. Wasn't competition supposed to be *competition?*

Besides, the last time I looked, neither Prudential nor MetLife bought a lot of life insurance from ITT Life. Why should I be worried about making them look bad in the marketplace? Wasn't the best way to turn ITT Life around to develop better products to beat the big companies? I wanted to pummel those companies, not party with them. This was not what the rules called for.

If the Market Moves, Shouldn't You Follow?

There was something else I noticed. The growth of the life insurance industry seemed to be slowing down; profits were narrowing, and competition from banks and investment firms was becoming a reality. In fact, the percentage of disposable income spent for life insurance was in decline. This situation compounded the uneasiness I had with the industry rules, because it meant ITT Life would be getting a smaller piece of a steadily declining market. Normally, in a free market environment such as this, one would seek to discover the reason for the decline in sales, offer a solution, and then grab as much market share as possible.[2]

Significant social and economic changes were beginning to have a major impact on the industry. Among these changes, banks and investment firms were beginning to offer competitive financial products more aligned with consumers' needs. Prior to the late

---

[2]Author's note: If you find that all of this stuff about life insurance bores you to tears, then congratulate yourself—you are a normal person. However, if you find this information to be so exciting and riveting that you can't put it down, please do not operate heavy equipment, and call a doctor immediately. This material is not included here to test your mental state (that was done when you purchased this book), but to offer a real-life example—a case study, if you will—of the reaction and impact caused by cheating on industry rules. These could apply to any industry; I just happened to find them in insurance. So forgive me. I promise not to sell you a policy. However, I do have an idea that has helped many of your friends and may be of interest to you.

twentieth century, consumer options for financial products were a little like Henry Ford's color options for the Model-T—you could have any color you wanted, so long as it was black. In addition, the U.S. Census Bureau was now reporting that a male child born in any state except Arkansas, could expect to live well into his eighties and spend as much as a third of his life in retirement.

Within a very short period of time, the needs of the consumer shifted from a concern about the economic cost of dying too young to the economic cost of living too long in retirement. Some say that the prolonged male life expectancy from forty-two to seventy-four years could be the single most significant event of the twentieth century. (However, this advancement clearly disappointed a lot of women, who kinda liked the idea of the male head of household gone, just not his money.) Yet few leaders in the life insurance industry took note of this change; or if they did, they ignored its implications. As a result, what should have become a new opportunity for the life insurance industry—very much akin to the opportunity of one hundred years ago—instead became a threat to the industry's very survival.

Consumers began buying more of the products offered by banks and investment firms instead of insurance products. Collectively, the insurance industry seemed to believe that if they simply ignored the problem, it would go away. The battle cry of the industry became, "All will be okay, if we just get back to the basics!" Everyone was encouraged to band together to fight the Visigoth bankers and investment scoundrels. It struck me at the time that the "get back to the basics" strategy might sound nice, but what if the basics had changed? In such a case, the get-back-to-the-basics strategy would make a bad situation worse.

The mainstay and most profitable product sold by the life insurance industry up until this time was something called "whole life." This was "permanent insurance" (as opposed to temporary, or "term insurance"), which meant that once you bought it, you paid the premiums permanently or at least until you died.

For almost a century, whole life had been a good product for the consumer and a super product for the industry. But, by the late twentieth century, the product had simply become outmoded. This was neither good nor bad, just a fact. It was a little like the airline industry when the advent of jet engines rendered the reliable piston engine obsolete. The outdating of whole life would not have been a problem if the industry had buried whole life and welcomed the changes taking place as harbingers of opportunity, the way the airline industry quickly grounded prop planes once jet aircraft came into service. The insurance industry took a different approach, however. Industry leaders decided they knew better than the consumer. They were very content to sell whole life and wanted to continue doing so.

Think the airlines are in deep trouble today? Imagine the shape they would be in if, at the time jet engines became available, all the airlines decided collectively to stick with the piston aircraft? Wouldn't that be stupid? Well, believe it or not, that's exactly what the insurance industry did. Only they went one better; they tried to have the new products outlawed and almost got away with it.

The Answer Was as Obvious as an Insurance Guy at a Fashion Show

In assessing this environment—and desperate to turn ITT Life around—we determined that we would never be successful by allowing others to define our success or inhibit our options, especially when the directives we were being asked to follow were so obviously out of touch with what the market called for. Once we accepted this reality, everything seemed to open up, and it was clear what we had to do. In fact, it was quite simple. *We had to cheat on the industry rules.*

The Enemy Within

We viewed the larger insurance companies as our competitors, not our compatriots and we were determined to beat them in the market with better products and service. This may sound like an obvious approach, but in the life insurance industry at the time, it was truly heresy.

First, we focused on the products we offered. What chance did we have trying to build ITT Life on the basis of selling an antiquated product that no longer met the consumer's needs? Instead, we committed ourselves to a development plan predicated on a new type of life insurance product called "universal life." Universal life was a new idea being developed by some in the "underground" of the industry.

Yes, wherever an oppressive culture exists, you'll usually find an underground of resistance trying to change the system. The life insurance industry was no different. Under the cover of geek-ness, a group of actuaries had been conducting clandestine meetings in calculation-filled rooms, trying to develop new insurance products. Actuaries are critical to the insurance industry; but if you've never met one and wonder what they are like, just imagine a person who wanted to be a CPA but flunked the personality test. If you saw Jack Nicholson in *About Schmidt*, you get some idea of what an actuary is like—except that Nicholson exhibited far too much charisma.

Universal life is a hybrid product, accumulating value like an investment while still offering a death benefit. It was designed to compete with bank and investment products and to reward people for living, rather than dying. Of course, this approach conflicted with the unspoken industry rules not to compete directly with other companies and for everyone to sell the same product. From my perspective, however, we had little to lose.

We felt that if we were going to make a run against the big companies, we might as well go all the way. We put all of our resources, limited as they were, into a plan to take on the mighty insurance industry and its beloved whole life product. Like any good war, we needed a battle cry. For that, we turned to the creative, if somewhat unorthodox, minds at the Minneapolis advertising agency of Fallon, Inc. to come up with two themes for our campaign.

Our message to the industry was, "Are You Married to a Lower Form of Life?" And to the consumer we suggested that "Your Whole Life Is a Mistake!"

To show you how pervasive the "no compete" rules of the life insurance industry could be, Fallon was the only advertising agency we approached who was willing to take our account. The other agencies worried they would offend the other companies and lose potential business.

We recognized that our approach violated the generally accepted operating tactics of the insurance industry, but our mission was to build ITT Life, not the other companies, so it seemed logical to us. It seemed so, well, so *American*.

General Quarters, General Quarters, This Is Not a Drill . . .

Although we expected to stir up a little controversy, we were not prepared for the firestorm that was ignited by our actions. The first resistance came from what we thought would be an unlikely source—our parent company, The Hartford. Hartford was big in the property and casualty business, not the life insurance business, and we felt the leaders of Hartford would be less concerned with our tactics. After all, our success would only benefit The Hartford.

Not taken into account was that Pete Thomas, the CEO of Hartford, and the other top executives were all members in good standing of the insurance club. They not only played by its rules, they helped formulate them. While the leaders of Hartford may have agreed with our logic and strategy, they did not want to violate industry rules.

Then we got a break. Out of the blue, Prudential announced they were going to enter the property and casualty business. (Prudential was beginning to struggle with whole life and seemed to adopt the strategy that you might as well compound your problems by trying to sell something you know nothing about. Sometimes I wonder who puts these people in charge!) In any event, the property and casualty sector was Hartford's bread and butter, so the actions of Prudential put Pete Thomas in a twit. He felt they were invading his territory, and he did not like it. His response was to turn us loose—not because it was the right thing to do, but to tweak Prudential.

So, with Thomas's spurious blessing, we launched our plan. Of course, this was not the end of our troubles with the clubbies at Hartford. The bureaucrats constantly tried to rein us in closer to the industry norm. As nascent cheaters, however, we simply ignored most of the "suggestions" made by those at Hartford, who were trying to thwart our efforts.

An attempted coup de grace came the day before we were to launch our new marketing plan. I received a call from the public relations department of Hartford, telling us we had to call off our plans "until they could be further reviewed." Bureaucrats never simply say "no." Instead, they will inflict you with so many nitpicking cuts that you eventually bleed to death. And, typically, the prolonged and agonizing process begins with a statement containing a phrase like, "until further review …"

Pete Thomas had initially given his blessing; we had expended tremendous resources to develop the program; we were ready to pull the trigger; then we get a call telling us all was off. Now I had a dilemma.

Well, as a student of history, I first thought of an incident that occurred during the resolution of the Cuban missile crisis. In 1962, the CIA discovered incontrovertible evidence that Soviet nuclear missile installations were under construction on the island of Cuba, a scant ninety miles off the Florida coast. In response, President John Kennedy initiated a naval blockade against Soviet ships carrying missile equipment. We were on the brink of a nuclear war.

While our crisis at ITT Life was certainly not as cataclysmic as that faced by Kennedy, there were similarities. President Kennedy had received a letter from Soviet Prime Minister Khrushchev offering an acceptable compromise to the crisis in Cuba. Just as the United States was about to announce acceptance of the plan, however, Kennedy received another letter from the Soviets backing off the plan. Faced with the apparent dilemma, Kennedy simply ignored the second letter. The rest, thankfully, is history.

We took the same approach with Hartford. First, we knew we were doing the right thing. Sure, we were cheating on life insurance industry rules, but these were rules that *needed* to be cheated on.

Even more important, we had marshaled all the resources, people, and ideas of ITT Life to develop this plan. The people of ITT Life were enthused and committed. Company morale was higher than it had ever been. To pull the rug out now would have destroyed any chance the company had for success. So, if we were going to cheat on the industry, we figured we might as well cheat on Hartford too.

Also, by this time, I knew full well that doing the unexpected and going against the grain of tradition and rules was not only fun, it was usually the right thing to do. And the potential cost for violating the rule was not nearly as penal as success was rewarding. The next day I flew to Washington, D.C., to launch the rebirth of ITT Life, violating all of the accepted rules of the life insurance industry.

At the national meeting of the Consumer Federation of America, we held a news conference to announce that whole life had become obsolete and no longer met the needs of the consumer. To put teeth in our declaration, we said that ITT Life would no longer sell whole life insurance (not that we sold that much anyway) and would introduce an entirely new form of life. We invited the industry to join us in developing new products that focused on meeting consumer financial needs of the next one hundred years, not the last century.

The reaction was amazing! The *Wall Street Journal* and *New York Times* both did major stories announcing that ITT Life was challenging the industry by withdrawing the sale of whole life insurance. This was the company's first national exposure in the media. Within a few days, *USA Today* followed up with a feature story. We were energized. In a very short period of time, ITT Life became the darling of the media and consumer groups—not something that many insurance companies could claim.

My, My, Aren't We Being a Little Paranoid?

The reaction from life insurance industry stalwarts was not quite so warm and welcoming nor, for that matter, even civil. The first retort was to dismiss ITT Life as a small, insignificant company in the industry. The industry giants encouraged the media, consumers, and others to ignore ITT Life on the grounds that we were simply an insignificant industry malcontent. Next, the industry began a series of personal attacks aimed directly at me. I was shunned by industry leaders, expelled from industry associations, and eventually referred to as the "anti-Christ" of the life insurance industry. One guy suggested my actions were the result of some genetic defect. Really, it's true. They took it that seriously.

Mass Mutual Life Insurance Company arrogantly launched a national advertising campaign that declared, "When new products are good for you, we will offer them." It may be hard to believe, but Prudential actually tried to have universal life outlawed by state regulators. That's a little like trying to win a race by shooting all the other runners. The executives at The Hartford received more than a few calls from angry club friends telling them that they had to "get that crazy MacDonald under control." The reaction from the leaders of Hartford was to hide behind a commercial version of plausible deniability and wash their hands of me.

No Matter What, the Truth Hurts

There was one very significant and telling component missing in the life insurance industry's reaction to ITT Life and its attack on me personally. While the industry claimed we should not be doing what we were doing, they never said we were wrong. They argued among themselves that we should not be doing what we were doing—we were cheating on the rules of the industry—but they never charged that what we claimed was erroneous. Only that it should not be said! They knew we were telling the truth. They just didn't want us to tell the truth because it fractured the camaraderie of the industry. If ITT Life were allowed to get away with this type of approach, then who might be the next to try it? Even worse, will the industry itself have to change?

In his book *Unsafe at Any Speed* (1965), Ralph Nader claims that GM's Corvair was unsafe because of its design flaws. The auto industry was immediately up in arms and quickly attempted to portray Nader as not only wrong, but as a rabble-rousing interloper. They pooled their considerable resources to try to discredit him. But the one point to remember is that Nader was an industry outsider. He could be dismissed. Or at least the auto industry hoped so.

Or consider ecologist and author Rachel Carson who, in the 1960s, railed against the unrestricted use of pesticides, including DDT. Both Carson and her book, *Silent Spring,* were labeled by the chemical industry and government officials as "alarmist." But again, Carson was largely an outsider, having given up her post as an editor and writer for the U.S. Fish and Wildlife Service.

Can you image what would have happened if the president of American Motors had called a press conference and announced that the internal combustion engine was polluting the world's atmosphere with poisonous gases and that people, therefore, should not buy cars powered by them? Or suppose a senior officer of Monsanto or American Cyanamid publicly excoriated the chemicals industry of the 1960s for using DDT and other dangerous pesticides.

That is exactly what we did at ITT Life. We went against the rules as an industry insider. We said that whole life, the industry mainstay, was no longer consumer friendly and that we refused to sell it.

Certainly there had been critics of the insurance industry and its products. However, because the criticism always emanated from those outside the industry, the industry could easily dismiss the source as biased and ignorant. The real dilemma for the industry now was that the criticism was coming from someone who could not be so easily dismissed—the president of a life insurance company. The difficulty was further compounded by the fact that the criticism was true!

An Honest Confession

To be honest, I loved the reaction we received. Sure, it was an ego boost for me to think I could actually influence the industry, but the more the industry attacked the position of ITT Life, the more credibility we gained. If the industry had just ignored us, I doubt we would ever have exerted such influence. But such a visceral reaction made people take notice. Industry newspapers and magazines carried spirited polemics written by the top "old boy" execs lampooning our strategy.

We became the whipping post for a score of "industry observers," who had no better way to spend their time than to criticize what we were doing. They were so furious with our approach that they never took the time to realize we were not the problem; rather, we were attempting to find a solution to a problem that had existed for some time.

One incident in particular still brings a smile to my face. I received a letter from a fellow by the name of Barney Barnhill. He was the president of another insurance company. He wrote that I was wrong about whole life and to prove it, he was going to buy another whole life policy. To Barney's credit, and indicative of the type of quality guy he was, fifteen years later he came forward and said that I had been right all along—right to challenge a complacent industry and right to build ITT Life with a product that addressed the consumers' needs. (There is a quirk of fate in this little story. In 1982, when Barney criticized my position on whole life, he was president of North American Life and Casualty, which soon became Allianz Life. In 1999 I became president of Allianz Life after it had acquired LifeUSA.)

The irony is that some of the most severe attacks came from the bureaucrats of Hartford. As charter members of the insurance club, they were more concerned about getting in trouble with their friends than in the success we were achieving for the organization. Of course, our response, as with our other critics, was simply to ignore them.

But, a funny thing occurred while we were being ostracized by the rest of the industry. In less than five years, the small and insignificant company known as ITT Life became one of the best-known, fastest-growing, and most successful companies in the life insurance industry. Part of this was due to the constant publicity we received. Virtually every national publication and hundreds of local media outlets published favorable stories on ITT Life, and our challenge to industry tradition.

As a result, ITT Life became recognized as a company with a different message. For the first time, not all of the companies in the insurance industry were the same. Sure, we were still hated and despised by the industry's traditionalists, but we accomplished what we had set out to accomplish. We shaped a new environment where our success could be possible, fashioned a different marketing approach, and began writing quality, competitive products that addressed consumers' needs.

At the same time, ITT Life began to build a different kind of distribution system. Suddenly, agents who, just a few months prior, would not have been caught dead with an ITT Life rate book in their briefcases began to call and contract with ITT Life. They were out in the field every day trying to make a living selling a product that was becoming increasingly difficult to sell. Soon, ITT Life had thousands of agents telling our story and selling our new products.

The most encouraging reaction of all came from the consumer. Despite that fact that ITT Life was neither an industry giant nor a household name, consumers, who had been underestimated by the industry for years, were smart enough to know what they wanted and were willing to buy value when it was offered. Soon, sales and profits began to skyrocket. ITT Life became a leader in the life insurance industry—not for the power of our portfolio, but for the power of our ideas. It was a heady and rewarding time.

A Personal Epiphany—Cheat to Win Comes to Life

While the campaign was quite successful for both ITT Life and The Hartford, the impact this experience had on my life was utterly irreversible. What seemed like a simple, logical marketing plan ultimately provided me with a structure for my evolving *Cheat to Win* philosophy.

I learned from the experience with ITT Life that if you understand and study the rules, find them to be defective, and are able to develop alternatives, then you can be extremely successful. Most people are unwilling to question or to challenge rules openly. Yet only if you cheat on the rules openly can you have a chance to win. And if you are going to cheat to win, it is not enough to simply mock the rules. You've got to do more than merely challenge authority.

The guiding lesson I learned from my early experiences with ITT Life is that the only honest way to cheat to win is to offer an alternative—to be innovative and create an alternative to the rules that have become obsolete and irrelevant. It is one thing to proclaim that the Corvair is unsafe, but quite another to build an alternative car that is safer. It is one thing to say your "whole life" is a mistake; the key is to offer an alternative and to make it work.

And the Moral of the Story Is . . .

If you pick the right time and the right rules and you have the right plan, then cheating to win can be both a powerful and rewarding strategy for success. You do not have to be a Fortune 500 executive. You don't have to be a Harvard graduate. You don't have to have an MBA or huge stockpiles of money. All you really need is vision— not only to see things as they are, but as they could and, perhaps, should be. The path to victory lies in challenging and subsequently changing habits that are ineffective.

If you find rules that have become irrelevant or ineffective, then you *should* cheat on them. It's the mindset of Sam Walton when conventional wisdom held that nobody could compete with Sears. It's the outlook of Apple's Steve Jobs when the business world believed that the behemothic IBM mainframe was the wave of the future. It's the attitude of Fred Smith when he founded FedEx and made monkeys out of the naysayers who insisted that no one could compete with the U.S. Postal Service. What people did not understand was that Fred Smith was talking about *24-hour* delivery, not *24-day* delivery. Steve Jobs was talking about creating a computer for the *desktop,* not the warehouse.

When a rule needs to be broken, it takes a unique individual to step forward and break it, and an even rarer individual to replace it with a new and better rule. This is the essence of the *Cheat to Win* philosophy. We all have a choice. It's up to us to step forward to expose bad rules and write new ones that can make life better. Or we can become one of those millions of faceless people who "go with the flow," most of whom will someday look back and realize their "whole life" was a mistake.

4

Reminiscing about the Future

*If one uses their power to live in the future
as others live in the past, then the future
becomes as present as the past for all to see.*

Homo sapiens are the only living species to think about the future. In fact, we are so preoccupied with what might happen in the future, it could be called an obsession. A huge, billion-dollar industry feeds this obsession by purporting to offer a sneak preview of the future.

There are so many fortune tellers and palm readers plying their trade today that they should have their own registered lobbying group in Washington, D. C. No respectable newspaper in America goes to press without an astrology column. Psychics make millions with their own "psychic hotlines" and infomercials. More than a few presidents, kings, aristocrats, and dictators have sought out psychics, stars, or signs before making decisions that would impact millions. Hitler would not send reinforcements to Normandy until he consulted his personal psychic (who, by the way, was out of town, since he didn't know Hitler would need him). Nancy Reagan would not allow "Ronnie" to travel until the astrologer was consulted.

The desire to see into the future is not limited to the occult. There are hundreds of metrics to predict the future. The PSAT and SAT attempt to predict how well high school students will do in college. We have all taken aptitude tests that attempt to predict our career aptitude. Not to be outdone, otherwise serious-minded business people believe that the fastest and surest way to manage a company is to create a multiplicity of business plans based upon forecasts that attempt to prophesize the path the company will tread over the next one-, five-, or even ten-year spans.

Why are we so obsessed with the future?

Because, as inventor Charles Ketterling has suggested, we will have to spend the rest of our lives there. If we can discern what the future has in store for us, we can better prepare for it. We can take advantage of what the future holds for us—we'll know what decisions to make, what actions to take, and what course to follow.

Of course, the problem is that no matter how mystical or psychic we may be, no matter how much money we spend or how much we plan, it simply is not possible to predict the future. And despite all the wonderful things you might learn by reading this book, I can't predict the future for you, either.

But do you know what? Even if the future could be predicted, that may not be the best thing. Why? Well, if we can actually predict the future, then we are at the mercy of the future, good or bad. To seek a prediction of the future is actually an attempt to gain knowledge of something that is essentially beyond our control.

I have a better idea. It is a concept that may be even more worthwhile and powerful than the ability to predict the future. And that is the ability to *create* the future. When you think about it, isn't that what we all really want? We want the power to shape our own future and live our lives according to that fruitful vision, as opposed to being helpless victims of fate.

Getting Your Cheating Off to the Right Start

That's why a cheat-to-win philosophy starts, quite rightly, with creating an all-important vision of your future. It's your mental roadmap that funnels all of your physical and intellectual energies toward your single, all-important purpose. And by creating this vision, you improve your ability to concentrate, plan, and, in turn, to stay motivated until you achieve your vision.

Not only is the power to shape our future more valuable than the ability to foresee it, it's something we can all do. The rule says to use plans in order to try to predict the future. This is a rule to cheat on and, instead, use your powers to project the future. Rather than spending time and money on a fruitless attempt to predict the future, we should learn to nurture the capacity to "reminisce about the future." If we learn to reminisce about the future, we can achieve virtually anything.

How Do You "Reminisce about The Future"?

To reminisce about the future means to develop the ability to visualize the future *as if* it were the past. We already reminisce about the past. We visualize significant previous life events—graduation, marriage, the birth of a child—with a vision that allows us to see the past and almost relive it. We can even tell others about it and take them with us as we tell the story.

Now, think for a moment what it would be like to possess a form of intuitive reasoning that would enable us to reminisce about and visualize the future as clearly as we do the past. I mean drawing in our minds a picture of what we seek to achieve by this, so clearly, so distinctly, that it shapes our present reality to the point that it actually begins to take on the characteristics of our vision.

Skeptics will argue that that's the sort of pie-in-the-sky fantasy practiced by the Harry Potters of the world. The "rules" say that no one can possibly have the power to predict and actually influence the future. And the skeptics will be proven right, if we join the masses that nestle like couch potatoes to dream about the past and watch the true opportunities of life pass by like scenes on a TV sitcom.

I am not suggesting that we spend our time idly dreaming about the future. If we have a concrete vision of what we'd like the future to look like, our present actions will help us transform the vision into reality. Simply put, although it is not possible to see the future, it is possible to take actions that will allow us shape it.

A Case in Point

If you had visited my office after I was elected president of ITT Life, you would have seen a pyramid of twenty-one different business cards, all bearing the name Robert MacDonald, framed and hanging on the wall near my desk. Some who observed this carefully framed career history might have considered it nothing more than an executive ego trip. Kinda like the top dog has your attention and his wall hangings brag about his "meteoric" rise from rookie agent to company president. That wasn't my purpose at all. Rather, it was a symbol of something decidedly more important, and not unlike the purpose of a book I wrote some years back.

A few years before founding the company LifeUSA, I wrote *Control Your Future*, a book about achieving personal success in the insurance industry. Years later I was sitting in the office of David Carpenter, the president of Transamerica, discussing the success of LifeUSA. While Carpenter headed up a large, established company that was among the leaders of the insurance industry, he seemed fascinated with the rapid growth of LifeUSA. During the discussion, he casually said, "Mac, the first time I read your book I took it for simply a discussion about the life insurance industry. The second time I read it, I could see that you had painted the exact picture of LifeUSA as it is today. How did you know ten years ago what LifeUSA would be like today?"

The question was as good as my answer was simple. The business cards on the wall and the book about "how it should be done" were my way of cheating to win. All of those business cards had been saved because early in my career I had "reminisced" about how it would be to one day become president of a company. And that visualization was a guide, a roadmap if you will, that helped me realize my goal. The business cards mounted on the wall of my office served as a confirmation that the power of reminiscing about the future really does work.

I was motivated to write *Control Your Future* for the same reason. My real intent was to *visualize* how a successful insurance company should operate. The book served the same purpose as a filmmaker's storyboard creating rich images (visions others could see and understand) of the future LifeUSA and the success the company would achieve. With this type of tool in place, decisions become logical because they are measured against a specific mental picture of the objective. It is actually possible to work back from that vision to create the specific framework and activity that transforms vision into reality. Forget the predictions about the future that never happen; reminisce about the future and *make* it happen.

Defining Our Own Success

Both of these incidents, the business cards and writing the book, confirmed a long-held suspicion that all of us have a power that few of us use to our full advantage. And that power is the ability to create success as we define it, simply by reminiscing about the future. But defining success has never been easy.

Possibly the most abused word in the English language is "success." Everyone talks about success, but for too many people, success is a cliché-riddled idea that embodies power, fame, title, and money. True achievement cannot be measured in dollars in a bank account, plaques (or business cards) on your wall, cars you drive, or epitaphs chiseled in your gravestone. True success is not defined for us by others.

Success and winning are defined and achieved when we live life on our own terms, whatever they may be. Success is the ability to exercise the right and power to decide and control our own future. This kind of success can only be achieved when we have a crystal-clear vision burned into our psyche and work steadfastly toward turning the ephemeral image into a tangible victory. But to be in a position to achieve this goal, we have to be ready to cheat on the rules that tell us we can't reminisce about the future.

Winners Reminisce

All successful people habitually reminisce about the future. They have a vision that, when combined with experience, they use to build their futures. Jack Nicklaus, arguably golf's greatest player, was once asked the secret to his remarkable success. "It's simple," he said. "When I stand over a shot, I visualize exactly what's going to happen. And then I make it happen." Chris Evert, one of the world's greatest tennis players, is reputed to have once said, "I could see the ball hit the line *before* I hit it." Quarterbacks renowned for pulling out a victory in the last two minutes of a game—players like Joe Montana, John Elway, and Peyton Manning—have all have expressed the same idea. They describe an ability to see the field opening up before the snap of the ball, and visualize the play unfolding.

George Patton is remembered as one of the most successful fighting generals of all time. He seemed to have the uncanny ability to anticipate the actions of his foes. And it's no wonder. Patton was one of the great students of history. For years prior to World War II, he studied the battlefields of Europe and envisioned all the battles that had gone before and all that would come after. When queried about his success in battle, he said, "I see the battle before it happens. I've been there before." And of course, he had. He learned to reminisce about the future.

We Are All Winners

It's important to remember that all of us have been winners at one time or another. Each of us has a reservoir of successful experiences, a template that we can use as a guide. These experiences not only remind us of how we achieved success in the past, they lend texture to our visions of how success will feel in the future.

But the business world doesn't ask us to do that. It's sending the wrong message and leading us in the wrong direction. Modern business suggests that we'll achieve our goals only if we have drawn together a sufficient number of business plans, complicated proformas, and other financial planning busywork.

Poppycock!

How much time and money is wasted chasing the grandiose dreams of five-year corporate business plans? Have you ever seen a plan even come close to achieving one of these "forecasts"? Of course not—because these plans, even though they are among the proper rules of business management, attempt to predict the future, when what is needed is the vision to *make* the future.

Successful individuals, whether they are the mailroom intern or the CEO, share at least one thing in common—they have always carried a true vision of what they were trying to achieve. They know exactly how their personal vision of success looks and feels—even know what it smells like. Without such vision, all is lost. And all the business plans and corporate busywork in the world won't save your sorry behind. Here is a case in point.

Reminiscing about Capital

In 1987, we were negotiating with Transamerica Life Insurance Company to provide financing for the start-up of LifeUSA. Over several months and scores of meetings, we were slowly moving forward in the proposed partnership. I met with everyone who would see me, including the chairman of the company. I desperately wanted to tell our story and elicit the support of Transamerica.

Finally, after the idea had been presented to Transamerica's board of directors, I received the call we had been waiting for. The board had approved the recommendation of management to support LifeUSA, but with one condition. We had forgotten to submit a five-year business plan for the development of LifeUSA. This was hardly an accident. We simply didn't have a five-year business plan. However, it was clear that we would not receive funding from Transamerica until we translated our vision into a specific prediction of numbers. Our CFO promptly assembled a business plan, and we submitted it to Transamerica. Of course, we knew that set of numbers and forecast would never see the light of day again, but Transamerica was happy.

Is there a moral to the story? Only that outstanding results follow from a well-defined vision, not vague predictions and meaningless forecasts. Don't get the idea that I am against planning. I still abide by a valuable lesson I learned as a rookie life insurance agent in 1965: "Plan your work and work your plan!" However, it is important not to confuse the vision one builds by reminiscing about the future with a "forecast," which is what most business plans are.

The Lesson of ITT

The Transamerica episode surely added to my existing distrust of the rule that claimed you must have a formalized business plan in order to succeed. This doubt was hardened to steel during my years as president of ITT Life. Under the leadership of the legendary Harold Geneen, ITT, the far-flung "conglomerate" (a buzz word used to describe companies with many parts but no whole), developed a business planning and forecast system that could have put the Pentagon to shame with its detail and complexity.

Every year legions of financial people in the units of the ITT universe would spend months putting together the ongoing five-year business plan. Then, in early November, all of the ITT unit leaders would flock to New York for a show-and-tell. Each would be given their fifteen minutes of fame (shame) to predict the future. The presentations were required to focus on the "what-ifs" and numbers. Never was there any focus on an actual vision for the company. If strategic positioning was discussed at all, it was in the context of "peer group" comparisons, a nonproductive exercise companies seem to enjoy. (See chapter fifteen—Be Peerless in the Face of Peer Groups.) Discussions that revolved around an actual vision for the company were considered too "soft" to attract management interests.

So do you know what happened? We devoted tens of thousands of dollars and a jillion hours of manpower putting together business plans. Then we all trooped off to New York for the dog and pony show. Then, as expected, after all the handshaking and back-slapping was over, everyone would return home, put the plans on the shelf, and forget them—until the whole damnable process would start again the next year.

A Plan in Search of a Circular File

Traditional business plans are a waste of time, money, and effort—and a rule we should cheat on. Don't get me wrong. Sound business plans have their place. It is important to have an educated "guesstimation" of sales, revenues, expenses, and income; but recognize that they are nothing better than a guess. Business plans are best used for budget planning and measuring the progress of a company, but should not be relied on as a basis for predicting the future performance of a company.

At LifeUSA, our formula for developing business plans was very simple. First of all, if the plans submitted were more than two pages, they were too long. Each division or department would be asked to list ten operational priorities for the upcoming year. From that list, they would have to pick the five most important actions. From that list, they would indicate and "guarantee" which of those would be completed and implemented during the year. Once those items had been established, the leaders were then required to develop a plan for implementation and report the progress each month. In effect, this process forced managers to "reminisce about" the year ahead of them. They were not asked to predict results in the form of numbers, but rather performance in the form of implementing their vision.

We learned that when we became proficient at reminiscing about the future of the company, and were able to identify the actions and activities that would enable us to achieve the vision, then the activities necessary for success and the numbers fell neatly into place.

Achieving Specific Results

Reminiscing about the future is not limited to the broad schemes of corporate or personal planning. The concept can be a useful technique to produce some very specific results. One example is IT development.

The traditional approach for IT development calls for the user to meet with the IT business analyst and programmer to explain the requested new program. After a few meetings, the analyst and programmer would go off to develop the new IT service. Every once in a while the programmer would call the user to ask a few questions or offer a suggestion. Eventually, the project is completed and delivered. The problem is, more times than not, that the program delivered was a different animal from what the end user really wanted, or, worse, the requirements actually changed as the program was under development. The result is wasted time, effort, and expense for all concerned.

The reminisce-about-the-future approach to cheating on this rule is to reverse the process. Start in the future and work back to the present. Ask the end user to spell out a clear vision of what they expect to accomplish with the new program. To do this, the user would be forced to develop and produce the exact output reports they expected to receive. If the user could not do this simple act, then they probably did not know what they wanted. If the user could not actually create the "report" they sought to receive, then it was obvious that they didn't have a specific vision for a solution to the problem, if indeed they really had a problem.

By forcing the user to clearly and concretely outline their vision for the project, they provided a specific guideline for the technical people to follow and a basis for measurement as the project progressed. By applying the concept of reminiscing about the future to cheat on the traditional rules of IT development, the company was able to develop more efficient programs faster and with significantly less cost than they otherwise would have using the conventional approach.

What Reminiscing Isn't

Reminiscing about the future should never be confused with forecasting, dreaming, or planning. Forecasting is an effort to predict what will happen in the future, like picking the winner of the Super Bowl three years from now or predicting what sales volumes for a company will be three years from now. Dreaming is a naive hope for something to happen in the future—such as being happy, achieving riches or success. Planning is compiling a list of specific actions to take in an effort to achieve a stated objective.

Reminiscing about the future encompasses none of these ideas. There is nothing soft or mystical involved with reminiscing about the future. Reminiscing about the future is, in fact, a hard, serious, effective management technique that is made more effective because so few cheat on time-honored rules and actually practice it. Dreams are what others wallow in while you move toward your goal.

Making Reminiscing about the Future Work

To reminisce about the future, we use the sum power of our experiences, creativity, imagination, desire, and commitment to create a simple, specific, realistic mental image of what it is we seek to achieve. My vision to become the president of a company by age forty or to build a new life insurance company that could compete with the industry giants are examples of reminiscing about the future. The key is to make sure the "reminisce" is specific, attainable, and focused. Once the future has been visualized, decisions regarding planning and forecasting are much easier and more realistic.

It is surprising that this technique is not used more often, since the law of imagination is now recognized as a universal principle by those who study successful people. The mental images and ideas we hold in our mind tend to manifest the physical reality to which the images correspond. A human being tends to act in accordance with the mental images of the future that she or he holds. "The imagination," according to motivational author Napoleon Hill, "is literally the workshop wherein are fashioned all plans created by man. The impulse, the desire, is given shape, form and action through the aid of the imagination faculty of the mind."

Before we achieve something worthwhile, we must first have an image of it already alive in our thinking—our reminiscing. Once the image or the specific inspiration of the future has been created, then we have installed the guide for transforming the vision to reality. What's more, our brain has the power to do this automatically. When we reminisce, our brains will automatically provide us with the specific actions necessary to make the vision a reality, much like a guided missile seeks its target.

There is evidence of this everywhere. When we have an idea—when we reminisce about the future—our minds cannot help churning out ideas and actions to turn that vision into reality. In short, if we can reminisce about our future, we can successfully *program* our future.

Reminiscing with Desire Wins the Day

Passively reminiscing about the future is not enough, however. Hundreds of golfers practice more than Nicklaus. Scores of failed generals have read books before a battle. Obviously, to reminisce about the future effectively, there must be more. There has to be a true deep-seated desire to, as Nicklaus said, "make it happen!"

Winners have profited from this technique time and again and many books have offered further proof of its effectiveness. In the best-selling book *Psycho Cybernetics*, Maxwell Maltz recounts the miracles that many men and women have experienced by achieving success through reminiscing. Maltz offers empirical evidence that reminiscing will fan the flames of your desire, fortifying your will with new determination and resoluteness. These visions, rich with desire-supporting emotions, become, in effect, synthetic experience, new "tapes," if you will, that you can replay again and again when your focus needs to be sharpened.

And the Moral of the Story Is . . .

The fastest, surest way to achieve your goals, whatever they may be, is to learn to reminisce about the future. Through this simple yet powerful strategy, you can visualize your future and then, working back to your present state of affairs, develop the plans and programs to make your vision come true. This principle works because, when you reminisce about the future, your mind automatically begins to produce the reality of your vision. And the more you concentrate on your vision, the more motivation and willpower you develop to achieve it.

Every person reading this book has access to powers that will allow them to peer into their future. Your future need not just happen. It can be made. And if someone is going to make your future, shouldn't it be you? You don't have to be a famous or special person to achieve the power to reminisce about the future. You can become famous and special, if that is your choice. And there is no better time to start than now.

The world is changing rapidly and dramatically. The business world and the attitudes of consumers, employees, the government and society are in a state of flux. Accordingly, the opportunity for a new brand of success is available in this country, but it's going to take a special type of person to recognize and take advantage of it. In order to be successful, you must be willing to think and act differently than most. You've got to forget about the past and liberate yourself from the tethers of previous defeats.

You cannot allow yourself to be constrained by the ideas and attitudes—*the rules*—imposed on us by others. Like the novelist who is only successful when life is examined from more than one perspective, success will never be achieved if we allow our approach to a career or, for that matter, life, to be one-dimensional, especially when that one dimension is prescribed by others.

As you go through life, there is one gauge you can use to measure how you are doing. It is a simple question: Do I feel comfortable? If your answer is yes, then you are probably not following your true path to success. That warm sense of comfort is generally the body temperature at the center of the crowd. And—make no mistake—it is the crowd that will ultimately suffocate your dreams.

Start today and have the audacity to write your own rules and create your own vision of the future. As someone once said, "Failure is the curse of complacency, but success is the child of audacity." Remember, he who dares, wins!

If you want to fashion tomorrow in your image, you must be careful not to let the agenda of others dominate you and your thoughts, and thus confine your visions. Frame concrete, specific choices. Make sure that your vision is realistic and clearly focused. The future belongs to those who get there first! By learning to reminisce about the future, you can be the one waiting there when the rest arrive.

Once the vision is in place, you can set about making all manner of *Cheat to Win* changes in your business and personal life. And it starts with what may be the most important principle you'll learn in this book: the miracle of parallel interests. This strategy can transform your every reminiscence into reality.

5

The Perspective of Parallel

People who have the ability to add value to your efforts will be encouraged to do so if they are allowed to share in the value created.

Have you ever noticed how astrologers always coach their "clients" to take important actions only "when the stars are aligned?" Dreaded things happen when the planets are not in proper alignment. Astrologers use this approach because they are playing to a fundamental law of nature. This natural law dictates that events and activities aligned in parallel are more powerful and effective than those that are divergent or conflicting.

It's natural. Horses to a wagon or dogs to a sled are harnessed in parallel so their power can be combined into a single, dynamic force. A football team may have eleven individuals on the field at the same time, each with different talents and assignments, but the team will only be successful if all eleven work in parallel to achieve a common goal. The wheels of a car are aligned in parallel for efficient operation. When one wheel is out of alignment, the car becomes difficult to control and inefficient, if not dangerous.

Humans are impacted by this law of parallel as well. As the least solitary species of all in existence, we are driven to associate, relate, and cohabit with one another. We join clubs, fraternities, sororities, churches, and just about any organization we can find because there is strength in greater numbers united by a common cause. Despite strong personal egos, most of us desire to be accepted, to belong, and to feel we are part of something larger than ourselves. We are more comfortable when we are *with* something as opposed to being *against* something. The bottom line is that we are happy when we associate with others who have interests we can relate to, interests that are *parallel* to our own.

If It Works, Why Ignore It?

While few argue with the natural law that things go better in parallel, there is one area where this principle is not only ignored, it is often scoffed at. For some reason, in business there seems to be a rule that says things go better with conflict.

Employer-employee, management-shareholder, seller-buyer, and vendor relations all seem to be based on the rule that getting what we want is best achieved by actions based on divergent interests and conflicting objectives. Too many approach relationships or business negotiations with an attitude of, "What is mine is mine and what is yours should be mine." Businesses seem to adopt a strategy of exploiting divergent interests and working in conflict as the way to win. This approach is counterproductive and simply wrong.

How parallel were the interests of management and workers in the sweatshops of the early industrial revolution? Violent strikes and the rise of labor unions in the 1920s were the obvious result of conflicting, not parallel, interests. It's the appearance of conflicting interests that causes customers to distrust companies. Were the problems of Enron, Adelphia, Tyco, WorldCom, and other rogue companies the result of parallel or divergent interests? Would these problems have been prevented if the interests of all stakeholders had been in parallel? Why is "jungle" a popular synonym for the world of business? And why do people accept that, in business relationships, "the law of the jungle" should prevail?

The reason is simple—stupid, but simple. There is a set of traditional business rules that dictate the proper course of action in relationships is to gain leverage and take advantage of a situation whenever possible. Many corporate cultures foster competition between employees, seek leverage with vendors, and opportunistically exploit advantages at the expense of customers. There is no doubt that the practice of gaining leverage and taking advantage of opportunities has its proper place. My complaint is with the traditional technique of achieving this objective at the expense of, rather than in unison with, the interests of others. It's a rule we should cheat on all the time.

Success in business should not be achieved by stepping on, over, or going through people, but by aligning our interests with theirs in parallel. Follow this one simple philosophy, and it will lead to the instinctive ability to build on the natural power of parallel relationships: *People who have the ability to add value to your efforts will be encouraged to do so if they are allowed to share in the value created.*

I know this is a straightforward, basic, and maybe even mundane philosophy, but it works. You've heard the expression, "You can accomplish a great deal, so long as you are willing to share the credit." By aligning parallel interests, the individual interests of many are powerfully directed toward the welfare of the whole. For example, if employees stand to gain personal benefit from the success of the company (beyond simply keeping their job), it stands to reason they will contribute more toward the success of the company.

Unfortunately, this is not the prevailing attitude in business today. Too often, company management acts in a way that suggests the interests of the employees are at odds with the interests of the company. However, when parallel interests are established, the company and employees are joined together like links in a cooperative chain—all sharing and working together toward a common goal. The same philosophy should be applied to relationships with the distribution system, customers, suppliers, and shareholders.

If you cheat on the traditional practice of fomenting conflictive relationships and make it your objective to align parallel interests in both your personal and business dealings, then you will achieve power and success far greater than those individuals who define relationships within the context of a power-and-control dynamic.

Parallel in Action

LifeUSA's success is a good example of the power of parallel interest. In 198, LifeUSA was a new company in a mature, slow-growth industry dominated by century-old financial giants. With no "silver bullet" such as a unique new product, a dramatic leap in technology, or a deep financial base, the very idea of starting a company such as LifeUSA violated all the rules. Few gave LifeUSA much of a chance to survive, never mind achieve success.

Yet, as old-line insurance companies suffered from declining sales, reduced profits, and shrinking value, LifeUSA established itself as one of the fastest-growing, most successful, and talked-about companies in the insurance industry. What was the secret to the success of LifeUSA? There are many reasons why the company survived, but the secret weapon for the company's success was the philosophy of parallel interests.

Taking advantage of the law of parallel interests gave LifeUSA an incredible leg up on its competitors and it was an advantage that no other company shared. The core concept was to build true parallel interests with all stakeholders of the company. These included employees, agents, customers, vendors, financial backers, reinsurance companies, and shareholders. Fostering a culture alive with true parallel interests marshaled the inherent powers of each distinct group to achieve a single purpose—the shared success of LifeUSA.

The heart of a parallel interest culture is predicated on equality. The goal was for employees and agents representing the company to have a vested interest in its success, beyond simply keeping their job. To accomplish this objective, employees were required to allocate 10 percent of their gross, pretax income to purchase stock in LifeUSA. This was not a choice or an option, but a requirement for those who wanted to work with LifeUSA.

The employee ownership participation was not in the form of stock options, restricted stock grants, phantom stock, or employee stock ownership plans (ESOPs). No freebies here. The employees were required to purchase, with their own hard-earned money, actual stock in LifeUSA. Employees purchased the same class of stock at the same price as the management of the company. This structure placed all of us in parallel, causing all of us to want the same thing: for our stake in the company to grow and multiply.

Our employees were not mere passengers on the LifeUSA ship of fate; they were partners in every sense of the word. They could affect the outcome of their investment by their hard work. This unique dynamic created the purest form of parallel interests. At LifeUSA, employees had their own money on the line and truly understood the concept of ownership. The bottom line was that employees were taking a significant risk that would only be rewarded if LifeUSA became successful.

This is the essence of the parallel interest concept: to share *both* risk and reward among all players. This concept is at the cornerstone of the cheat-to-win strategy, the key motivator that serves as the mainspring to the whole process.

Keeping Parallel in Parallel

A critical aspect of maintaining parallel interests is to make sure that the model becomes a way of life and not just a gimmick. If it doesn't come from your heart, it just won't work.

Northwest Airlines is a perfect example of what happens when you're disingenuous about parallel interests. In the 1990s, Northwest Airlines was buffeted by rising costs and plummeting net income, not an unusual phenomenon in the airline industry. Even after a series of bandages, like cutting employee salaries, the company was headed pell-mell toward bankruptcy. As a final desperate action, Northwest Airlines turned to an employee stock ownership plan.

The concept was sound, but the implementation was guileful and insincere. It was doomed to fail from the beginning. Why? Because management brought the employees in as "owners" of the company not because they thought it was the right thing to do, but because they had no other choice. Accordingly, employees were never truly perceived or treated as owners of the company, so they never acted like it, either. The plan never bore the fruitful abundance that parallel interest offers, and the airline continued to struggle.

If stock ownership, options, or other such plans are to build successful parallel interests, there must be a sincere and heartfelt desire to create the reality of parallel interests, rather than the mere perception. Management must recognize and respect employees as both employees and owners of the company. Likewise, employees need to understand they have two roles with a company—as an employee performing a specific task and as owners participating in the overall performance of the company.

Spreading the Gospel of Parallel Interests

Because the concept of parallel interests and employee stock ownership is so foreign to most people, LifeUSA worked very hard to promote the concept. I have to admit we stole a page from *The Communist Manifesto* to make this brand of capitalism work. The word "owner" was used the way Communists used "comrade" and for much the same reason: we wanted to remind our partners constantly of their ownership and rightful position within our corporate culture.

When employees entered the parking lot each morning, they pulled up to signs that read "LifeUSA Owner Parking Only." Employees walked into the building through a door marked "LifeUSA Owner Entrance." When they picked up their coffee mug it read "I am a LifeUSA Owner." The personnel department was not called, "Human Resources" (a term I loathe even more than "comrade"), but rather "Owner Services." When meetings were called, they were "Owner Meetings." I think you get the idea. It is one thing to talk about parallel interests; it is another thing to *live* the concept.

Equity, Not Equality

It's vital to understand that using stock to cultivate a parallel relationship with employees offers the benefits of ownership, but not the right to run the company. Nor is it a requirement that the benefits received from parallel interests must be equal. However, they must be equitable. At LifeUSA, not everyone owned the same amount of stock, but that was okay because everyone acquired it the same way—by buying individual shares at the *same price* as everyone else.

Owners were entitled to share in the value of the company, receive information about their investment, and have a say in how the company was managed, but not to manage the company. It would be a mistake to confuse parallel interests with egalitarian democracy, equality, or the brotherhood of the mob. Like the football team with eleven different players with eleven different talents, playing 11 different positions, there still needs to be someone who calls the plays and provides the leadership.

I may have had more LifeUSA stock than anyone else, but, like everyone else in the company, I purchased my shares, rather than acquiring them through stock options or other grants. Our employee stock ownership plan was equitable because everyone had the same class of stock, and—most important—no group could benefit unless all benefited.

The Great Payoff of Parallel Interests

Using parallel interest as a basis for LifeUSA's corporate culture created the dynamic environment in which what was good for the company was also good for the employee. Likewise, what was good for the employee was good for management and, in turn, the company as a whole. Instead of employees feeling as though they had just a "job," they felt as if they owned their job.

The people of LifeUSA viewed themselves more as capitalists than captives—timecards and punch clocks were not needed. Time and again, the employees of LifeUSA proved that people take better care of what they own than what they rent. Chances are that if I arrived at the office after 7 A.M. it would be difficult to find a parking place. Not to be irreverent, but some compared the LifeUSA experience of parallel interests to the religious experience of being "born again." Once baptized in the concept of ownership and parallel interests, it consumed you. If a little effort was rewarded, then more effort meant greater rewards. If computers crashed or work backed up, there was no need to request extra effort; employees instinctively put their shoulders to the wheel.

Recruiting Became Infinitely Easier

No corporate manager needs to be told how employee turnover can devastate net earnings. It is not unusual for some companies to have 10, 20, and even 30 percent annual turnover of employees. And when you realize that the loss of each employee can be valued at approximately 150 percent of their wage or salary, you're talking huge dollars in lost productivity, new employee training, and a host of other exorbitances.

LifeUSA had no such problem. The LifeUSA culture was self-perpetuating in that we rarely had to recruit for new employees. Existing owners almost fought with each other to see who could bring in more of their friends, relatives, and even spouses looking to join the LifeUSA team. Today, many children of the first generation of owners are working at the company. The turnover rate was usually less than 2 to 3 percent, and most of that was because one spouse moved outside the area for another job.

Ownership Is Not for Everyone

As effective as the LifeUSA system of creating parallel interests may have been, it was not perfect. Not everyone subscribed to the concept of parallel interests through ownership, but it was interesting to observe how the culture responded to those who missed the point. Rarely did management have to counsel or chide an employee for not working hard. Believe it or not, the culture of employee-owners was much better at that task.

The owners developed a type of self-policing or cleansing of their culture. Much like the way our body rejects foreign tissues and organs, the LifeUSA body politic would purge itself of counterproductive employees. The owners adopted the attitude of, "I'm working my tail off to make this thing work for all of us. If you're not willing to do the same, you better find work elsewhere."

When confronted with the company's "can do" culture, complacent employees were forced to either participate or leave. Sadly, many of those employees who left the company later came to understand the intrinsic value of the parallel perspective when they joined companies without such a culture.

Taking Stock Is Not the Only Way

There's no doubt that stock ownership is a powerful way to create parallel interests between a company and its employees, but it's not the only way. The stock ownership plan was simply one manifestation of a broad management philosophy of shared interests. Even if it is not practical to share actual ownership of the company with employees, it is possible, in any size company, to create the feeling of ownership by fostering the concept of parallel interests.

The key is for the employee to feel in parallel and not in conflict with the interests of the company. There are a number of ways to achieve this result. Parallel interest strategies such as compensation, performance bonuses, communication, participation, recognition, and respect for the value of the employee can all be used to communicate (or kill) the concept of parallel interests. Chapter fourteen, Hothouse for Humanity, will illustrate some of these strategies for building parallel interests in an entrepreneurial organization.

Pay for Performance

Employee compensation is an effective way to promote parallel interests. However, sometime in the foggy history of corporate governance, an obscure management guru specializing in the esoteric study of corporate time in motion came up with the rule on compensation philosophy, now in place at virtually every major company in America. The rule is: Employees should be paid for the value of the job, not the worth of the employee.

That's a rule that ought to be broken.

The rule relies on the use of grade and time levels of compensation. The federal government is the poster child for this foggy bit of regimentation, which should tell you a great deal about its effectiveness. In government service, your public relations job, for example, is a Public Information Specialist G-1035-14. Or if you're a doctor, you are labeled as a Supervisory Medical Officer GS-602-15. It's no wonder the government pays $300 for a screwdriver and a week's pay for a toilet seat.

The underlying idea is to place a range of value on the job based upon how long the employee has been in the position and the value assigned to the position by some geeky human resources consultant. No matter the extent of real value an employee may add to an organization—all employees are compensated at a predetermined value for the job, not the value added by the individual. In addition, once the employee reaches the top of the scale, they are blocked from any future increase in compensation in that job.

Is this dumb or what? Think about it. If an employee has been with the company long enough to reach the top of their "pay grade," isn't it logical to assume this person knows the job better than anyone else in the company? And that the experience of this individual may be adding significantly more value than other employees in the same job? Yet, to receive an increase in compensation (other than cost of living increases), this employee must resign and move to a new job. Sure, it may be a job that pays more money, but one in which the employee has little experience and can add less value. What sense does that make for a company? Wouldn't these employees be more inclined to work hard if they were being paid for the value added by their experience rather than just time in grade?

Adding Parallel to Your Shop

LifeUSA developed a pay-grade system that established certain ranges based on the minimum expectations for the job. If someone did the job but little more, simply went through the motions, so to speak, they received the basic wage. However, another factor to the compensation system was to measure and pay for *extra value* brought to the job by a talented person doing more than was expected to add company value. And this extra value had no maximum level.

The result was that two employees slotted in the same job for the same amount of time could be paid significantly different levels of pay. The theory was simple—if one person brought experience to the job, made twice the effort of those doing the minimum levels, and offered greater productivity, then it was equitable to pay them more. I will not claim that this system was easy to implement, but the employees appreciated the incentive and the company benefited from it.

In general, employees fared far better when they hung on to their job and added value, rather than job-hopping for higher wages. The employee learned that hard work and added value would be recognized and rewarded. In the end, the company received exceptional effort. This approach put the employee and the company in a parallel position—and was more efficient and less expensive than the traditional system.

The Trickle-Up Theory of Bonuses

Once LifeUSA became a publicly traded company, it was more difficult to use stock as a way to create parallel interests. In its place, a bonus plan was designed to accomplish the same objective.

Implementing this bonus system required us to cheat on a couple of established corporate compensation rules. Instead of starting at the top of the organization and allowing financial perks to (maybe) trickle down, the LifeUSA bonuses started at the bottom of the organization and worked their way to the top. Instead of the CEO being the first person to receive a bonus, he was awarded a bonus only after everyone else had received one. And, equally as important, the CEO bonus was a factor of bonuses received by other employees.

The LifeUSA bonus plan was also unique in that it was not one single plan for the entire organization, but rather specific "niche" plans structured to the peculiar activity of each division. The standard corporate bonus plan is based on the company achieving certain sales, profits, or stock price levels. These may be effective measurements for the senior management of a company, but not very effective for the vast majority of employees who find it difficult to measure their impact on the profits of an organization.

By isolating specific activities that, when pooled together, created discernible value for the company, each division created their own "bonus pool." At the end of the year, this bonus pool was distributed among all members of the division, based on the value of their contribution.

To illustrate the concept, when trying to build the securities division of LifeUSA, a bonus plan was designed to encourage and reward specific activities that ultimately would increase the value of the division. These were simple but concrete measurements that everyone could understand and affect. For example, for every registered representative recruited to the company, $25 would go into the bonus pool. When a new registered rep produced the first piece of business, $50 was added to the bonus pool. For each $100,000 of business produced by a rep, $100 was put in the pool. These factors would then be balanced with control of expenses, so that if 1,000 reps were recruited, but expenses exceeded budget, then the bonus pool was reduced by a specific factor. By the same token, if there was record recruiting activity, but expenses were below budget, the bonus pool was increased by another factor.

The idea of this type of bonus is to communicate directly to employees that their activities are inextricably related to *enhancing the value* of the company and that their extra efforts will benefit both the company and themselves *directly*. Everyone was able to relate to this parallel interests system of compensation.

With this program in place, when a potential rep called for information, they were never seen as a "nuisance" to the person taking the call, but rather an *opportunity* to add to the bonus pool. With the potential to make money when a new rep submits business or when an established rep writes more business, employees are motivated to fight for that business.

The important point is that parallel interest plans such as these can be instituted in companies of any size. The critical element is that the plan be effectively communicated, fully understood, and structured so that employees feel they have direct power to influence results. Most important, the plan must be equitable.

Does Any of This Parallel Stuff Work?

The concept of parallel interests worked wonders at LifeUSA, thrusting a young upstart in a highly competitive industry to a position of superiority in just a decade. And while the concept of parallel interests has fallen on deaf ears in many corporate environments, savvy management teams are slowly catching on. A recent study by Columbia University, for example, demonstrated that companies that share profits and gains with employees have significantly better financial performance than those that don't. Unfortunately, there are still too many companies that don't understand or accept the concept and continue to follow the traditional system designed, to give the most to those who already have the most.

I know of one fast-growing company led by a young, talented, and aggressive management team. Shortly after a successful initial public offering, management was pushing for a way to stimulate incentives and tie employees to the growth of the company. In essence, the objective was to align the employees' interests in parallel with those of the company. Unfortunately, the senior management of the company missed a golden opportunity to add an element of parallel interests across the board to all employees.

The proposed plan was to grant a block of "restricted stock" to certain employees. The employees would then vest in the ownership of the stock based on certain performance objectives established by the board. Incentive plans using performance targets that can be arbitrarily moved (like the strike price for stock options) to set qualifications for bonuses are a recipe for trouble, but the concept of restricted stock can be an effective tool in creating parallel interests.

However, the value and effectiveness of this particular plan were undermined from the onset by its flawed structure. Not only were the grants limited to only the higher echelons of management, but even this group was stratified by the percentage of grant received. The top two officers of the company received a grant equal to 100 percent of their salary, the next group 50 percent, and the bottom third received stock grants equal to 25 percent of their salary.

Everyone else in the company received no incentive to put forth the extra effort needed to drive the company's profitability. This approach is far from being equitable, let alone in parallel.

The CEO and the CFO are exceptionally talented and motivated to see the company grow because they have a vested interest in the success of the company. But they can't do it alone and, with a plan like this, they may have to. There is no incentive for most of the company's employees to go the extra mile to add value because they don't get to share in that value. Even those in management who participate in the program are not in parallel with the top two executives, because the grants are not equitable. It is sometimes necessary to limit the participants, but, at the very least, it is important to keep the plan equitable for those who are participating; this is easily accomplished when all stock grants are based on the same percentage of salary.

Yes, I have heard the argument that these programs are too expensive to include everyone. Well, if that is the case, then find one that is not too expensive to include everyone! I don't argue for equality but for equity. If everyone in an organization is directed toward the same objective, the ultimate reward is greater for all involved.

The point of all this is that with a little effort, creativity, and willingness to cheat on the traditional rules of corporate management and compensation, you can build a powerful culture that is in parallel with the objectives of your organization.

Getting Customers in Parallel

Still another way to build parallel interests is in the relationship with customers. Companies often give lip-service attention to customers' product needs and to providing excellent service, but few are willing to align themselves in a true parallel relationship with their customers. Lines not in parallel will eventually diverge or intersect. Either way, this will create distance or conflict between the best interests of the company and those of the customer.

We often hear about such conflicts of interest in the news. When the CEOs of seven major tobacco companies told a congressional hearing that "nicotine is not addictive," they were not only belying established medical fact, they were encouraging their customers to commit suicide on the installment plan—not a real parallel interest. When another said, "We don't smoke the crap. We just sell it. We reserve the right to smoke for the young, the poor, the blacks and the stupid," it is not difficult to espy a lack of parallel interests.

In most businesses, once the initial sales transaction is complete, there is little incentive for continued contact. The widget is sold, the customer takes it home, and the profit is booked. In fact, continued contact with the consumer can actually cost the company money and reduce profits. In the life insurance business, however, the company actually loses money in the first few years after the policy is sold, so the company can only recover the initial costs and make a profit if the policy is kept in force for a number of years.

The longer a policy is in force, the more profit the insurance company makes. Aware of this, LifeUSA designed products that rewarded those policyholders who purchased policies and then held them for a number of years. The longer the policyholder held the policy, the greater the benefit and reward offered by the policy. By contrast, those who purchased a policy and kept it for a short period of time were penalized with lower values in their policies. This type of policy structure aligned the interests of both the policyholder and the company in parallel. What benefited one party also benefited the other.

This approach may seem logical, but believe it or not, most insurance companies at the time designed policies to function in exactly the opposite manner. Illogically, many policies were designed to reward short-term policyholders more than long-term holders. This approach sent the wrong message to policyholders, and the result was a conflicted relationship between the company and the policyholder. With products structured in this manner, is it any wonder companies suffered?

Why would the companies be so stupid and act against their own best interests? Well, no one has ever accused the insurance industry of attracting the best and brightest of business leaders, but even an insurance guy should be able to recognize when the odds are being stacked against them. The real reason insurance companies—as with other companies in many industries—were willing to accept this is because, at least in the short term, it's sometimes easier to do the wrong thing than the right thing.

Insurance companies were having a difficult time selling their traditional products, which had become largely obsolete. To compensate for this, they attempted to make their products more attractive by moving the benefits to the front end of the policy. While short-term sales increased, the ultimate effect was to double the losses for the companies when customers cashed in their policies after only a few years.

This is what happens when the interests of all parties are not aligned. The result? The customer is encouraged to take action that conflicts with the best interests of the company, and the product they're buying does not fully meet their needs. The managers of the company have no incentive to remedy the situation because there is no incentive plan in place to align their interests with those of the company. The best hope for most of the insurance executives who took this path was that they would be long into retirement before the true results of their actions became apparent.

At LifeUSA, management and employees were bound together by a concept of shared ownership—parallel interests—and there was no incentive for anyone to take actions that would undermine the long-term profitability of the company. This point was dramatically brought home to me when one of the owner/employees who was charged with underwriting and approving new policies said to me, "Mac, I'm really in the middle here. As an employee of LifeUSA, I want to get the policy issued so we have more premium income but, as an owner and shareholder, I don't want to issue what may turn out to be unprofitable business."

Not many companies have employees who are just as concerned about the welfare of the company as they are with their own. That is the "double benefit" of being in parallel. All interests are aligned for the benefit of all—the customer, management, employees, agents, and shareholders.

And the Moral of the Story Is . . .

I am absolutely convinced that in today's highly competitive world—filled with well-educated employees and savvy consumers—the secret to achieving lasting success is a conscious, conscientious effort to cheat on traditional rules of leverage and conflicting interests and replace them with the concept of parallel interests.

Regardless of whom you are dealing with, whether the subject is personal or professional, you should approach every business relationship with the objective to "get in parallel." Whether it is managing a company, division, job interview, promotion, pay raise, or acquisition, your chances of winning are virtually assured when you ensure that the other party wins when you do. By using the benchmark of "Is this in parallel?" you will develop a natural inclination to cheat on outmoded business rules and your stars will always be aligned—even without the help of your own friendly astrologer.

6

Taming the Bureaucracy

*The danger inherent within a bureaucratic culture is
that failure is not identified and risk is not rewarded.*

The **principle** of parallel interests, as effective as it is, runs hard aground when submerged in a bureaucratic organization, whether large or small. The perception of bureaucracy usually brings to mind an organization with an institutionalized set of cumbersome rules that dictate employee behavior and company procedures. Often these rules and regulations are embodied in employee handbooks and operating procedure manuals. However they come about or are communicated, the objective is to ensure that employees follow company procedures in a uniform way.

Do such rules work? Of course they do, otherwise we wouldn't have them. And when business procedures work, they help coordinate the forces of many different departments together into one, unified, dynamic whole. But there is a downside. When rules are obeyed simply out of tradition—without ever asking *why?* — they often evolve into an endless river of paperwork that can clog the system and make life difficult for all employees. This is particularly so for the creative, entrepreneurial types who are inclined to take the very actions that make an organization better.

Enter the "bureaucratic quagmire," which is a prodigious nightmare of initially well-intended rules that hamstring employees and suppress creativity, causing detrimental results. Once given the opening, rules spread like a spiderweb of restrictions to trap the spirit of the organization in a way that ultimately causes slow death to new ideas, innovative actions, and the excitement of growth. Incarceration by rules may provide security and protect against risk, but it also suffocates the vitality of change.

The federal government is obviously the poster child for this kind of senseless bureaucracy. How bad is it? Consider this: The Ten Commandments endorses morality in a mere 297 words. The Bill of Rights is postulated in 463 words. Lincoln's Gettysburg Address touched the masses with only 266 words. A recent federal directive to regulate the price of cabbage contains 26,911 words. It's this kind of bureaucracy that produces those $300 screwdrivers and pricey toilet seats. I rest my case.

The Mac Renaissance

It took me a while to understand bureaucracies and their devastating effect on productivity. But as bad as governmental officialdom can be, there is another type of bureaucracy that is equally, if not more, pernicious.

Such an environment runs counter to everything discussed in the chapter on parallel interests and is created when the organizational culture is founded on the "mentality" of bureaucracy. A bureaucratic state of corporate mind arises when businesses develop a proclivity to punish failure, while failing to reward success. Such a cultural bent saps an organization's strength and vitality because it enmeshes employees in an ever-widening net, like a domino theory gone bad (to mix a metaphor). One by one, the key elements that bolster employee productivity are bridled, including:

- Accountability
- Responsibility
- Reward for accomplishment
- Sense of urgency

Bureaucracy As Thick As the Mind Can Create

This kind of bureaucracy exists to some degree in nearly all businesses. And the more tangled in bureaucracy a company becomes, the greater its loss in productivity and, therefore, its potential for profitability and success.

It starts as the consequences for individual action begin to move out of balance. When accountability is neither identified by management nor embraced by the employee, and the fear of failure overpowers the reward for success, then the organization is wandering down a path that leads to a paralysis of analysis. In such an environment no one will assume the ownership risk of an action because there is no reward of equal value. As true accountability vanishes from an organization, decision making becomes constipated through the body culture, leading to missed opportunities and ultimate failure.

Allow me to clarify the concept of reward in an organization. Most assume that when "reward" is mentioned in the context of an organization that it only refers to financial incentive. While pecuniary reward is important and valued, it is not the only type of recognition that will motivate an employee to add value to an organization. Action as simple as giving the employee appropriate credit for a good idea, or recognizing employees in front of their peers for the work they do, can provide incentive to add value. The important element to reward is recognition—in an equitable fashion—for the value contributed by the employee.

Of course, most businesses purport to have some sort of "employee review" procedure that periodically provides the working crew with "accountability" and critical feedback on their performance, but as the bureaucracy grows so does a lack of credibility for this exercise. This sort of activity has always given me a bad feeling because it takes me back to the report cards I would get in school. (I tried to convince my parents that all the "Ds" stood for "dedicated.") All too often, these performance reviews become perfunctory bureaucratic acrobatics designed to protect the legal rights of the company, rather than promote creative behavior.

It's not that I am against management or guidelines for activity, but that's only half the apple. The problem is that when leaders abdicate the management of the company to the rules, then a fertile environment for the cancerous growth of bureaucracy is created— and that eventually eats the life out of the organization.

Controlled Anarchy for All

Leaders should cheat on the traditional rules of creating rules and eliminate most rules altogether. The rule should be, "We have no rules!"

But don't get me wrong: anarchy and mayhem may be apt descriptions for my golf game, but not for my management beliefs. A competitor once offered an excellent backhanded compliment when he said, "Having observed your company from the outside, I have wondered how a company headed up by someone as wild and crazy as you, could be so successful. Now I know that LifeUSA is one of the most tightly controlled and managed companies I've ever seen." Yet if questioned, I believe the employees of LifeUSA would describe a culture of freedom, not control. If anything, a lack of controls might be the theme of their feelings. Those who worked with LifeUSA are more likely to tell you that what they liked most about the company was the freedom to do what they felt needed to be done to make the company grow. Especially the freedom to try and fail. How can this seeming inconsistency be explained?

Let the Guidelines Rule the Rules

Understand that there is a difference between *guidelines* and *rules*. Rules are for those you don't trust. Guidelines are for those you respect. You give a person a rule, you take away thought. You give a person a guideline, you stimulate responsibility.

As a company grows, it's a tradition to set up rules to tell people what they can and cannot do. Left unchecked, these rules become a crippling bureaucracy that stifles the reason why the rules were needed in the first place. The experience of LifeUSA demonstrated to me that making it a rule to cheat on the bureaucracy rules offers the best chance to foster the vitality and flexibility of a growing company.

This approach took root at LifeUSA by establishing a number of "guidelines" for company direction and "rules of engagement" for each department or division. Once the guidelines were communicated and the rules of engagement agreed upon, individuals were free—actually encouraged—to operate in a way they felt would best achieve a specific objective. Those who responded with creative approaches and succeeded in adding value to the organization shared in the value their creativity fostered. There was no punishment for trying and failing; only for failing to stay within the guidelines and rules of engagement established as boundaries. (Only if someone felt they had good reason to violate a guideline or rule of engagement did they have to go to management to secure approval.)

This does not mean that people were not held accountable for failing, but there was a "get out of jail free" card for them to show that they had learned from failure and would not repeat the same mistake twice. (Actuaries got three cards because they were a little thicker.)

The corporate guidelines for LifeUSA were not very complicated or numerous. Nor should they be. LifeUSA operated under the "guiding principles" of never give up control of distribution, product development, administrative support, or customer service. Sure, these four guidelines do seem simple and wide ranging, but you'd be surprised how many companies (in all industries) either don't have guidelines such as these or violate them (usually by adopting some form of "outsourcing," but more on that later).

Requiring the company to always control distribution may have limited some opportunities in the short term—such as selling products through bank distribution—but the future of the company was protected. Even though using another distribution system may be a quick and inexpensive way to grow, in the long run, if a company does not control distribution, it does not control its future. Thus, our marketing people knew that they were free to develop any distribution model they desired, just so long as they never gave up control over access to the distribution.

After guidelines were in place, we all agreed on "rules of engagement." A "rule of engagement" is simply a specific exposition of what is allowed and not allowed within a guideline. An example of a "rule of engagement" employed by LifeUSA stated that the company would sell only "value-added," not "commodity" type products. Under this rule of engagement, our actuaries and salespeople were free to develop any product their little marketing hearts desired, just so long as it was not a commodity. Due to this rule of engagement, LifeUSA never sold term life insurance, because that product was based on price, not value.

Another rule of engagement impacted customer service and was called the "48-Hour Challenge." This was a straightforward rule designed to quantify and identify standards of customer service. The "challenge" was to guarantee that new insurance policies would be issued within 48 hours of having received the application from the agent. If the company failed to accomplish this goal, the agent was paid $100 to compensate for below-standard service.

Implementation of the challenge accomplished a number of management objectives. It signaled to our primary customer—the agent—that we were committed to providing outstanding service. (Believe it or not, the average issue time for other companies was 48 days, not 48 hours. In an industry that views copycat as spectacular innovation, not one competitor attempted to mimic the 48-hour challenge.) The challenge also communicated the internal benchmark for customer service and was a way for management to measure the productivity of the company.

Working with this approach, management only established the guideline for the 48-hour challenge and left the details up to the employees. Of course, such a "rule of engagement" was easy for a new company receiving 50 applications a week to implement. Yet today, 18 years later, with the company receiving thousands of applications per week, the same 48-hour challenge is in place and being met at Allianz Life.

The point of these examples is to underscore that bureaucracy thrives when the environment is complicated and confusing. (That's one reason why government gets bigger and bigger.) The way to defeat bureaucracy—or to never let it take hold—is by fighting to keep things simple and clear. Simplicity to bureaucracy is like sunlight to a vampire. You don't have to be small to be simple and clear—but you do have to be good! As organizations grow larger it is more difficult to keep things simple, but the reward for the effort is a clean, efficient, growing culture—and the dearth of bureaucracy.

Feeling the First Headwind

Prior to 1975, I'd never been exposed to a real brand of naked bureaucracy, because as an agent or agency manager I was my own bandleader, dealing directly with issues and finding resolutions. If a financial management system was required, I could do it myself. There was no bureaucracy or fixed rules that prevented me from taking a needed action. But that all changed with my first official corporate job, when pure, unadulterated bureaucracy slapped me upside the head—without me quite understanding what it was. Getting from one decision to another became a little like running into a stiff wind. It couldn't be seen, but I sure could feel the resistance.

In order to learn this lesson, I moved my family from beautiful Orange County, California, to wonderful Worcester, Massachusetts (not exactly at the end of the world, but you could see it from there), to join State Mutual Life. (Just how smart was I? Orange County—where Richard Nixon was born, the airport is named after John Wayne, and Ronald Reagan is considered a liberal—was supposed to be the bastion of conservative thinking. Trust me, Orange County could not hold a candle to the conservative lifestyle of western Massachusetts, where you were not considered a local unless your ancestors were on the *Mayflower*.)

I walked into the halls of State Mutual Life, a thirty-two-year-old, freshly minted second vice-president charged with developing a new marketing system to bolster the company's lagging sales. This seemed a fairly easy assignment and not too far afield from what I had done as an agent and agency leader.

However, I soon found myself embroiled in what felt like a perpetual "groundhog day" of meetings. Every day was the same—

rush to work, drop my briefcase in the office, and head to the nearest conference room for the first committee meeting of the day. I could have made a few extra bucks renting out the office, since most of my time was spent in some conference room for what seemed to be unremitting meetings.

That would not have been so bad if we accomplished something, but that wasn't the case. It seemed the easier the task, the longer it took to get action. Had I lost my touch in decision making? What was happening here? I didn't realize it at the time, but I had run smack-dab up against one of the best bureaucracies this side of the Bureau of Labor and Statistics. If I had understood what was happening, it might have crippled my attitude (just as it had most others in the meetings), but remember, I was new to this corporate stuff and just continued to do what I knew best, which was to do something.

What seemed confusing to me was that even though I was a junior member, other participants began to readily agree with my proposals, and we actually started to get things done. Suddenly I was the team leader, and this invigorating new responsibility inflated my ego tremendously. I flattered myself into believing what a wonderful guy I must be. Here was this great young leader, making all these executive decisions. Surely, I was the chosen one to lead State Mutual to victory! Pretty heady stuff!

What a dummy I was. It took me a while, but I finally figured out the real game. The committees were formed not so much to take action, but to study, delay, and obfuscate. Committees were like bunkers that provided members with a bureaucratic bomb shelter under which they could hide in an arbor of anonymity. But aha! If someone was willing to step out and assume responsibility for decision making, the committee was happy to oblige, since they could not be blamed. And that someone, of course, was good old naïve MacDonald.

What I had unwittingly discovered was the rule in a bureaucratic business that encourages hiding in the herd because there was only risk, not reward, for stepping out in front of the crowd. If you have ever seen the *National Geographic* pictures of (no, not naked natives) a herd of water buffalo—each trying to fight its way to the center of the herd avoid predators—then you have some idea of what these bureaucratic committees are like.

Stumbling Into Bureaucratic Success

Inadvertently, I had cheated on the number-one rule of bureaucracy, but it was to my ultimate benefit. By doing what seemed right and natural, I stumbled onto the fact that if you do step out and assume responsibility in a bureaucratic organization, you can accomplish a great deal. Just cheat to win. Ignore the rule. Take responsibility. The committee "herd" will always follow you because you're the point man; you will protect them from shouldering any blame.

In other words, much as we might denigrate the bureaucratic system, there is an upside. A bureaucratic culture is fertile ground for those willing to cheat to win. It opens up the potential to provide leadership and superior decision-making opportunities while others are afraid to act.

Why Being Point Guard Works So Well

Resisting bureaucracy was easy for me, only because I had yet to be intimidated by the threat of some dark punishment lying in wait for those who fell off the corporate decision cliff. One of the ways bureaucratic organizations attempt to control members is to use intimidation to convince them that failure to follow the rules will call down some type of excruciating accountability punishment. (Somewhat like a mystic witch doctor who maintains his power over the villagers by convincing them that there is a vicious monster in the cave at the top of the hill, that only he can tame.) That is just not true!

The irony is that the very nature of the bureaucratic organization makes it difficult, if not impossible, to hold people accountable for their actions. The monster has no teeth because the bureaucracy of rules allows—actually encourages—people to play hide-and-seek with accountability. This is exactly the reason why most bureaucracies ultimately fail—if you can't keep track of what is happening, you can't involve people in the process with either accountability or reward. The organization ultimately expires suffering from an acute case of internal inertia.

Cheating on the bureaucracy rules was not an issue for me because I had been out in the field hunting and missed the monster meeting. I was like the kid who naïvely wandered into the monster cave as the other villagers stood by and quaked—convinced the kid would be eaten. For me, ignorance was bliss. I was no more worried about catching hell from the bureaucracy monster for making a mistake than I was about getting tossed out of the Democratic convention of 1960.

Yet the bureaucratic system fosters this fear of failure. And for many employees, it's a fear that paralyzes. I remember offering a promotion to an employee and he refused to take it because it made him "too visible." He wanted to keep a low profile and stay unknown. His worry was that if he became too visible, he might make a mistake and get blamed and canned for his failures. That's the kind of corporate paralysis that a bureaucratic culture can unwittingly create. And you wouldn't believe just how deep this paranoia embeds itself in the culture, or how expensive this stupidity can become. Thankfully, our friends at Hartford Insurance can offer delicious examples of both.

The Residue of Bureaucracy—Stupid Is As Stupid Does

Soon after being elected president of ITT Life, executives of Hartford (the parent company) came to me and said, "We want to get out of the credit insurance market and sell the existing block of business." Credit insurance, for the uninitiated, is the type of insurance you might purchase when you buy a car. If you die and you've got credit insurance, the car loan gets paid so your kids can drive to the funeral in a car that is free and clear. (I won't even bother going into the problems that develop if you die *in* your car.)

ITT Life was heavy into credit insurance because the company had previously been owned by a consumer finance company. (There is a partnership from consumer hell!) When the finance company made a car loan, they'd try to write the credit insurance as well. That's the same thing the credit card companies are doing today. They sell you the credit—then they try to sell you the credit life.

In the good old days, credit insurance was a highly profitable shtick. Customers seized on the blessing that their car would be paid off if they died—but they largely ignored the fact they were being hugely overcharged for the insurance. The party was spoiled only after the government stepped in and made this asinine rule that you could not gouge the consumers with prices that were usuriously unfair. Can you imagine the gall? Here the finance company applied the highest interest rates possible, and the insurance companies were charging a buck for what cost them ten cents. And the government was crying the blues that we were being unfair to customers.

After the regulators got serious about monitoring the industry, the companies had to charge fair prices for credit insurance. And worse yet, they had to disclose (in four-point, fly-speck type, of course) what those prices and terms were. Naturally, once the playing field had been leveled, consumers got wise and the business became not only very competitive, but, ultimately far less profitable. And that's why Hartford wanted ITT Life to jettison the business.

After analysis, we figured that—at best—our block of credit life insurance was worth, maybe, $20 million. Fortunately, we found a subsidiary company of Mutual of Omaha that was interested in buying the business and was willing to pay $25 million for it. Hartford said, "Go for it."

So we went through all of the negotiation, all the due diligence, and were literally at the closing table ready to sign the purchase agreement when The Hartford's second-guessing bureaucrats sprang into action. They called and told us to raise the price.

I was in shock. Here was a deal that *guaranteed* we could bag Mutual of Omaha like they were ducks in the wild kingdom, and that was not enough for Hartford. They wanted us to *raise* the price! Their utterly absurd thinking was this: If Mutual of Omaha was willing to pay $25 million, and we think it's only worth $20 million, maybe they knew something that we didn't. In other words, maybe we were being taken. "Raise the price to $30 million," Hartford demanded.

My suggestions that this was a silly and stupid bureaucratic misstep (or other such types of words) fell on deaf ears and minds in an apparent vegetative state. We were forced to troop back to the negotiating table, and hand-delivered The Hartford's demand: "We'll sell for $30 million." Not surprisingly, our friends from Mutual of Omaha pawed at the ground, sniffed into the wind and said, "Screw you!" (or other words to that effect), and got up and walked out. End of deal.

The Bureaucratic Error

In this seemingly simple action, things went wrong from the moment The Hartford bureaucratic culture took over the process. At The Hartford, and hundreds of other companies like them, employees have little incentive to take risks and a huge downside for making mistakes. And it's a rule that's ass-backward. The Hartford execs calling the shots of this "sale-that-never-happened" would reap no reward whatsoever for successfully dumping this dying business. But there would be hell to pay should it prove that Mutual of Omaha made money on the deal.

It seemed to make no sense—and for good reason. Here was a business that Hartford did not want to be in. Credit insurance was not core to our future, and we were losing money (which was difficult to do in the credit business) and market. Yet, when someone was willing to bail them out—at a profit no less—they were paralyzed.

The safe way out—the bureaucratic solution, if you will—is to do nothing. In our case, that meant putting up continually higher hoops for our negotiating partners to jump through. And when viewed from anywhere outside of the negotiating room, nobody would be the wiser.

The sad part of all this is that, by keeping a business that was not wanted and not profitable, eventually the entire block had to be written down for a multimillion-dollar loss. Yet no one—especially the shareholders—ever knew of the stupid decision. You see, the bureaucratic response to this situation is always, "It's not our fault.

We wanted to take the action, but they would just not meet our price." No foul—no harm! Except for the shareholder. For me, it was one of those defining moments when you come to understand where bureaucrats are coming from—and the compelling need to resist it.

To be fair, I had the same type of experience after Allianz AG acquired LifeUSA. Allianz Life was involved in mass marketing of insurance products, which can be very efficient and profitable, so long as the process is tightly controlled and managed. Unfortunately for Allianz Life, neither had been done and the company was losing literally millions each month on this business.

After determining that the business could not be resuscitated and made profitable, it was agreed by all that the company should exit the business. On the very day we were to announce this action, I received a call from the chief bureaucrat of Allianz North America (a really good guy, but the epitome of a bureaucratic citizen) who suggested we think the decision over a little longer! What? You mean till we lose another $100 million?

By this time I had been dealing with bureaucracies for almost twenty years and any cartilage of patience with them had been rubbed very thin. I had learned their secrets and how to cheat on their rules. This time my reaction—compared to what happened with The Hartford—was a full fifteen-minute diatribe on how stupid bureaucrats were, followed by the announcement that we would move ahead with the decision.

One of the advantages you have when dealing with a bureaucrat is that they will never risk taking action to stop you. For the very reason they are bureaucrats, they do not want to be held accountable for any action.

Hartford Lesson Two

Now, you would think a $20 million pummeling would be sufficient to convince Hartford management that accepting responsibility and rewarding good behavior is the way to go, but noooo. (With all this talk about Hartford, you may think I am being unfair and too critical of the company, but trust me, I'm not.) To be fair, Hartford is certainly not the only bureaucracy to act against its own best interests; it's just that they do it so often and so well. (If you want to hear some real horror stories, ask me about some of the actions Hartford took in an effort to keep LifeUSA out of business, only to ensure our success.)

In fact, the same thing happened again when we tried to buy ITT Life from Hartford in 1986. Like I say, this kind of corporate bureaucracy seeps into a business and calcifies thought, making the organization inflexible to change and entrepreneurial creativity. And it *stays* that way. I knew that Hartford, basically a property and casualty company, did not like the life segment of the market and was interested in selling ITT Life. (There was a little motivation from the fact that they did not like the way we stood out from the crowd of other life companies with our "radical" position on product and marketing.)

Knowing they were interested in dumping ITT Life, I, and other members of the management team, approached Hartford and offered to buy the company. At first blush Hartford was willing—even eager—to negotiate. The management group had valued ITT Life at somewhere around $80 million and had found a financial backer to support our bid.

We started the ball rolling by offering what we thought was a fair value for the company, but every time an offer was made Hartford would raise the price. That was frustrating, particularly because Hartford had previously indicated to me that they were willing to accept even less than $80 million for the company.

But that's not the way negotiations went. If we offered $80 mill, they would come back and demand $85 million. If we agreed to pay the $85 million, Hartford would one-up us again. No, we want $90 million. No, we want $95 million, and on and on.

This tit-for-tat went on for several months, and although frustrating, it did serve one useful purpose: It taught me the wisdom of learning how to confidently walk away from a deal that isn't working: to draw a line in the sand and say, "This is it. I go no further." (You will learn more about this in chapter 17—"Negotiate to Procreate!") Frankly, we were on a slippery slope, falling in love with the company like a kid with a schoolboy crush. With intimate knowledge of the company and believing in its potential, the romance began to cloud our vision and limit our ability to walk away—but not quite.

We went through this charade multiple times for at least six months. When we finally got up to $115 million, they rejected it. That's when our attorney (bright guy that he was!) said, "This is not going to work." We were offering Hartford $115 million in cash to buy this company that we thought was worth about $80 million and that they thought was probably worth even less. Just who is being more stupid here? We told The Hartford to keep the company and their darn credit business.

Bureaucracy in Action

Of course, the reason Hartford wouldn't sell ITT Life to management was the same dumb reason why the credit life sale fell through: the bureaucracy of their system held a two-edged sword of Damocles over their heads. Hartford's top dogs would get no reward, no bonus, no nothing, for selling ITT Life. There was no cultural incentive for them to try and get this deal done. But there was a definite downside. They would be open to ridicule if it could ever be said they sold the company—especially to management—for less than it was worth. And in this case, the Hartford negotiators had no committee to hide behind.

A Painful Lesson Learned

I am convinced that no matter what we had offered, Hartford would not have sold the company to us. They could not sell the company to us because there existed in Hartford this bureaucratic mentality, this inbred, institutionalized fear of failure that offered no reward for determining the right thing to do.

As a result, we left ITT Life as a management team and started LifeUSA. In the meantime, Hartford hired a caretaker president who ran the value of the company down to virtually zero dollars. Eventually the company was disbanded and the shattered remnants were folded into Hartford. Instead of having $100 million to put straight on the bottom line, plus getting rid of all of the liabilities, problems (not to mention some rule-cheating entrepreneur), and the hassles, their actions (or lack thereof) probably cost the shareholders of Hartford $200 to $300 million simply out of the blindness of bureaucracy. It was a shame. It was incredibly dumb and incredibly expensive.

And yet, this kind of idiocy goes on all the time at businesses big and small. When the organization is small, this stupidity sticks out like a sore thumb. But the larger the corporation, the greater the likelihood that the problem will be subsumed by the bureaucracy. Like so much sand on the beach, granules of thick-headedness get lost. You have to be inside to understand what is happening.

But make no mistake: The corporate rule that loses touch with accountability and fails to reward success is a rule you must cheat on if you are going to give yourself and your company a chance to prosper.

Isn't That a Trifle Cavalier?

To some, the cheat-to-win attitude about bureaucracy may seem a tad cavalier, as if there's some loose cannon calling the shots. But I would argue that is not the case. As with any kind of cheating, you have to know that you are doing the right thing. You can appear to be shooting from the hip, but your intellectual aim must be straight, true, and above all, correct. You have to break the bureaucratic rules effectively and successfully. And if you're reading this book with a yellow highlighter in your hand, get ready for the bottom line:

Bureaucrats can do nothing to a winner. Bureaucrats have no power over success—only over failure. You have to be willing to challenge their power over failure (the pointing-the-finger, "I-told-you-so" kinda thing), because they have no control over your success. The most effective way to beat a bureaucrat is to be successful.

Beating the Bureaucracy

We've discussed the need for both accountability and reward as ways to fend off bureaucracy in an organization. There is one other tool that can be used to prevent suffocation by the bureaucrat and that is imbuing yourself and the organization with a continual sense of urgency.

When bureaucracy is allowed to fester, ownership is shunned, no one is held accountable, and an acute lack of urgency takes hold. Bureaucracy is molasses in the gears of urgency that slows down, and eventually kills, forward momentum until any vestige of creative ingenuity simply withers away. It happens all the time.

A sense of urgency does not mean making fast decisions: it means working quickly to get the information needed to make a decision. For the bureaucrat, the rule is to do what can be done to delay the decision. Cheating on that rule requires constantly pushing for the information that allows a decision to be made. The bureaucrat waits for all the answers that will never come. The cheater searches for all the answers needed to make a reasonable decision.

This question of a sense of urgency is not—as you might think—the quintessential difference between a small company and a large company. There is this mistaken belief that small businesses can stop on a dime and change strategies overnight because they're small. Not necessarily. Smaller companies may seem less bureaucratic because their structure is more visible, and they are often driven by a palpable sense of survival, hence a sense of urgency. In addition, smaller companies may seem more entrepreneurial in spirit and have fewer tiers of approval.

But a sense of urgency has nothing to do with size or being an entrepreneur. It is more about accountability and reward. Entrepreneurial organizations tend to have a sense of urgency, but it does not mean that the biggest of organizations, including the most unwieldy of them all—the federal government—can't have a sense of urgency.

For example, at the beginning of World War II, the United States possessed a miserably small arsenal of weaponry; it had very few ships, planes and troops and even less matériel to make war. The events of December 7, 1941 (when the Germans bombed Pearl Harbor), electrified this huge bureaucratic organization and imbued it with a sense of urgency. The United States transformed into a fully armed nation primed for war faster than anyone could have imagined or predicted.

When Franklin D. Roosevelt directed that 50,000 aircraft would be built in a year, everyone thought it would not be possible, especially when industry was only turning out 500 aircraft per year at the time. Less than a year later, America was building planes at the rate of 50,000 a year. The point is that no matter how big or small the organization you manage or merely work for, bureaucratic inertia can be overcome. A strong sense of urgency is a high-octane fuel that can be used to burn away the stifling levels of bureaucracy. If you need to get it done and there is a sense of urgency, you can do just about anything you set your mind to.

Getting the Ball Rolling

The challenge, of course, is motivating people to respond to all issues with a sense of urgency. There is a difference between having a sense of urgency and shooting from the hip. Having a sense of urgency does not mean that you are not organized and does not mean that you are not planning—nor does it mean that you are running off at the cuff. It means that you have a sense of determination to get things done, and that frustrates the hell out of bureaucracy. A company without a sense of urgency will soon have a sense of bureaucracy.

The Bureaucratic Challenge

The challenge facing management today is to instill or retain a sense of urgency in the organization. Taking a singular action just won't cut it. Success requires a variety of exploits. You must identify and build an entrepreneurial culture (see chapter 14). People need (and want) to be held accountable for the results that they achieve— both good and bad. Priorities need to be clear, consistent, achievable, and staunchly supported. Deadlines must be set—held to and met. And those charged with responsibility must be given authority, held accountable, and rewarded for success. With this attitude and approach embedded in the culture of an organization, bureaucracy will never be given a chance to take root.

Busting the Bureaucracy

It's one thing to start a new company such as LifeUSA and fight off the intrusion of bureaucracy, but can an infected culture be healed? Outsiders often asked if the culture of LifeUSA could have been transferred to a company like Prudential Insurance. (See, I didn't pick on Hartford here!) My response was that it would have been more difficult; but with strong, persistent, unequivocal, and committed leadership, it is possible to move almost any organization. (Well, maybe not Hartford!)

Bureaucracy survives by creating, implementing, and protecting a complicated body of rules that suppresses creativity, hides accountability, and inhibits action. The kryptonite of bureaucracy is simple, easy-to-understand guidelines and rules of engagement.

A bureaucracy is busted by the straightforward acts of involvement and fair reward. Bureaucracy is busted when employees are encouraged to identify a problem, explore options, make a recommendation, and empowered to implement a solution.

Keep in mind that, even though organizations are often rife with bureaucracy, there are also employees everywhere who are yearning to be free of the yoke of mindless rule-making and bureaucratic thinking. In fact, one recent survey reported that "getting rid of organizational bureaucracy" was the most important factor employees would change to boost their productivity. When these employees are given the opportunity to be in parallel, to be entrepreneurial, held accountable, and rewarded for the value added, they will respond as if you have given them a huge dose of freedom. And you have.

And the Moral of the Story Is . . .

Few forms of institutionalized bureaucracy can rob your business of its productivity faster than the traditional rules of business. My rule is that rules ruin. Guidelines guide. Accountability rewards.

It's bad enough when employees have to buck an inflexible tradition of mindless rules and regulations, but when they aren't rewarded for creatively breaking these rules, the whole enterprise suffers. Eventually, bureaucracy encourages all to hide behind committees, pass the buck, shirk responsibility, sulk, and sit idly by as the organization rolls over and sinks. The brave steps needed to make a business a true success story are never taken.

The antidote for the ravages of bureaucracy is a culture that operates with a sense of urgency to encourage risk-taking, freedom from fear of accountability, learning from failure, and rewarding success. Cheat on the rule that says people need rules to control them and understand that, as a rule, people will perform to their potential when they are encouraged to make their own rules and are rewarded when they succeed. Defeat bureaucracy the right way and you will create a culture that builds success right from the start.

7

Intimidate the Intimidator

If someone tries to intimidate you,
but you don't know it, are you still intimidated?

You've got that feeling in the pit of your stomach. Again. The milk you had for breakfast has churned into butter. Your palms are sweaty. Your Arrid Extra Dry deserted you hours ago. You get this way every time you are going to meet with the Big Boss. And this time the feeling started to build yesterday when you were informed of today's meeting.

Hesitantly, you push the button for the executive floor and the elevator crawls up toward the top of the building; the questioning eyes of other passengers wonder, "What right do you have to enter these rarefied heights?"

Alone in the elevator as the doors open, you are greeted by the steely glare of a security guard who visually scans your person as if he were expecting an Al-Qaeda terrorist. He says nothing. You sidle by, turn right, and walk down the long corridor festooned with precious art. Up ahead, you see what everyone in the lunchroom refers to as the "two Dobermans." Actually, they are Janice, the pretty one, and Marian, who could easily double for Owen's momma (Anne Ramsey) in the movie *Throw Momma from the Train*. They are his secretaries and gatekeepers. You think to yourself, "Impressive. It took me three weeks just to get on the company e-mail system, and this guy has two secretaries of his own."

As you stand there, feeling somewhat like a schoolchild sent to the principal's office, Marian peers over her Ben Franklins and opens with, "May I help you?" In a shaking voice you sputter your name and acknowledge your appointment. In a distracted voice she says, "He has you down for 11:15, but there are some people in his office now, so if you can just wait a few minutes." You give your best impression of nonchalance and sit in one of the reception chairs. After just enough time to allow the knot in your stomach to inch its way into your throat, the paneled doors swing open and three very executive types move out and past you.

There is a bit of encouragement when one fellow in the departing group actually seems to offer you a nod of recognition. The Big Guy looks at you just as Marian is announcing your presence. He motions to you and then shakes your hand with the warmth of a politician who wants your vote but knows he will never see you again.

You are led into his office. It's cavernous. Your whole apartment would fit it here. And yet, it appears almost uninhabited. It's more like a showroom than a workspace. Nothing is out of place.

In one part of the office you notice two couches arranged to face each other. Financial magazines and newspapers are neatly stacked on a coffee table between the couches. There are framed photos everywhere, including a picture of him with the mayor and another with the governor shaking hands at some party. There are several pictures of your leader cutting groundbreaking ribbons with those oversized scissors. On the corner of his desk is a picture of him shaking hands with the president of the United States.

But all this is foreplay. The centerpiece is the desk. Taking up almost one whole side of the office, it looked larger than your bed. (I wonder if he has ever . . .? No, don't even go there!) It seems a waste to have such a large desk, since there is so very little on it.

You are not invited to sit on the couches. Moving behind the desk, he motions you to one of the two padded chairs placed in front of the desk. As you sit, you begin to sink to a level where your eyes barely clear the Boss's desktop. It's as if it wasn't a chair at all but one of those silly bean-bag things.

He begins by asking some questions about a special project you've been working on. This is your baby and you know more than anyone else about the details, the ins and outs along with the potential. But a strange thing happens as the discussion moves on to some of the problem areas. Your mind almost goes blank. You wonder, "What is he trying to get at? What does he know? What answer is he looking for? Can I be honest with him? Why am I sitting way down here? If I'm injured in this meeting, is my underwear clean?" Soon, you don't even know what you know.

Somehow, you get through the meeting without the knot in your throat becoming an unwanted gastric spill. In fact, he actually seems pleased with what you've told him. As you leave, he shakes your hand and thanks you for meeting with him. Perhaps it's more relief than anything, but you feel pretty good about yourself and the meeting. That feeling lasts till you are riding down the elevator on the way back to your desk.

Suddenly your mind is awash with all the things you *should* have said. Bright ideas and salient points that were nowhere to be found when you were in his office now flow freely. You could kick yourself for some of the answers you gave him. Now you are really sick thinking about the meeting. If only you had not been so scared and could go back and start again. You would not only look better, but you could give him better information to make informed decisions. But, you can't go back. The opportunity is lost. Forever.

Sure, this story may seem a bit far-fetched for today's world, but not that far. We've all found ourselves in a place where the situation controlled us more than we controlled the situation. That's called intimidation. Whether others aggressively apply it in a crude effort to influence or control our actions, or if we bring it on ourselves, intimidation saps our ability to perform at our highest potential.

Let's face it: intimidation is a fact of life. It joins death and taxes as one of the few certainties of life. Like a Stephen King horror story, intimidation comes at us in many forms and faces. If we're going to have to live with intimidation, we might as well learn how to deal with it, resist it, and even use it. The key is to make sure that intimidation and those who wield it never control us.

Intimidation can be blunt and blatant, or it can be subtle and surreptitious. Intimidation comes to us with the face of our parents, teachers, bosses, leaders, friends, and foes. But no one can hold a candle to the real masters of intimidation, our friendly religions. If you are looking for intimidation, you need look no further than your organized religion. Could anything be more intimidating than being threatened with becoming a human marshmallow for all eternity if we don't follow the rules set down by religion? (Jews and Catholics may disagree on a lot of things, but one thing we share in spades is the application of "guilt" as an all-encompassing intimidator for our actions.)

The question is not or whether we will face intimidation—we will. The real uncertainty is how will we deal with intimidation. Finding the right approach to thwarting intimidation may not be easy, but it is important that we do so, because how we respond to the application of intimidation in our life will go a long way toward determining just who it is that will control our life.

Intimidation Is a Thief

Intimidation robs its victim of the ability to perform at peak levels. In turn, this deprives the intimidator of the best the target has to offer. Yet intimidation—and ways to implement it—is still considered by many to be one of the most effective management tools in the bag. And many pursue intimidation with disheartening vengeance.

Why Does Intimidation Occur? Simple. We allow it. The sad fact is, we are conditioned from early childhood to accept different forms of intimidation. Whether it's from our parents, church, school, the military, or business, we are never far from those who try to control our lives through intimidation. They perpetuate and allow this kind of bully-power to surface, escalate, and endure. And that's true whether the manager is working for a school, a bank, a hospital, or a corporation. Any fear of reprisal becomes a synonym for intimidation.

Moreover, the rules say that we *should* allow ourselves to be intimidated. Business cultures lead us to believe that it's OK to be intimidated by power, authority, position, and status. Respect for authority, position, and status is fine, but being intimidated by it is quite another thing.

I was fortunate as a youth to have some experiences that fortified me against indiscriminate intimidation in the business world. I've already related some of my exploits with John Kennedy and others, but, for me, the best experience was meeting Dwight Eisenhower. As a boy, Dwight Eisenhower was my hero. (That may show you just what kind of life I had!) Anyway, here was a guy who had done it all, from West Point to the White House. He had defeated the Nazis and held the Russians at bay. If anyone deserved to be intimidating, it was President Eisenhower.

During my senior year in high school, just after President Eisenhower left office, he was visiting Los Angeles and was scheduled to appear at a rally in the old Olympic Auditorium. I decided to see if I could meet my hero. After arriving at the Olympic Auditorium I soon discovered that Eisenhower had been ensconced in a trailer set up behind the auditorium. Positioning myself just inside the back entrance (don't ask me how you do those things, you just do it) I didn't have to wait long, as Ike soon entered the waiting area and stood off to the side by himself.

I seized on the opportunity and walked up to the "all-everything" former president and introduced myself. He could not have been nicer or friendlier. Here was this guy who had done it all, taking time to talk with a teenage nobody who had done nothing. If ever anyone had the right to be intimidating for who they were and what they had done, it was Eisenhower. Instead, he acted as though he was happy to meet *me*. That experience taught me that those who have a right to use intimidation rarely do, and those attempting to use intimidation usually do so out of weakness or insecurity.

Lessons learned from meeting great and powerful people like Eisenhower and Kennedy helped me all my life and convinced me— right then and there—that the intimidation rule is one that should be repealed. It's a bad rule. It's a rule we should cheat on, because if we allow ourselves to be intimidated, someone or something else is able to control our future. And if we try to win through intimidation, we limit how other people can help us win. A long life of encountering attempted intimidation has taught me that using intimidation to manage and control people is a rule to cheat on. Allowing others to control us through the use of intimidation is even worse.

Of course, some forms of intimidation are fine. I see no problem using a large dog to intimidate a burglar or an aircraft carrier to get attention of nations that pose an imminent threat to our national security. However, intimidation used to belittle and control others has no place in our relationships, either the office or at home. And yet, this crippling intimidation seems to be everywhere. It's evident in corporations of all sizes, in small businesses, in law offices, even in hospitals.

A St. Paul Travelers Insurance Company study recently reported that, all too often, hospitals and clinics are a festering source of intimidation. Doctors intimidate nursing supervisors. Supervisors intimidate line nurses. Nurses intimidate each other and those farther down the pecking order. The same is true in other businesses, where CEOs intimidate VPs and VPs browbeat managers, and managers malign office staff and office staff beats up anyone in a lesser station. And everybody loses.

Employee relationships on all levels become strained. Lines of communication are muted. Absenteeism and turnover rates rise. Productivity diminishes. Customers get the short end of the stick (and if you're the "customer" in a hospital, this kind of intimidation reduces the quality of patient care you need to stay alive).

Making Cowards of the Brave

Intimidation makes cowards of the brave resulting in wasted time, talent, and opportunity. The idea that you could command people to do things because they're afraid of you—and expect them to perform without having to convince them it's the right thing to do—makes the use of intimidation a pretty tempting commodity. It sounds like it would be nice—efficient and easy—but there's a problem with that. It doesn't work.

In fact, trying to intimidate others is one of the most self-destructive actions you can take if you are trying to lead yourself, or anyone else, to success. The intimated:

- Become less valuable to everyone. To themselves. To the people they work with. To the success of the company.
- Become afraid to speak up and to offer their ideas and share their concerns.
- Become wary of taking the initiative and, accordingly, their doubts become self-fulfilling.
- Become drones, mindlessly carrying out a sort of genetic blueprint cloned by the intimidating figure on high.

It's no secret that most people are basically underutilized. We use only a small fraction of the capacity of our brains, scientists tell us, but it's more than that. You don't have to be an Einstein to do as much as you can. And one of the big things standing between most people and full utilization is intimidation. They're afraid to be great. Instead of leading people to greatness, most managers use intimidation to purposefully frighten them and limit their effectiveness.

Remember the words of Shakespeare: "Our doubts are traitors that make us lose the good we oft might win by fearing to attempt." If you intimidate people, they're going to be afraid to act boldly and confidently. They'll be too fearful to talk to you. They'll become too chary to tell you about roadblocks that are coming, known only to them.

Don't Let It Happen

You never want your team, whether it's a major corporation or the fellow staffers in your small business, to become intimidated. That is a bad situation to be in, but it's one that many so-called powerful people bring on themselves by thoughtlessly, and unwisely creating an atmosphere of intimidation.

There's an actual syndrome (or at least there is now) called "power-man syndrome." It occurs when a leader is so isolated from unfiltered outside communication that he or she never learns what is *really* going on. (Maybe it should be called the George Bush Sr. syndrome.) When everything is learned from "yes-people," nothing is really learned at all since nobody is willing to proclaim the emperor has no clothes. As a result, the leader inevitably begins to make almost unbelievably bad decisions and often destroys the enterprise he or she is trying to lead. And a major factor in the power-man syndrome is the element of intimidation.

Thomas Jefferson recognized this problem when he wrote, "Men by their constitutions are naturally divided into two parties: (1) Those who fear and distrust the people, and wish to draw all powers from them into the hands of the higher classes. (2) Those who identify themselves with the people, have confidence in them, cherish and consider them as the most honest and safe... In every country these two parties exist; and in every one where they are free to think, speak and write, they will declare themselves."

The Press Makes Matters Worse

This business of intimidation is also fostered by the popular press, always on the lookout for a new fad, whatever its value. Scores of best-selling management books have touted the use of intimidation. Remember *Winning Through Intimidation*? Here was a national best-seller that claimed the best way to cow the competition, and those with whom we do business, was to apply ruthless, unbridled intimidation.

Then came the *One Minute Manager*, and corporations and career-minded supplicants by the millions were taught that a one-minute manager was the guy who sat in lofty judgment of anyone who paused in the shadow of his greatness. And your job, this slender primer told you, was to deliver sixty seconds of intimidation from your bully pulpit to be followed by a strategic but patronizing pat on the shoulder.

The problem with books like these is that they suggest that bosses, from whatever lofty pedestal they may rule their kingdom, can use their power and authority to intimidate to win. And I believe, most assuredly, that this is a rule that is wrong, wrong, wrong.

How I Learned My Lesson

I wasn't born knowing that intimidation in the office doesn't work and, in fact, I figured it out by the accident of my own ignorance (of which I was, in the beginning, generously endowed). My education came during the early tenure of my first corporate job at State Mutual Life. On my first day, someone from personnel escorted me to my office and wished me luck. I looked around my new work home and quickly came to the conclusion that as offices go, it wasn't much.

Clustered with ten similar offices, it was a plain, windowless cell located in the core of the building. In reality, the office seemed more like a cave than a place of power. The offices on each floor of the building formed their own inner sanctum. They resembled the image of covered wagons pulled up in a circle to provide protection from the wild savages. One benefit offered by this office was that it had its very own private washroom. (I was to learn later that those higher up on the totem pole not only had their own washroom, but a private shower as well.) Anyway, I did not think much of it because, except for the first few months in the business, I had always occupied a private office. One thing that did stick out, however, was that these were the only offices in the building. Everyone else working for the company was relegated to a ring of Dilbert-style cubicles surrounding and forming a natural barrier keeping people away from the core.

A couple of weeks later, I found myself participating in one of those interminable corporate committee meetings. (You know, those magical gatherings where people can go to hide in the safety of group decisions so as not to be exposed to blame for anything that happens.) I forget the subject matter, but I do remember pushing for some particular marketing program. Still new to corporate life, and learning the rules of engagement, I was impressed that everyone seemed to be agreeing with my recommendations. Little did this sacrificial lamb know that they were just happy to have me be out front on the issue and ready to take the poison arrows. (See chapter 6—"Taming the Bureaucracy").

However, there was one guy who simply would not agree with me. He challenged virtually every suggestion I made. It was like *"Point-Counterpoint."* I have to admit that he made some excellent points and caused me think about my conclusions. Still, I could not get him to give in on the project. With the prospect of lunch rapidly creeping up on our thoughts, the committee was happy to conclude its efforts without resolving the issue. Not me—I invited my challenging new friend to meet me for further discussions. He agreed and asked where I was located in the building. I said, "Fourth floor." We settled on meeting in my office after lunch.

An hour later I looked up to see him standing at the door to my office. I motioned him to come in and take a chair. I'll never forget the first words out of his mouth when he looked at me and said, in a hesitant voice, "Gee Mr. MacDonald, I didn't know you were in the 'core.'" Here was a guy at least ten years my senior now calling me "Mr. MacDonald." (Up to that time the only person who called me Mr. MacDonald was the vice principal in school when he said, "Well, Mr. MacDonald, welcome to detention . . . again.")

From that point on, my friend would do nothing but agree with me. While happy to have him recognize the greatness of my thoughts, even I was perceptive enough to recognize that this change was not due to my personal power of persuasion. Once he discovered that I was housed in "the core," the questioning, challenging, and the value of his ideas were all lost.

For me, this incident was the first clear example of intimidation's destructive nature. When this guy saw me as just the new kid on the block, he felt free to offer his candid and constructive thoughts. Once intimidated by my position and office, that contribution was lost.

It turns out that the "core" truly was the inner sanctum of the company power base. There were those who clawed and fought their whole career just to have an office in the core. Likewise, leaving the core meant you had either literally or figuratively died. The problem, of course, was that members of the core ended up simply talking to themselves. They had very little contact with, and therefore even less understanding of, what others in the company were thinking, saying, and doing. It may not have been intentional (although I think it was), but the entire atmosphere and culture of the core totally intimidated those who were excluded—and sometimes even those who were admitted to the core club seemed to be intimidated by the atmosphere.

Getting To the Core of the Problem

It didn't take long to figure out that the people toiling away in the cubicles were a lot more important to my success than those bunkered in the core with me. With my objectives still more focused on actual, rather than perceived, progress (an attitude change many corporate rules attempt to impose on new players), it was easy for me to make what seemed like a fairly simple and logical decision. I decided to move out of the core and camp with the people doing the work.

It didn't seem like a big deal when I walked into my boss's office and told him of my desire to move out of the core and take a cubicle. His first reaction was one of confused wonderment. It was that same searching look you get when you tell a joke and you can see the other person didn't quite get the punch line, but doesn't want to admit it. After this perplexed pause he questioned, "Say again?" When I repeated my desire, he just started to laugh and told me to get back to work because he was busy. Only on my third try did this guy come to fully understand what I was telling him. And from his reaction, you might have thought that I had offered proof that God was dead and that Osama Bin Laden had been elected Pope!

I didn't even come close to anticipating the firestorm of protest that emanated from the power elite of the company over my decision. Not only my boss but his boss and even the company president tried to talk me out of moving out of the core. They argued that no one had ever, ever moved out of the core—voluntarily, that is. Every manner of persuasion was used to impress upon me that it couldn't and (from their perspective) shouldn't be done. I was asked not to make public my request and to think it over for a couple of weeks. In essence, the core club members wanted to give me some time to come to my senses.

But when the two weeks were up, my decision stood and I moved out of the core. From my perspective all I was trying to do was create a better working relationship with the people who reported to me. What I did not understand at the time was that the other occupants of the core didn't care about me being in the core. They were upset because, by voluntarily leaving the core, I had effectively diminished their perceived power and ability to intimidate others. What they had worked so hard to achieve had become less valuable and sapped some of their bully-power. My action was a form of intimidating the intimidators.

My move to the cubes on the open bay floor provoked ire from the "core of cronies," but an even stronger response from my fellow cube denizens. At first the rumor was that I had been demoted, but when word seeped out that I had actually requested the move, an instant company folk hero was born. I had mocked and turned my back on one of the most intimidating symbols of power in the company. The lesson I learned from this simple act was that, by giving up that "sign" of power, I actually gained significantly more power from the entire organization. I felt like the guy who stood up to the school bully simply by staring him down.

For me, the action was no big deal, but by the reaction of others, you'd think I was David, who had slain the evil monster of intimidation. From most everyone else's perspective, my action was something they had always wanted to do—mock the core—but never could because they were too intimidated by what it stood for.

An indication of how those who reported to me felt about the move came as I returned from lunch on the first day of the move. There, sitting on the floor in the middle of my cubicle, was my personal little Port-A-Potty. They knew I had given up the private washroom in the core office and they wanted to show how much they appreciated it. When I left the company a year or so later, it struck me that virtually every department offered me a memento to take away from the company. Every single one of them made some reference to moving out of the core.

Learning from Intimidation

It became obvious that using intimidation as a management style was a rule that must be broken. Intimidation applied from the perspective of fear should be cheated on because it garners neither respect for the intimidator nor performance from the intimidated. It is a waste of time. As the process of intimidation was observed, it struck me again that those who attempted to use intimidation were doing so from a position of weakness, not strength. From then on, every time I encountered intimidation, used to create fear, my reaction was to mock it and resist it. I made it an objective to do all I could to reduce the influence of intimidation in all future management dealings.

Over time I also learned that every company has its own "core"—even the one you work for—to establish rules many will use to instill fear and intimidation in others in the company. The key to defeating this strategy is to learn to recognize the basis of the intimidation rules and then cheat on them.

Fighting Fire with Fire

Some forms of intimidation do have a place in management and can be very effective in accomplishing goals and leading people. The first of those forms is what I think of as reverse intimidation. Remember the old saying, "Fight fire with fire!" That is turning the intimidation back on the intimidator. Like a mirror used to reflect and increase the power of the sun, intimidation reflected back on the intimidator magnifies its impact. The person who consciously uses intimidation in an effort to gain control over you is like the school bully. He will keep pushing so long as he thinks he can get away with such action. On the other hand, as soon as the intimidator realizes you will not be intimidated, then the whole relationship will change.

I remember working for one guy who specialized in institutional intimidation. He tried it all, including not allowing those below him to ride on the same elevator. One of his big tricks was to bring all of the company managers together for quarterly meetings. It was a true "me versus you" type of meeting. This executive and his eunuchs would sit at a large table on one side of the room, and everyone else would sit across from them. One by one, managers were called to come forward and sit in a lone chair positioned in front of the intimidator. From there it was all downhill. Many did not survive the process.

The key to surviving this type of situation is to recognize it for what it is; a crude attempt to intimidate. Once you recognize the situation, you are well on your way to thwarting its impact. While many of my colleagues were made to feel like Galileo facing the Inquisition and reflected that with their body language, I've found that the only effective response is to turn the experience into a star performance. You know the old saying, "If you are being run out of town, get in front of the crowd and make it look like a parade."

In other words, when you can get outside the situation and recognize that the purpose of the setup is to intimidate you, not to stimulate your best performance, you can use that knowledge to rise above the intimidation and turn it against the intimidator. One thing you will soon learn is that, once the person who attempts to use intimidation to control you discovers that such tactics will not work, you have turned the tables and have the real power.

Turning the Tables on Bully-Power

When I took over as president of ITT Life, the distribution system was totally out of balance. One organization produced more than 60 percent of the business written by the company. This state of affairs was unhealthy and, by its nature, placed the company in a very weak position. This problem was compounded by the actions of the organization's leader, who attempted to use his leverage to browbeat and intimidate the company. This had been the tactic he used on my predecessor and he tried the same with me.

The scenario was always the same. Whenever there was an issue or something he wanted, the technique was to bluster and threaten. This went on for a number of meetings until finally (out of frustration and not some deliberate plan) I was fed up and said, "Bob, it is obvious you are not happy. We can't satisfy your needs, so why don't we just agree to disagree and you take your business to another company." I knew that if he called my bluff (it was not a bluff, though) and moved the business, the company would be decimated. But I also knew that if we continued to succumb to his intimidation, the company would never succeed.

At first, he could not believe that I was serious, but he soon discovered just how determined I was to thwart his intimidation. Once this guy understood that I and the company would no longer be intimidated by his actions—that I would not only let him move the business, but help him—his entire attitude changed. After that encounter we still had issues and conflicts, but they were always resolved on a mutually respectful basis. I gained his respect, because he knew that I would not be intimidated by his actions, and we had a very positive relationship going forward. I had dealt with the issue out of pure frustration, but it turned out to be a wonderful lesson in dealing with and fighting intimidation. Intimidation should never be allowed to make you do what is not right to do.

It's important when using this approach to have your ducks in a row—know the right thing to do and be confident so you can be brave. You see, while it may have been a short-term disaster for this guy to move his business away from the company, it would have been cataclysmic to allow him to continue to intimidate the company. Understanding this situation made my decision much easier. You'll discover that the benefits from this approach to dealing with intimidation are much better than the feelings you will have if you cower in the face of such activity.

Eschewing the Imperial Throne

In another situation, I was dealing with a big boss who believed that "closeness to the throne" should be considered a great reward and one that people should fight for and be intimidated by. We should feel privileged to sit with the King!

This guy was in town one day and a large dinner was planned in honor of his visit. He was arrogant to the level of imperialism.

However, there were managers who would have killed to have the opportunity to sit at his right hand. For some reason, I was invited to sit at the head table with the potentate. Without saying anything to the planners, I asked one of the guys I worked with to take my place in the spotlight. While he was a little nervous, it was an opportunity for him to meet the King and he agreed. (He agreed not out of desire to kiss-ass with the big guy, but because he was such a good guy and wanted to help me make a point.)

At the dinner it was obvious to all—as I held court in the back of the room—I had spurned the opportunity to mingle with the potentate and all the other "important" people at his table. This action sent two messages. One message was meant for the intimidator, suggesting that I did not need his recognition to feel good about myself. The other message was for those who would have killed to be at his table. By clearly mocking that which they craved so badly their hair hurt, I was sending a very powerful and intimidating message.

The Power Cruise

That's why, years later, I deliberately reversed the power of intimidation when we arranged an ocean cruise for the top salespeople and employees of LifeUSA. The cruise was a reward for the first billion-dollar year in sales. (Amazing how time changes things. Or is it new management? The company now does a billion a month in sales.) From experience, we knew that some of the sales people would attempt to flex their egos and stoke the fires of their self-worth by complaining about their accommodations and attempting to intimidate the staff into upgrading them to a larger suite. The logic, of course, is that the more luxurious one's shipboard accommodation, the more important they were.

We countered this activity by assigning me—the chairman and CEO of the company—to the least desirable cabin on the entire ship (something akin to steerage). When some, as expected, attempted to intimidate the staff into improving their cabins (no matter how sumptuous the cabins actually were) the staff was ready and offered them the opportunity to switch cabins with me. When they discovered the cabin I occupied, the complaints evaporated.

The point is that when the supposed value to be gained from the application of intimidation is debunked and eliminated, then the impact, power, and value of intimidation simply evaporate.

Breaking the Intimidation Rules as a Way of Life

If you had visited LifeUSA when I was CEO, you would have noticed the absence of the traditional corporate portrait of the CEO, but you might wonder who the guy is pictured in the silly bumblebee outfit. That was little ol' me.

And my office was not what most expected. No massive oak desk. No hand-carved credenzas. No sterling coffee server. Over to one side, you would see a desk pushed up against the corner. There was no way a meeting could be conducted across the desk in this office. In the middle of the workplace was a casual conference table. Anyone who came into the office for a meeting would settle around it as if sitting at a kitchen table having coffee with a friend. Missing would be formal chairs and the executive couch.

As any LifeUSA owner will tell you, my office of stuff was really weird stuff. A small flock of pink lawn-ornament flamingoes peeked out from behind the potted plants. Bookshelves with souvenirs circled the office walls and bric-a-brac covered every surface. Most of it was cheap kitsch, gaudy, and basically silly. All of this was designed to make *anyone* visiting me feel at home, unintimidated, free to speak, ready to offer insight, and willing to join a team of equals. (That is as soon as they stopped looking around and laughing!) One thing about my office followed the pattern of other CEOs: The walls were covered with pictures of famous and important people I had met. The only difference was that in my office these were all pictures of LifeUSA owners. There were scores of pictures of LifeUSA owners working, having fun, and being with "Mac."

As LifeUSA grew to be a larger company, there was pressure to change my office décor. Many viewed it as not appropriate for someone in my position. I remember an interior designer who came in with a plan for new furnishings and a layout that was elegant, refined, tasteful, and, as you probably figured out by now, utterly opposed to what I wanted and needed. I'm not blaming the designer. Most CEOs follow the rules of intimidation they have learned and want the big desk they can stare over. Although this designer didn't suggest it, some CEOs even recommend sawing the legs off the chairs placed in front of the desk, so they can loom like some kind of medieval inquisitor over everyone seeking an audience. All that's missing is an iron maiden sitting ominously in the corner, a trap door, and a few muffled screams emanating from somewhere below.

So why did I fight so hard over a bunch of yo-yos, squirt guns, snow domes and action figures? The reason is that most people, seeing this stuff, are going to drop their "sent-to-see-the-principal" nervousness and anxiety, and be their real selves. The general tendency on seeing a guy with a pinball machine in his office is not to feel too formal. People relax. They can think better, be more creative, and willing to make suggestions, accept challenges, and take chances. That's what I want them to do.

The sole objective for an office like this was to take the edge of being in the office. The goal was for people to be comfortable and natural—so they could be at their best. No one should have felt intimidated coming into my office. One of the best tests to measure the success of this effort was that Owners always wanted—and felt comfortable enough—to bring their friends, spouse, and children by to visit the office.

One thing you wouldn't find, inside or outside my office (or anybody else's office) when I ran LifeUSA was a secretary. We didn't have them. I answered my own phone, I typed my own letters, and I was responsible for organizing my own information. I had a PC on my desk and I used it, just like everybody else, almost, in the company. Not having a secretary is part of not being intimidating.

Those new to LifeUSA had a difficult time learning how to obtain an appointment or meeting with me. The usual question to other owners was, "How do I set up a meeting with Mr. MacDonald?" Or, "Who arranges Mr. MacDonald's schedule?" They could not quite accept that the way to meet with the CEO was to call him or stop by his office. All of this was planned—a hammer to knock down the barriers of intimidation. When people see you fetch your own coffee, open your own mail, and personally answer your own voice mail, they're going to think, "Hey, this guy is just like me. He's not some member of the ruling elite. I can trust him. I can work with him." That's what I'm looking for.

And the Moral of the Story Is . . .

If you were to learn nothing else from this chapter but one thing, it would be this: Those who use intimidation as a tool to dominate and control others do so out of weakness and insecurity, not from strength of leadership.

Breaking the intimidation rule starts with YOU—no matter what your station, no matter what you're calling. Sure, the CEO of a corporation is ultimately calling the shots, but every employee can invoke the No-Intimidation zone and use it widely in his or her division or department.

Just think: what if—instead of scaring everyone—you inspired and encouraged people to be brave? What if, instead of trying to make people feel small, you were able to make them feel big and powerful? What would happen is that you would begin to create an open society where people were comfortable coming to you with whatever was important to them. Communications would open up, new ideas would flow, and people would be willing to step up with their best efforts. The intimidation bully would be vanquished forever and for good!

I'm no Pollyanna. But I do believe that looking for the best in your employees and coworkers and breaking down the walls of intimidation is a system that benefits everyone. There are lots of things we can do to fight intimidation.

When you encounter someone trying to follow the rule-by-intimidation theory, set yourself up to be better than this person—if only because they are trying to intimidate you. You may not necessarily be smarter, faster, or more knowledgeable, but you can certainly be better. The general rule in the corporate world is to make the intimidator appear godlike. There are many ways corporate titans assume a mantle of superiority. They ride around in limousines (if not helicopters). They have private parking spaces, personal entrances, executive lunchrooms, and offices as big as Utah with desks the size of Rhode Island. Even private bathrooms have their own zip codes.

All of these trappings have a single purpose: to elevate the person who has them to a superior status, to promote the attitude to become *better, more deserving , more powerful* than the mere mortals who toil beneath them. Accordingly, many still believe those on top should wield greater power to coerce both submission and better performances from the rank and file. (When I encountered that attitude I would always remember my experiences with Kennedy and Eisenhower to bring these pretenders down a few levels.)

My experience is that you can be much more successful by doing exactly the opposite. The objective should be to demonstrate to those we work with that we are there to support their efforts, not the other way around. The simple fact is that if people view you as an asset, not an ass, they are going to be much more comfortable working with you.

I am reminded here of Steven Spielberg's powerful movie, *Schindler's List*. There's a scene in the movie where *Untersturmfuhrer* Amon Goeth is chatting with Oskar Schindler on the balcony overlooking Goeth's concentration camp.

Speaking of the Jewish prisoners, Schindler says to Goeth:

> "They don't fear us because we have the power to kill, they fear us because we have the power to kill arbitrarily. A man commits a crime, he should know better. We have him killed, we feel pretty good about it. Or we kill him ourselves and we feel even better. That's not power, though, that's justice. That's different than power. Power is when we have every justification to kill—and we don't. That's power.
> "That's what the emperors had. A man stole something, he's brought in before the emperor, he throws himself down on the floor, he begs for mercy, he knows he's going to die ... and the emperor pardons him. This worthless man. He lets him go. That's power. That's power."

And that's the power you want. Depending on your station in corporate or business life, you have the power to arbitrarily fire, demote, punish, embarrass, humiliate, and intimidate those employees you work with and for. You can delight in gleeful *schadenfreude* at the peril of your minions as you exercise your power in a vain attempt to coerce and control.

Or you can use that power to invite and encourage more openness, honesty, hard work, and sincere support from those on whom your very success depends. The choice is yours. Intimidate the intimidator, and exorcise fear from the culture, and you become an enabler for the power of people, not a governor.

8

CYA—The Paper Moon

*Most businesses would easily become more successful
if management would spend less time trying to
cover its collective ass and accept responsibility for
their leadership, good or bad.*

Throughout history, all social orders developed their own distinctive set of accepted mores, customs, and rituals, activities that evolved as the society developed. As innately inquisitive humans, we look back on our past to better understand where we've been, how we got here, and where we are going.

Archaeologists, for example, study relics and artifacts to learn about past human life and activities. Anthropologists examine history to glean information as to our origin, cultural development, and interactive relationships—the fibers that govern and bind social groups together. (Like why did man stop eating apples for a period of time?)

These professionals have discovered activities that seem quite natural and understandable. Prayers to the god of pecuniary power were especially popular. Fighting with tribal neighbors has always been fairly a routine occurrence. But other activities—like sacrificing perfectly wholesome virgins to the deities—seem strange to us.

As odd as many of these ancient activities appear to us today, my bet is that the anthropologists of the next millennium are going to have an even more difficult time trying to understand one of the unique customs and beliefs of corporate organizational society. It is a practice that goes against the very grain of human development.

From the earliest of times, man has sought to leave his mark—to let those who came after him know he was there. For eons it has been a natural human trait to hand down some type of sign in a symbolic search for immortality. As soon as man could find something to write on (is that where tattoos started?) he left his mark—man wanted others to know he had been there and done that. Cavemen decorated their caves for all to see. We sign paintings, declarations of independence, and rocks at the top of a mountain. "Kilroy was here," is everywhere.

What the anthropologists of tomorrow will have a difficult time explaining is why man involved in commercial affairs (corporate animals) of the late twentieth and early twenty-first centuries worked hard to hide not only their activities but to place blame for anything and everything on somebody else. (You know—the classic management rule taught at Harvard: "When you make a mistake—blame someone!") No longer do individuals seek recognition for their contribution; they don't even want it known they were there.

This is distinctly a modern business "achievement." I know of no petroglyph that says, "It was Thor who chased the buffalo from our hunting grounds. I know, because I was in the bushes with my main squeeze, Grindyl, and saw him do it." Or, "I warned Pebbles not to paint here, but just look what she did to our cave walls! Punish her, not me."

Pointing the finger at the other guy, denying culpability, and failing to accept responsibility, seem to be the unique aspects of the way most businesses, and employees, operate today. We even have a name for this phenomenon. It's called CYA—Cover your ass!

My bet is that if employees were asked to list the most important rule for survival in the corporate jungle, at the top of the list would be, "the ability to effectively cover your ass." Ask anyone in a corporate organization what the term "CYA" means and they can answer without hesitation. In the corporate world, no rule seems more inviolate than CYA. Like fledglings out of the nest, it's amazing how many corporate people learn this rule as soon as they walk in the door. It's as if the rule has a genetic legacy.

Generally, the CYA philosophy is manifested in the form of the written memo. This conjures up visions of the experienced CYA practitioner churning out reams of memos to form a papier-mâché barrier intended to fend off the slings and arrows of corporate blame and accountability. While CYAers do produce enough memos to frighten any tree-hugger, the CYA attitude takes many insidious shapes.

Think of CYA as a type of mind game in which the players use all forms of bob-and-weave, now-you-see-me-now-you-don't, yes-I-do, no-I-don't techniques to play hide-and-seek with responsibility. For the CYAer, any tactic that can be used to confuse and delay is fair game. The ultimate accomplishment for the CYAer is to accomplish nothing. (One upside to this activity of appearing to do a lot but actually doing nothing is that if you are really good at it, you can run for president of the United States.)

For those of us with a bent toward making things happen, the CYA philosophy becomes both an interminable frustration and a Godsend of a gold-mine-sized opportunity. Under the same physical rule that says a force leveraged against itself magnifies the power, CYA turned back against itself magnifies the potential to get things done. Only one thing is required to take advantage of this situation—you know what it is—you have to cheat on the CYA rule. You have to do it early and often.

Precisely because this rule is so universally accepted, people who cheat on it will exercise power that is far beyond that of mortal men. Cover-your-ass mentality is based on the belief that if you let your ass hang out, someone will bite it off. In reality, it is more likely that it will be kissed. What the faint hearts of the corporate world fail to realize is that very little bad happens to people who go commando to make decisions and accept responsibility for the results.

Contrary to the CYA premise that any business decision is a bad one and should be avoided, there really is no "right or wrong" decision. Invariably, taking action in a corporation involves multiple options. Unless all options are followed (which would be impossible), there is no way to prove the option selected is right or wrong. Those who have made a choice, *any* choice, have, in fact, done the right thing.

Remember, there is no need to hit a home run with each decision. Babe Ruth may be immortalized for his home runs, but in the process he won the American League title for most strikeouts *six times*. If he had been afraid to pick up the bat, he would not have failed so many times, but also, this example wouldn't be such a cliché.

Sure, some bad decisions can cost you your job. John Casey's decision to frantically expand Braniff Airlines after deregulation, for example, was wrong and earned him a pink slip. But most of our decisions, especially those made on the way up, are not nearly so life threatening. As we move up the corporation making decisions, we become like the magnet drawn through a pile of iron particles attracting those who will follow us anywhere.

People are attracted to, and are willing to follow, an individual who can, and will, make decisions. These people are soon referred to as leaders. Such people, even if not always "right," will find they are very popular and will not be eliminated because of a few stumbles. If, as our career develops, an anti-CYA philosophy is embraced, then by the time we are in a position to run a company, decisions will come easily and usually with very good results.

A Committee of Asses Have a Lot to Cover

Work with executives by Dr. Siegfried Streufert (could a true behavioral scientist have a better name?) showed that the most successful people do not overplan, but approach important decisions with a general strategy, and assume that decisions would become clear as events unfolded. (These are called guidelines, rules of engagement, and parallel interests, techniques that are discussed in other parts of the book.)

Elsewhere in this book, my travails at State Mutual Life are recounted, as I was tortured with a mind-numbing parade of committee meetings. But I quickly learned that taking responsibility at these meetings was my ticket up the corporate ladder, because the remaining committee members were too busy covering their asses to do much else. The sports theory of management was adopted in corporations—when you have a losing record it is a lot easier to fire the manager than the whole team. From the perspective of the professional CYAers, individuals could be fired, but it was very difficult to fire a committee.

Covering Your Butt Can Be a Corporate Way of Life

The CYA rule is not limited to the corporate committee room. As mentioned, it is most often used in the form of the corporate memo. I love CYA memos because the receipt of one signals that the sender is (or at least they think they are) weak. You know the person sending it will be no threat when it comes down to real decision time.

If you are willing to cheat, it is possible to use CYA memos to your advantage. They are especially useful when you encounter someone who simply won't move off the dime (which is different from a paradigm because then you have two people with two dimes who won't move), because they're concerned about being blamed if the project goes wide of the mark. To these people the best response is, "I recognize the concern you have. Why don't you just send me a memo?" You don't have to say, "CYA memo" because everyone knows what you mean. The files of those who cheat to win on the CYA rule are replete with memos from others that start, "As you decided and requested, I am going ahead with the plan to . . ." If you are willing to put the responsibility on your shoulders and let the other person follow the CYA rule, it becomes quite easy to get people to do things they otherwise would not. (Presidents of the United States have found this technique quite effective in achieving both good and bad results, such as assassinations and coup attempts.)

It Makes No Difference Whose Ox Is Al Gored

You'd be right to surmise that with my attitude toward rules, I have been the subject of a good many CYA memos. A couple of good examples would be one memo written *about* me and another that is addressed *to* me.

The first one came from the Hartford Insurance Company's head of public relations and was sent to my boss with copies to almost everyone in the universe. (You should understand that most corporate PR people have PhDs in CYA techniques.) The memo is archetypal and deserves examination:

"On Monday I had a call from Bob MacDonald who reported that his appearance last week before the National Council of Consumer Interest in Columbus, Ohio turned into a debate with Dale Gustafson, an actuary with Northwestern Mutual.

"As Bob recited the sequence of events to me, this was originally going to be a speech and the people assured him there would be no confrontation. The situation apparently seesawed back and forth, and then, I believe, a day or two before the meeting Bob was informed that he and Mr. Gustafson would be facing each other.

"I told Bob that in line with our instructions from ITT in New York he then should have cancelled the appearance. I also said he should have contacted us to discuss the change in plans.

"I reminded Bob that our instructions from Ned Gritty (ITT's chief PR officer), from Pete Thomas (Hartford insurance's CEO) and from you are that he is not to participate in public debates. ITT does not want a confrontation. There can be no equivocation on this point. I thought all of us had made it abundantly clear, and I cannot believe that Bob still went ahead with a debate when his instructions are to the contrary."

Making Effective Use of CYA Tactics

God, I love memos like this—what a classic! Even today, twenty years later, as I sit here writing this chapter, thinking about that memo gives me goose bumps. This masterpiece of an archetypal CYA memo announces to whomever it might concern (or anyone who's the subject of one of these inane missives) "I'm not to blame— It's Bob's fault. I warned him." (Even British Prime Minister Neville Chamberlain could not have written a better CYA memo about Hitler after the 1938 Munich "peace" conference.)

Yes, the writer was correct—I had violated one of the rules. But for me the action was more than worth the risk. There was so much more to be gained by breaking this rule than by following it. Sure, there was a risk, and if I had been wrong there would have been problems, but the potential upside was much higher than the downside.

ITT Life had just initiated the attack against the life insurance industry and its pet product, whole life. Here was the opportunity to make our point before a national consumer group, obtain some highly favorable publicity. It was a risk that no self-respecting rule-cheater could resist.

By the way, the guy sent to debate me was from Northwestern Mutual Life. The stodgiest of stodgy companies in the industry. (They called themselves, "The Quiet Company." And for good reason; there was a lot they didn't want you to know.) To put ITT Life on an equal plane with Northwestern Mutual was akin to the upstart Arizona Devil Rays defeating the New York Yankees in the World Series. We know that could never happen.

Dissect this memo and discover the classic CYA format.

"I told Bob . . . he should have cancelled . . ."
"I also said he should have contacted us . . ."
"I reminded Bob . . ."
"I cannot believe that Bob still went ahead . . ."
"I leave it to you . . ."

It's obvious from these negative mea culpas that the writer is the consummate rule-knower, -disseminator, and -follower. As with the classic rule-follower, he leaves things to others and, once covering his ass, exits from the scene. It's interesting to note that the writer, as with most CYA writers, takes the position of only being a messenger. The rules he is reporting on are those of others, not his. He takes no position on the rules. Why take a chance and put your ass on the line?

In fairness to the memo writer, I think he liked what we were doing and wanted us to be successful, but rule-following had become so ingrained into his psyche that he had simply lost the ability to take a risk and preferred to watch the game from the protection of the tunnel.

Fortunately, my appearance was a success. ITT Life gained some excellent exposure and highly favorable publicity. We were placed on the same level as a company that had been doing business just short of one hundred years longer than we had. Of course, I never heard another word about the memo. That's the way it is with CYA memos. But I knew that, somewhere in a file at Hartford (my God, I bet it's still there to this day!), that memo was collecting dust, and if I had ever tripped over one of the rules out it would have come. It also helped that in the intervening years ITT headquarters in New York presented our advertising and PR department a number of awards for doing exactly this type of rule-breaking activity.

Always Be Accountable

With any luck at all, you will be the subject of CYA memos. If so, be proud—like a red badge of courage. Be cheered by the fact that when CYA memos are targeted toward you, it is a clear indication that progress is being attained. Generally, CYA memo writers don't want confrontations, so they will try to use these missives to cover a lot of ground at one time—like the old-fashioned "kitchen sink" memos. Certain employees issue these memos on an annual basis, as if they were renewing an umbrella insurance policy.

One of the better ones read, "Bob, just in case you have not seen a copy of the attached ITT Hartford policy re procedures and guidelines for public relations activities, I thought you would like to have a copy. This is our bible and we have to make every effort to conform." Whew! Now rule-following had become a religious experience. This bureaucratic, CYA rule-follower didn't fool around with specific regulations like the other writer. This guy just dumped the entire rulebook on my head.

We were not immune from these types at ITT Life, either. One guy followed a similar philosophy with our salesmen. His job was to keep the sales force up to speed on new insurance regulations. So every time a state passed a new law, out would go a memo and attached to it would be a Xeroxed copy of the law. Little did it matter that few of our agents could read, let alone carry a law degree in their briefcase. Yet if an agent happened to stumble over a state regulation, this guy could claim he had done his job.

This whole situation reminds me of a conversation I had with one of the corporate mucky-mucks at the Hartford headquarters. As usual, I was being chastised over some rule that had been violated. Being in a good mood (which rarely happened in Hartford),I acknowledged my transgression but argued that common sense dictated that we had done the right thing. His response (probably one of the few times he had ever been candid and open with his thoughts) was one of those lightning-bolt flashes that startles and burns in your psyche. He said, "Bob, you are right and that's fine for you, but I won't sacrifice principle on the altar of poverty." Beautiful. Almost poetry. Can I rest my case now?

One of the benefits of being a practitioner of the cheat-to-win philosophy is the innate ability to recognize the CYA mentality. When you are able to do that, you can use CYA attitudes to accomplish your own objectives. Remember, people who write CYA memos are those who take no actions. They are no threat. If they took action, it would violate their basic CYA philosophies. Those CYA memos are most effective when gathering somewhere, collecting dust and growing like a tumor, but so long as we are successful (and usually even if we are not) these memos will never be seen again.

As I pointed out, the real value in the CYA memo is providing "cover" for people afraid to act of their own volition. Thus, a properly placed "reversed" CYA memo from you can provoke action from people who would not otherwise act. Offering up a memo taking responsibility for any action will inoculate these people with immunity from accountability and free them to help implement our plans.

The Line Between Respect and Renegade

There is a line between being respectful to authority, recognizing the need to be part of a team effort, and being a renegade. Recognize that being a renegade is not the same as being a rebel. A rebel has a cause; a renegade is a rebel without a cause. Breaking rules for a good can be good; breaking rules to break rules rarely is good. From our perspective today, Washington, Jefferson, and Hamilton are heroic rebels. In order to improve the common good, they cheated on bad rules imposed by established authority. To the British, however, they were renegades worthy only of death for their actions. Was John Brown of the Civil War era a rebel or a renegade—or both? Jesse James broke rules; was he rebel or renegade? Did General Douglas MacArthur cheat on rules imposed by Truman? Or did he violate guidelines established by our constitution? The point I am trying to make is that cheating to win is predicated on a rebellion against bad rules, not the blatant, self-serving disregard for authority exhibited by a renegade.

At The Hartford, both my boss and the CEO had approved the concept and general guidelines of the ITT Life marketing plan to attack the status quo of the life insurance industry. My attitude was that once the objective and guideline had been approved, it was appropriate—indeed necessary—to cheat on some traditional corporate rules that would —if obeyed—prevent us from achieving our objective.

If Pete Thomas had said, "No, you can't follow that marketing approach and must develop another," then it would have been inappropriate to move forward. However, once he had approved the concept, the rest of the rules were fair play.

Speared on My Own Petard

Certainly, as a leader of a company, I had no desire to see the tables turned on me by having people cheat on my rules, but I never felt that the way to avoid this situation was to have even more rules and tighter controls. My belief was that people could not cheat on my rules—so long as there were no rules. The strategy was to establish, communicate, and enforce guidelines and rules of engagement, but not operational rules. If people wanted rules, then they should make them—not me. Only if the guidelines needed to be changed or the rules of engagement adjusted did I expect people to come to me. This approach encouraged accountability and action while discouraging CYA tactics.

CYA can invade a corporate environment like infectious mold when leadership does not establish, promulgate, or protect honest guidelines and rules of engagement that give direction to activity. To fill this void, a whole body of rules emerges in an attempt to define the specifics of corporate action. However, if you know where you want to go, but are not especially concerned how you get there, then you don't need to have rules that reduce accountability, inhibit creativity, and cry out to be cheated on. Allow the doers of the organization, make the rules and you won't have to worry about CYA attitudes infecting your future.

Am I Still Free to Continue?

Your cheating-to-win arsenal requires understanding of yet another variation of the CYA rule. It's called the "checking back" rule. This rule requires that even after approval has been given for a project, you are compelled to stop several times to get continued approval. As with most rules, there is a rational basis for the implementation of this rule: checking back allows others to provide input if the situation has changed. But such rules also give those who have cold feet multiple options to block your efforts.

Gaining overall approval for a project is 90 percent of the effort to see it implemented, so why go through that process over and over? Cheating on the checking-back rule is not difficult because corporate animals rarely *want* you to check back. They actually fear that every time you check back there is the scary potential that responsibility could be transferred from you to them. (How wacko is that?) By cheating on the checking-back rule, you can keep your project on track and avoid the chance of it being killed by one of the rule-followers. It is important to pick your spot, but cheating on the checking-back rule can provide some early and large benefits.

Rosabeth Moss Kanter, writing for the *Wall Street Journal's* "Manager's Journal," called those who violate the checking-back rule "lone rangers." She wrote, "They have strong value orientation and are willing to battle the system for what they believe is right, even if they are alone in doing it. Outlaw as well as hero, these innovators may be ready to break minor rules to reach a greater goal. These people plunge ahead despite the roadblocks set-up by checking back."

A good example of this was IBM's development of the 360 System. If there were ever a company that belonged in the Guinness Book of Rule Makers it would be IBM. But a research lab in charge of developing a critical part of the 360 System moved ahead despite direct and persistent efforts of headquarters to control the program. Ultimately, the success of this effort ensured the success of the entire 360 System. If the group had checked back they would have been stopped and IBM would have lost millions—if not billions—in sales.

Closer to Home

In the summer of 1981, I presented my boss with the concept of a marketing plan for ITT Life that would break the two cardinal rules of the life insurance industry. The thrust of the plan was to attack the traditional product of the industry and to compete directly against (as opposed to with) other insurance companies. (See chapter 3—"Your Whole Life is a Mistake".) Following a frustrating number of meetings and presentations, tentative approval was finally granted. That was all I needed to be off and running without looking back.

In late August we began to marshal the forces of ITT Life (meager as they might be) in order to be ready to launch the program in January 1982. With such a short time frame to accomplish this objective, we would have to cheat on the checking-back rule. We knew there were CYA people who felt we were taking a major risk and would do what they could to stop us, despite corporate approval. To counter this risk, a special effort was made to ensure that all details and contingencies were covered and reviewed. The only real way to successfully cheat on the checking-back rule is to make sure there is little the checker can criticize when they check on you for not checking back.

The marketing plan was brought up with the Hartford people again at the annual ITT business plan meeting. (One great advantage of a bureaucratic and CYA environment is, "out of sight, out of mind." CYA rule-followers never go looking for trouble.) At these meetings, attended by over one hundred highly paid people, the only thing worse than the boredom was the horrible waste of time and money. We would sit in a room for two full days (that's one hundred people just from the insurance division of ITT), presenting and talking about plans that everyone making effective use of CYA tactics had already reviewed several times and few believed had even a modicum of reality.

True to form, this being my first such presentation, I managed to violate the two basic rules of the meeting:

1. Make sure there are no surprises.
2. Keep the meeting very serious.

During the meeting I surprised most in the group by announcing the details of our new marketing program—and managed to do so using bits of humor and language that caused other attendees to actually laugh. I am not sure which violation drew the most concern.

I must point out (cover my ass) that the surprise element of the presentation was not due to an attempt to undercut my superiors. Well in advance of the meeting I had provided full copies of the presentation well in advance of the meeting. While I did not deviate from that presentation, I will admit the humor was ad lib. The apparent bolt from the blue stemmed from the fact that people either didn't read, understand, or believe what I was going to say. I prefer to believe the plans were not read.

With most of the people making the presentations being financial types, you can imagine just how much excitement electrified the room. There were more overhead slides than at an army budget presentation. The best part of the meeting was watching the people from New York, none of whom knew anything about insurance, trying to impress Rand Araskog (the CEO of ITT at the time) by asking seemingly intelligent questions. The flip side of the fun—if you can call a meeting like this fun—was watching the Hartford people trying to keep their cool responding to dim-witted questions.

Just before it was to be my turn, the head of our sister company—Hartford Life—got up to make his presentation. This guy was the perfect corporate animal. Well dressed, polished, serious, reverent, and full of bullshit. He got up and gave the classic business plan presentation. It was obvious he knew and followed all the rules. As was typical at these meetings, he used the early part of his presentation to explain all the raisons d'être for the goals of the last business plan that had not been met. The middle of the report detailed plans for what they were going to do (or not do) next year. In a classic finish, he listed the rationalizations as to why they were not ready and why it would be difficult to implement the plans he had just listed.

In one fell swoop, he had scored a classic corporate home run— he hit a triple. He was able to wash away the failure of the current year, lay grandiose plans for the future, and set the stage for the first part of next year's report. He got to third base, but, as with most corporate players, there was no real effort to score. It's a lot safer to be on third base and blame someone else if there is no score.

It startled me to hear The Hartford Life report because the groundwork laid out was exactly what we were planning to do. He mentioned the sad state of the insurance industry's products and how lazy the big companies had become, along with how ripe the industry was for real competition. My heart almost sank to the floor when he said they were going to take advantage of this situation. However, my spirits soon bobbed back to the surface as he got back to corporate reality by saying, "This is a great opportunity and we are developing plans to take advantage of it, but we are not ready now." Whew!

My report was fairly simple and straightforward. Not because of any great insight, but because the meeting was running long and everyone wanted to get to the cocktail party. During a break, the time allotted to my presentation had been cut from fifteen to five minutes. Can you imagine that? Three days away from my company. Lost forever would be the cost of salary, travel, food, and lodging all for a five-minute presentation to people who didn't understand or care what I was going to say.

I tried to make the best of it, even kidding about the time. Casually mentioning my concurrence with The Hartford Life presentation, audible gasps could be heard when I said the only difference between our plan and Hartford Life was that we were ready to implement the strategy immediately. Shock replaced boredom on the faces of the attendees. I could hear low whispering,

"Oh God, an actual commitment." I don't know if it was the lateness of the hour, the presentation, or the humor, but there was a round of applause when I finished. That didn't happen at those types of meetings.

Unfortunately, I missed the cocktail party that day because I was besieged by all the CYA boys who were running for cover by reacting as if they had never heard of or seen my plan before this moment. Even worse, they were mortified and anguished over the use of humor during the presentation. As one sage (who had been to the cocktail party) said, "People do not like to smile in those meetings."

I am still amused that, four years later, in November 1985, when my boss was giving me a performance review, one of his criticisms was the fact that I had used humor in the 1981 business-plan meeting. He said, "Sure, people acknowledge that you are the best at giving a presentation, but you can't make light of the company and its business."

Little did it matter that ITT Life had accomplished far more then even we could have wished; the point that stuck in his craw was that I had broken the CYA rules. It became obvious that these business-plan meetings had become nothing more than the great CYA rule run completely amok.

The reaction to our cheating on the checking-back rule was immediate and predictable. Our offices in Minneapolis were immediately flooded with schools of lawyers, public relations, government relations, and administrative people. And in the months that followed, it seemed the primary activity of many of the Hartford bureaucrats was running for cover. How could they get their ass covered?

Fortunately, we had followed the key rule for cheating on the checking back rule: We had done our homework. Much to the surprise of our visitors, all the questions raised had been anticipated and prepared for. It was the ultimate compliment when one of the lawyers sent out to "help" us actually violated the CYA rule and endorsed our plan. Yet, up until the eve of our press conference in Washington announcing the program, we were fighting off road blocks put up by the bureaucrats.

It was a risk to break the checking-back rule and leave my ass uncovered, one that could have cost me my job if we had not prepared properly. However, I am absolutely convinced that if we had not violated the rule, there is no way we could have launched ITT Life's marketing program in anything like a timely fashion. The fact is, if we had not cheated on the rule every time we reached a decision point our program we may never have launched the marketing program—and ITT Life would still be just another small life company struggling to survive.

My management strategy for eliminating the need for people who work with me to cheat on the checking-back rule is not to ask them to check back with me for approval. Rather, once a plan has been approved—it has been approved. All I want are reports on progress being made, so there is no need to cheat.

And the Moral of the Story Is . . .

If real, serious, and rapid success is to be achieved, we as individuals and the culture of our organization must be encouraged to cheat on the CYA rule and put our ass on the line. This can be done with total impunity so long as when we do put our ass on the line we have our "stuff" together. (Oh, it would have been so easy to plug in the other word, but that would have been too cheap.) If a culture properly assigns appropriate accountability, with rewards equal to the risk, there is no need for CYA attitudes.

Tolstoy never made it to a corporate boardroom, but with his attitude he could have probably would have been very successful. Over a century ago he said, "The people who bind themselves to systems are those who are unable to encompass the whole truth and try to catch it by the tail; it leaves its tail in your fingers and runs away knowing full well that it will grow a new one in a twinkling."

The true doers in business are those who are willing to step out from the crowd and fully accept the responsibility for their actions. When you're willing to leave your ass exposed, you can accomplish a tremendous amount no matter your level in the company, no matter how old you are, no matter your gender, your race, or your religion. When your cohorts are running for cover, you need to run for the open. If you are willing to cheat on that rule and not worry about covering your ass—and if you are doing the right thing—then you are going to be very successful. Even if that is not the case, you can learn a valuable lesson from cheating on the CYA rule. If efforts are not recognized or appreciated, you can learn that you are in the wrong organization and should seek more fertile ground for your talents.

Most people focus on the negative, as opposed to the opportunity. The paradox is that most people are trying to cover their ass from a downside risk that is virtually nonexistent. And that's the whole point: the upside potential to be achieved by cheating on the CYA rule is so much greater then the spanking you might get for failure that it is, pants-down, no comparison. Cover-your-ass rules prevent more good things from happening than they ever prevent bad things happening. That's precisely the thought I discovered in the *Economics Press*, "None of us likes to make a mistake. All managers worth their salt want to avoid errors, but who can tell for sure whether a new idea will work until it has actually been tried? If the possible gains far outweigh the potential loss, it's a mistake *not* to try it."

9

Look Down to Move Up

Ass kissing is such a contemptible form of attentiveness
it's a wonder so many stoop to do it.

One of the most cherished rituals of humankind is the adroit practice of ass kissing. Carried down through the annals of time, for many this activity has been raised to an art form designed to propel them to the highest levels of success, powers, and riches. It is believed this practice originated in antiquity when first described by the Greek root word, "assofmine," but the modern derivation comes to us directly from the German word "asinine."

That, for all our life, we should be titillated by elements of the human ass is not surprising. (Lord knows it's difficult to go through a day without meeting one.) After all, our first experience in this life is to have our butt slapped. (This initial encounter with authority—the doctor—is to let us know we are not in charge and that people in authority administer pain so that rules are followed.) Our rude welcome to the world is followed closely by having the nurse kiss our ass with kindness—a hint of good things to come.

Growing up, we are constantly conditioned to the benefits of ass kissing. Children learn early on that acting sweet and nice in front of adults, no matter how they act with peers or siblings, always gets the treats. The student who brings the polished apple to the teacher or stays late to clean chalkboards (politically correct forms of ass kissing) always wins the glowing smile and special succor of warmth. Conversely, it was a clear signal that we were falling behind in the ass-kissing department when the authority figure said to us, "Why can't you be like Johnny? He is so nice."

Most are so indoctrinated with this form of false flattery that by the time we graduate from college and enter the business world, we are totally schooled in the ways of ass kissing and ready to turn pro. This preparation is essential, since one of the most revered rules of business life is that admission to the elite inner sanctum comes only to those who are quite proficient at kissing the asses of those above.

At the same time, we are encouraged to accomplish this task by stepping on those lower in the pecking order so as to properly purse our lips. (All the while expecting those below us to perform the same function. Like a chain ass-kiss.)

This concept is ass backward. We should kiss this stupid rule good-bye and cheat to win—early and often. If we have the courage to break this rule, we'll not only move up the ladders of life faster, we'll also feel a whole lot better about ourselves. Let's follow the theory of the ass-kissing rule, and then learn why we should cheat on it.

Ass Kissing-—Theory and Practice

The presumption is that if we kiss enough big asses often enough then we will be pulled up the ladder from above, so we can continue to practice the act. The banner hung above the entrance to the Ass Kisser Hall of Fame situated just outside Harvard Yard reads, "Best Ass Kisser Wins!" While there may be the appearance of winning and short-term benefit derived from perfecting the talent as a practicing ass kisser, in the end (so to speak), it doesn't work.

Ultimately, not only will you feel bad about yourself for engaging in the act (or at least you should), your peers will see you for what you are and ridicule you. You'll get less respect than the late Rodney Dangerfield. Worse yet, those who are the recipient of your gluteus lip service will grow to distrust you—and you risk becoming the proverbial office "turd in a punch bowl." And even if the kissee falls for your effort, and believes your solicitous offerings, then you have bet on a loser who will surely fail and eventually drag you down to their odious level.

Ass Kissers I Have Known

Ass kissing is such a prevalent practice in business that after forty years of observing this activity, the examples available would make this the longest chapter in the book. I am sure you have great examples of true world-class ass kissers, but let me put forward one of the best (or worst) examples I encountered and the failure it can bring on. The names have been changed to protect the smell. This experience happened as Allianz Life had acquired LifeUSA.

Apparently ass kissing had risen to epidemic levels at Allianz Life. Just after the acquisition was announced, Herbert Hansmeyer, the head of Allianz operations for North America, asked me to sit with him to discuss senior staffing of the merged company. When the name of one of the very senior members of the existing Allianz Life staff came up, Herbert said to me, "Now, you are going to discover that this guy is just a politician (the loose German translation for ass kisser) and not very effective as an executive. You are going to want to fire him right away, but please don't because we like to use him in certain situations."

Sure enough, as I observed this guy, he spent almost all his time trying to kiss ass with anyone—especially the honchos from Germany—who he thought could help his career. This guy was good, in fact better than good. He was world class when it came to ass kissing. At the same time, he treated with icy disdain anyone below him who did not kiss his ass. (What really endeared him to me was when I discovered that he was constantly going to our German friends to either complain about changes being made at the company or to claim personal credit for company successes.) Those who worked for this man distrusted him completely: they knew that since he spent most of his time with his nose firmly nestled in the BC (figure it out) of those above him, he could not be counted on for support.

To make matters worse for him, the targets of his ass-kissing attention—the very people he was trying to impress—recognized him for what he was and had even less respect. (It was like watching one of those reality shows where the people don't know they are being watched.) The irony is that with his vision blocked, he was the very last guy to see any of this. He firmly believed that those below saw him as the great force in the company because he spent so much time with the big asses. He thought those in Germany viewed him as a real comer and ultimate company leader.

About eighteen months later, Henning Schulte-Noelle, the CEO of Allianz AG, was in town from Munich, visiting the company. As I drove him back to the hotel he said to me, "Bob, I thought you were a good executive." "Yes," I said, "what changed your mind?" "Well," he responded, "I thought you would have fired this guy by now. He is nothing but a politician." I didn't have the heart to tell Henning that I had been ordered not to fire the guy, but did decide that it was time to take some action.

A few weeks later I called this chap into my office and, none too gently (he was so delusional that only a two-by-four upside the head would get his attention), explained that not only did I and everyone he worked with think he was a poor executive, but the very people whose patooties he had kissed thought even less of him. While counting on the people in Munich to rescue him from me and his employees, those in Germany would just as soon see him working for the French. (Which turns out to be just about the worst curse the Germans thought they could dish up to anyone.)

Of course, he blamed me for his situation and felt I was out to get him because he didn't kiss my ass enough. Just goes to show you how cloudy your vision gets when you spend so much of the time with your eyes closed. Anyway, at least he was smart enough to leave the company and find an antiquated culture (a mutual life insurance company) that apparently encouraged and appreciated professional ass kissing, and he became a star.

Establishing a Natural Pecking Order

I am a firm believer in offering deference and respect to those with greater experience and higher in the pecking order—if they deserve it! Even then, I will show respect for their position, if not for them.

People we work for deserve our loyalty, respect, and support—until they do something to prove otherwise. But those qualities or attributes are best delivered honestly—face to face—not by bending over to find something good to smooch.

Over forty years of experience has convinced me that blindly following the "kiss ass" rule as a shortcut success is wrong. It will ultimately be your long dark tunnel to failure just as surely as Hastings Cutoff was to the Donner Party.

The Cheat-to-Win Road to Success

My experience tells me that the pathway to success comes most assuredly by helping others be successful—not the empty calories of ass kissing. If we look down the ladder, instead of up, and help the people below to be successful, then they will push us up. One of the great leaders in American history understood this point completely. As Bruce Chadwick wrote in *George Washington's War*, " . . . and he completely understood that the function of all good leaders was not to make the men under him . . . care about what happened to him, but what happened to them. His political genius was to understand that the successful leader . . . gains power and status not by assuming his own success, but the success of others."

I learned early on the rule of "power of numbers" in trying to accomplish my goals. There was a limited amount I could do myself—and even less if I spent time ass kissing. If I could please and motivate those below me, then a lot more could be accomplished and my fortunes would rise with the tide. Maybe that is why we hear about, "The hordes of Mongol marauders." If you kiss ass, in the end you are nothing but an old horde. But if your honest interest is to help and protect others below you to achieve success, then they become hordes of supporters that give you immense power.

One promise made (and kept) to people I work with is that if they will work their ass off for me, I will do the same for them. The philosophy to embrace is that it is our job to make it possible for those who work for us to concentrate on their job. They don't have to worry about protecting their ass—that's my job. They don't have to worry about the next promotion—I'll do that for them. They don't have to worry about the next raise—I'll get them what they deserve. They don't have to fret about working hard only to have someone else take the credit—they'll get all they deserve. And, if something goes wrong, I'll be ready take the blame. Early on I learned that great success can be achieved when I make it my job to create an opportunity and environment where others are free to do the best job possible. I want them to understand that I spend my time looking out for their best interests, not mine. That approach may cheat on the kiss-ass rule, but it works!

If the people who work for you trust you and believe that you really will take care of their best interests, then not only are they freed up to do the job that needs to be done, but they will be grateful to you and push you up the ladder ahead of them.

Ass kissing was a great art form at my first corporate job with State Mutual Life. Not only were you expected to kiss the ass of the people above you, but also, for more practice, those in the "core" took turns kissing each other's asses. Trust me this behavior caused bitter and deep resentment among the rank-and-file employees who hated it. Not having been properly schooled in ass kissing, I failed to catch on to the practice right away and my truculence (undeservedly) elevated me to near-hero status among my fellow employees. The power of paying attention to those down the ladder made a very strong impression on me.

Most of the people who worked at LifeUSA will tell you that they are grateful for all I did for them. Even today, I receive letters and comments from people thanking me for making their lives so much better. (That is, except for the guy I called on the carpet for ass kissing extraordinaire. He only sent me one note and it had some weird white power in it.) My response to these comments—and it's true—is that the only thing I did was create an opportunity for them to be successful. I did not make them successful. The fact is that all these people did much more for me than I ever did for them.

Fortunately, by cheating on the ass-kissing rule, I had learned that it's possible to achieve high levels of success by allowing others to share in the dream. I mention this not to hold myself up for what

I did, but to offer evidence that marshaling masses of asses to support your efforts pushes you a lot further along than one old ass can pull you.

Even if you are in a culture that tolerates or even encourages professional ass kissing, you can win by cheating on the rule. The bottom line is that if you are in a situation where ass kissing works, then you are working for the wrong company. If you work for a company with a culture that allows success only by ass kissing then kiss the company good-bye.

Instead, build or look for a culture that recognizes the power of people who are supported from above and are rewarded for accomplishment, not accomplished ass kissing. Ultimately, you will move up the ladder of success faster and farther by looking out for the best interests of those below you.

And the Moral of the Story Is . . .

Don't be beguiled by the value of kissing up to your superiors, regardless of how far you ascend the corporate ladder. Deferential? Yes. Toadying? No. Ass kissing? Never.

Break the culture of the corporate ass kissers by stepping out; concentrate on being the best at what you do, accept responsibility, and build on a solid foundation of helping those who support your efforts. Look down the ladder for support, not up. Build a parallel relationship with your staff, however humble, and believe me, they will rise to the occasion and help elevate you to any goal you desire. They are the wind beneath your wings.

10

The Secret to Gaining Power and Wealth

*If money is the root of all evil, then
surely power is the Viagra for all egos.*

No two motivators spur people to be successful in business more than attaining—power and wealth. They are truly the sisters of desire. With power and wealth comes the feeling deity—without them you are …. out of luck! Power is the ultimate! Wealth is not far behind. The only drive stronger than the drive to acquire power and wealth is the drive to keep power and wealth once acquired. Power and wealth are such all encompassing concepts that it would take volumes—not pages—to outline the rules that are in place to control their acquisition and retention. Not surprisingly, more rules are promulgated about how to acquire, use, and perserve power and money than almost any other human or business activity.

People will do almost anything to gain power and once they have tasted it, will do even more to keep it. (Joseph Stalin's proclivity to execute anyone who might be even the slightest threat to his power is a good example of the latter, but we will leave that tale for the history books.)

It's no wonder that power and wealth are so sought after. After all, most of humanity has, over time, been stratified along the lines of power and wealth. Virtually every human organization, such as schools, businesses, and governments—even families—exist in a hierarchical structure, largely divided by the "haves" and the "have-nots."

Not that there's anything wrong with seeking to achieve or actually acquiring power and wealth. The error of our ways is when we worship at the altars of power and wealth so that they melt into the ultimate vice described by the poet Shelley:

> *Power, like a desolating pestilence,*
> *Pollutes whate'er it touches . . .*

Somewhere between the vice and virtue of both power and wealth, however, is fertile ground for cheaters to advance their careers and business by learning how to cheat on the traditional rules dealing with these twin motivating engines.

Making a Difference and Making Choices

Please understand, when discussing power, I'm not necessarily referring to the horrific power wielded by presidents, emperors, or kings—not to mention wives. Power is relative. And when dealing with the subject of wealth, I don't necessarily mean the obscene wealth of modern billionaires. Wealth is artificial. For the purpose of our discussions, I would define power as having the ability to make a difference, and wealth as having the freedom to make choices. By these definitions we need not be corporate titans or political kingpins to wield power, and we need not be an Allen or Gates to enjoy wealth. (And if you don't know who these two guys are, forget it. Take this book back and exchange it for *"The Secrets to Winning the Lottery."*)

Since few of us would disdain the acquisition of some form of power or wealth, the proverbial $64,000 question is: What is the secret to getting them? Well, the real trick is to inherit them, but for those of us who were not born into families of power and wealth we will have to find another path. For most of us, that's going to mean cheating on the established rules for reaching levels of power and wealth. And there is a logical reason for the need to cheat.

Power Is Mine to Have and to Hold

People who already have wealth or power spend much of their time scheming to prevent others from obtaining the same. The cruel irony is that because they already have power and wealth, they have the wealth and power to establish the rules dealing with the acquisition of wealth and power. Not surprisingly, this makes it quite difficult for the "have-nots" to become the "haves"—for those without wealth to gain wealth. Or for those who are powerless to become powerful.

Virtually all society's rules in business, finance, politics, and even the social graces, exist to keep the rich wealthy and the powerful, more powerful. The American electoral system is a good example. (Forget that the blatant objective of the electoral college is to keep the wealthy in power. Need we talk about the presidential election of 2000?) For example, members of the U. S. Congress are not paid a lot of money relative to the responsibility inherent in their job, but they do have tremendous *power.* The rules, structure, and actions of congress are all geared toward creating a system that preserves their power. They call it incumbency; in Vegas they call it deck stacking.

Over the years, congress has established rules that result in an average of 93 percent of incumbents being swept back into (instead of out of) office. The rules are set up so that those in power remain in power. (And we said Saddam Hussein rigged elections!) It really makes no difference whether you are a Republican or a Democrat. (It doesn't make much difference for other reasons too, but that is again another story.) You see, power is power—no matter what form of government, political persuasion. or geographical area, those in power want to stay in power and create a minefield of rules to protect themselves. (Even God and academics get involved in this power trip. The College of Cardinals has been the scene of some great battles for power!)

Look at the John Kerry (if you can bear to) family, the Bushs, and the Kennedys, and you'll discover that these folks (and hordes of blue bloods like them), remain in power because of a set of rules that are designed to perpetuate their power and wealth—while keeping others out of the club.

This type of strategy trickles down into the corporate level and it seeps into the economic system. (Hell, it is the basis of the economic system!) It is the old story that you have to have money to make money. It's like the old saying: "I can get money from a bank if I don't need money from a bank." The rules are set up so that those who do not need the money can get the money, and those who need the money can't get it. In a nutshell, "Them that has, gets."

It Has Always Been That Way

It took some Italian guy of the 1800s (who, being Italian had nothing better to do) by the name of Villfredo Pareto (for those linguistics among us, the English translation of this name is "parent of Fred," but we don't know what happened to Fred) to quantify the obvious for us. Pareto, whom the Italians considered to be a mindless malcontent, was what we call an "economist" today. Pareto learned through research (I am sure with the help of some government grant) that most of the money and power in Europe was concentrated in the hands of a relatively small number of individuals. Duh!

Others studies he conducted during extensive subsidized trips abroad with his niece demonstrated that, not only was this true in Europe, but was also true virtually everywhere, including the United States. And not only that, the most telling point was that it had *always been that way.* (What a sharpie!)

This guy figured out that 20 percent of the population controls 80 percent of the wealth, and there is an 80 percent chance that you will not be part of the 20 percent. This perceptive discovery was so important to the understanding of economics that he got a rule named after himself (the very ultimate for economists) and it still exists to this day. This rule, known as "Pareto's Law," would later be dubbed the 20/80 rule (as opposed to the TV show *20/20*), and it has proved to be remarkably resilient in empirical studies as well as wholesale application to business.

The discovery and application of the operating rule, of course, was that the rule-makers had the power and they did all they could to perpetuate their superior positions. The rules have worked for generations of the "haves" who have wanted to protect their turf, power, and wealth from the "have-nots."

We make light of Signore Pareto, but the point is that rules regarding power and wealth are in place to maintain the status quo (as, frankly, most rules are) and to prevent the spread or diminution of power and wealth. Sure, you can play by the rules and follow along like a good ol' boy, hoping that before you get too old you might be admitted to the game; knowing full well that along the way a certain part of your facial anatomy is going to get quite brown. If that's not for you, and you want to sit at the table on your terms, then the logical conclusion is that you have to cheat on the existing rules to get there.

It Seemed Like a Good Idea

Any number of bright, mischievous, deceitful, and endearing do-gooders have attempted to come up with ways to cheat on the rules in order to shift the entire wealth and power curve, as it were, to the right: to favor greater equality for everyone. Pareto was one of these guys, and his idea was to shift the income curve through a progressive income tax that took the money from the rich and (theoretically) gave it to the poor. But all that did was penalize people for being rich and make others not want to work to be rich. (It took the U.S. Congress a while to discover this technique, but once they got the hang of it, they made it a science.)

Another guy with too much time on his hands (but apparently not enough time to shave) who attempted to balance out this powerful/rich equation was Karl Marx. This guy made our friend Pareto look like a right-wing piker! Wacko Marx came up with an idea that might have been a good slogan for the accounting department at Enron, but was not a very good economic theory. He said, "From each according to his ability, to each according to his needs." For some reason Marx got a lot of other people who didn't shave, either, to buy off on his ideas—and we know the rest of the story.

Beating Down Does Not Lift Up

All these great ideas offering to break through the barrier of wealth and power had one fatal flaw. The shared philosophy went something like this: To make poor and powerless people richer and powerful, take wealth and power from the rich and powerful and give it to the poor and powerless. The shorthand definition of this concept is called "class warfare." When these ideas are fully implemented, everyone becomes poor and powerless.

Simple Is As Simple Does

I would not dare to be presumptuous enough to put myself in the class of these great thinkers (except maybe in my own mind), but it seems to me that they all miss the point. You don't make people rich and powerful by reducing or transferring the wealth and power of those who have it to those who don't.

The problem with the rules that relate to wealth and power is that they are in place to prevent others from achieving wealth and power. The way to cheat on those rules is not to eliminate wealth and power, but to figure out how to create more wealth and power to spread around. It's only natural that if you are going to acquire wealth and power by taking it away from those who have it, they will fight you. The trick is to figure out a way to cheat on the rules in a way that creates new wealth and power so that the conflict is eliminated.

This situation was brought home to me as soon as I became president of ITT Life. As mentioned in the chapter on intimidation, one marketing organization at ITT Life had all the wealth and power in the company and were producing over 60 percent of the total new business. This state of affairs was unhealthy for the company and, in reality, for the marketing organization as well.

One of my first goals and challenges as the new guy was to strive to reach the point where no single source of business accounted for more than 10 percent of the total. When challenged to achieve this objective, the common reaction from the marketing department was to search for ways to control the growth of the existing organization or even divide it up into smaller pieces to reduce its size and power. (People who have never had real jobs running companies and think they are really smart or want to run for governor call this activity "anti-trust.") The dilemma created by this approach was that, while we might be able to achieve our objective by reducing the size of the marketing group, the company would be hurt as much as the marketing company.

We would not make ITT Life bigger by making this organization smaller. The challenge was: How do we continue to support the growth of this organization while reducing its percentage of total business? The answer was obvious: We had to attract and grow new sources of production at a faster rate than the existing organization was growing. The perfect scenario was to help the existing organization grow larger, while reducing its total impact on the company. By being successful in this endeavor both the organization and the company became winners.

This same simple concept applies to individuals seeking to gain some modicum of power and wealth. It is counterproductive to "steal" it from others. Yet the question remains: What can we as individuals do to overcome the rules that limit our access to power and wealth?

Lots of Little Together Makes Bigger

Contrary to existing rules, the way to gain personal power is to empower others. The way to gain wealth is to make others wealthy. Even though I am not an economist (heck, I am not even smart enough to read their magazine), I would like to have some laws named after me—like a MacLaw.

The first MacLaw: The amount of power you possess will be magnified and leveraged in incremental proportion to the power given to others. Only one with power can grant power, so the more power you grant to others, the more power you gain.

The second MacLaw: The amount of wealth you acquire will be a direct multiple of the wealth you share with others. So the more people you help to become wealthy, the more wealth you will gain. And people will come to you seeking to make you wealthy when word gets out that they get to share in the wealth they make.

A Lesson or Two from the History Books

History offers some wonderful validations of this approach. During the cold war, did anything seem stronger or more implacable than the political, economic, and social stranglehold the former Soviet Union and the countries of Eastern Europe had on their citizens? It was difficult to imagine that anything—short of nuclear war—could break the iron grip of the governments over the people. The West feared that this style of repression would spread, rather than recede, in the world.

Any individual who attempted to cheat on the rules and fight the system was at best ostracized as a "nonperson" and at worst institutionalized or eliminated. That's why the notion of one man against the system never bears fruit. (Nor does the one-man one-vote concept in Florida!) The system will always win. In totalitarian governments or dictatorships, one person who rises up to fight the system alone is going to lose.

In both politics and business, however, the appearance of power is almost always stronger than the reality. A dictator can remain in power only so long as he can maintain the appearance of possessing total power. In fact, power—any level of power—is a very thin veneer of gloss held in place by either trust or fear. Once these elements disappear, the hold on power becomes tenuous. Any time the masses of people share the same vision and rise up, the existing power becomes helpless to keep people under control.

In Berlin, Ronald Reagan was cheered for demanding that Soviet President Mikhail Gorbachev "Tear down this wall!" Notice that he asked the powerful to give up power, not the powerless to take power. I can't condemn Ronald Reagan for this approach; with the rules in place it seemed the only (if futile) thing to do. Everyone knew that Gorbachev would not abide by that request, because the rules had been put in place for everything but that.

The Polish government (despite what Gerald Ford believed) was as repressive as any government in the Eastern bloc. The Polish people had no power and barely more than potatoes to eat. (Can you imagine how much fun it would have been if Gerald Ford and Dan Quayle had been on the same ticket?) Yet the walls began to crack and crumble when an obscure and uneducated Polish shipyard worker by the name of Lech Walesa began to convince his comrades that they had the power to make things better for themselves and their country.

Rather than trying to gain power playing by the rules of the powerful—namely, join the party and support the status quo till it was his turn—Walesa gained power by rejecting and cheating on the rules. His secret was that rather than seek power for himself, he sought power for the people. In the end, Walesa became powerful—and the eventual president of Poland—by empowering other people. The Berlin Wall did not come down because Gorbachev decided to give up power, but when the proletariat joined hands and minds they became more powerful than the rules and together as a group they knocked it down.

What we do in our lives may not be as grandiose as overthrowing governments (although I know some that should be) and changing the course of the world forever, but the very same principles apply to changes in our lives and the lives of those in our world.

Building Power Blocs That Open the Way

Building our own power by empowering others is as easy as one, two, three. One, communicate. Two, respect. And three, trust. I have learned over the years that—no matter what level of power you may have—your power will be enhanced and strengthened if your efforts are used to enforce those simple points to share your power with others.

When a management philosophy employs constant, transparent communication, shows a need and respect for the talents of employees and trusts them to do the right thing, then an environment is created that is just right for the growth of the power and influence of the leader. It is a simple philosophy that works at the mailroom level just as it works in the palace. Experience has convinced me that people in their own world – no matter how large or small – can be more powerful if their first objective is to empower others in that world.

Information Is a Roadblock Or a Highway

If you are going to share power, the first rule to cheat on is the "information" rule. Think about how important information is to power, and how power is equated with information. People talk about society entering the "information age." Unfettered access to information will make us smarter, better at what we do, and yes—richer and more powerful.

Possession of information has always been an indicator of power in the business world. People are led to believe, "If I know something about the company and you don't, then I am more powerful than you." Remember how the Hartford powermongers got so bent out of shape when information about company plans and performance was shared with the employees of ITT Life? The powers at Hartford had the command of information and did not feel it was appropriate to share it with the employees. Hartford – and thousands of businesses like them—actually believe that theory. They deem that information is an expression of (quite rightly) power and power should not be shared. Information is to be hoarded, protected, and parceled out only to those in the power club. Most have the same attitude toward wealth: keep the cake and let others eat crumbs.

This attitude was no different than the pre-Civil War South, where citizens were prohibited from teaching slaves to read and write. Lawmakers knew that literacy was power. Accordingly, a literate slave was largely a contradiction in terms. This is a classic example of the powerful people making the rules. By breaking the information rule with ITT employees, their trust, respect, and support were gained—and along with that came more power.

Yes, information is power, but if you keep it to yourself and try to hoard it like a treasure, then information becomes like an unused battery hidden away in a drawer, slowly losing its power. There is more to breaking the information rule than just sharing specific facts. It also relates to the different types of communication given to those you seek to empower.

The Cornerstone of Corporate Power

The definition of power in the corporate world is the guy on the top floor in the corner office with two secretaries. The guy you have to fight through an armada of gatekeepers to see. If that's going on in a company where you work, you're getting a definite signal. A signal that the person in the big corner office on the top floor has a lot of clout and wants to keep it. That is the wrong signal to give, and as you move up it's a rule to cheat on.

If you had visited LifeUSA or Allianz Life when I was CEO, you would not have found a secretary in front of my office. The door was open and you could have walked right in. My office was cluttered with homey artifacts to put employees and visitors at ease. The signal I was trying to give was that power comes from a different source, or a different approach.

We wanted to send our employees (owners) an unmistakable message that *they* are the important, powerful people—and that's why they were placed on the top floor in the corner office. Employees make or break a company. They will work hard because of the respect you've shown them. Then, as a result of their work, you become more powerful than you ever would have been, hiding away on the penthouse level.

It's Sometimes Difficult to Go All the Way

Let me give you an example. The other day I met with a fellow who manages one of my investment portfolios. He's a good guy who means well. He mentioned that after following the LifeUSA story for years (at one time LifeUSA owned 40 percent of his company) he is trying to incorporate some of the "parallel interests" principles we developed at LifeUSA into his own business, particularly our program for sharing ownership and power with employees.

That was a great start, but he blew it all when he qualified his comments by saying, "Of course, I have to keep at least 51 percent of the stock so that I can keep control of the company." I was disappointed but not shocked. It was not an unusual reaction from others who mean well but can't quite come to grips with the idea that it is possible to give up legal control over something, yet actually increase power.

The in-vogue thing for business books now is to espouse the philosophy of people empowerment. They rightly argue that empowerment is the path to success, but they tiptoe around the crux of the issue without putting real teeth into their action.

What they and my friend don't quite understand is that the measure of your power and potential wealth is not based on the percentage of your ownership, but on the percentage of power and wealth you share. I admit it is difficult to break out of the old mold, but it is worth it—cheat on that damn rule that says you always have to have 51 percent! What you gain from others is in direct proportion to what you give to others. Trust me—it works! And I have the results to prove it.

Lesson Learned, Lesson Applied

Learning to share real information with those critical to the success of the organization is critical. So important, in fact, that one of the first actions taken at LifeUSA was to institute a series of communication forums designed to bring the power of the people to bear on what we were trying to accomplish.

Most businesses, and virtually all corporations, have remarkably efficient programs to share internal information. Employee Web sites, newsletters, memos, and the like quickly and accurately keep employees abreast of interoffice dope. You know what I'm talking about. All the news releases about new company hires, new members to the twenty-year club, anniversaries, awards, company softball teams, and babies that are made available to all employees. Naturally, I'm all for that. It builds camaraderie and corporate *esprit de corps.*

When I talk about sharing information, however, the objective is to go deeper and share information that empowers the employee. And oftentimes you can measure the degree to which it may empower an employee by the willingness of corporate managers to share it. The relationship is nearly always inversely related.

At LifeUSA, we were serious about sharing this kind of information. Our "Share the Wealth" meetings were typical of this approach. Basically structured as mini-shareholder meetings, they were held monthly as part of a program to build an entrepreneurial culture through communication.

We discussed the performance of the company, our P & L, corporate financial results—warts and all. Plans—yes, even secret ones—were discussed openly. In an effort to intermingle the functions of the company, presentations were made by various departments and everyone was kept abreast of certain important strategies such as new products and promotions.

Meetings like these were part of the *ongoing program* of communication that included meetings and conferences of all kinds: "Brunch with Bob" was a frequent meeting. Twice a month I would meet in the boardroom of the company for an informal bag-lunch meeting with twelve to fifteen employees. No managers were allowed, only owners! The meeting would open with me giving a report on the progress of the company—as if reporting to the board of directors—and outlining current plans. After my presentation the get-together was open to questions from anyone in the group. There were no limits or restrictions to what issues could be raised and discussed. Again, the objective of the meeting was not just to provide information, but to emphasize that the people in attendance—and others in the company—were important and respected for the value they brought to the company.

The concept of transparency was in vogue at LifeUSA before we even knew the word existed. The internal culture of the company was to share the wealth, the information, and the power with all employees. The belief was that for LifeUSA to compete with the giants of the industry, we had to cheat on the rules that exclude the rank and file from the total truth about the company.

Communication Needs to Be a Two-Way Street

You know how frustrating it can be to meet a person who only wants to talk about their issues? You can sit with some people for an hour and for a week of that time all they do is tell you their stories. What does that tell you? Obviously, they care more about themselves than you. They are showing no interest in you, and, even worse, no respect for you. You may have had something of importance to discuss, but after trying on numerous occasions to break in, you just give up the thought and let them drone on—and by that time you have tuned them out.

Others are empowered, respect is communicated, and trust is established when you are genuinely willing to listen to the thoughts and ideas of employees. Empowering communication is as much listening as it is talking. How would you treat someone who was famous, powerful, successful, and accomplished? With respect, interest, and attention? And would you express that by wanting to hear what they had to say and by learning all you could from them? That same attitude and approach can be used successfully when we seek to empower others we lead. Creating an environment that encourages openness and listening will make us the beneficiary (notice I just can't get away from the insurance business) of valuable information on an ongoing basis. At the same time, it will also constantly signal our respect and belief in the power of the person offering the information.

Of course, as a leader, you must differentiate between static and information. It is a bit like receiving messages from our probes in deep outer space. You cannot hear them unless you have your antennas up. You also need the ability to determine if this is black noise or if this is real information. If your culture has no antenna, then you're only going to get dead air, silence. You will only hear the sound of yourself talking. If you have an antenna, but you do not decipher the meaning of incoming information, you are getting data that will be useless to you.

The Power of Easy, Long-Lasting Lessons

I was fortunate to stumble onto the idea of gaining by simply showing respect for others when I moved out of the "core" at State Mutual. (See chapter 7—"Intimidate the Intimidator".) While that act of moving out of the "core" dealt with intimidation, it was also a lesson in gaining power. My move to the general work area sent a message to the people I worked with that they were more important than the executives I left behind. It transferred a sense of power to them when one who had power in the company (at least more than they did) choose to be among them. The act created an access to power they had not experienced before and made them feel (and in fact *be*) more powerful.

This form of respect from the leader resulted in increased efforts to reciprocate the shared power and respect. Soon our department was able to do more, more quickly and efficiently than other areas. As I say, this small example did not have a huge impact on the company—and certainly not the world—but it did make a mark on me. Slowly it became apparent that the department—and the people along with it—had become a powerful force within the company, simply because of small steps to empower the people in the department. In turn, I became more powerful and influential within the company than if I had tried to keep control of the power in the core.

This lesson carried over to ITT Life. The straightforward act of inviting all the employees to participate in a meeting to discuss the progress of the company empowered people to care about the company. Employees who care are very powerful. When you cheat on these power rules you will learn, as I did, that the leaders of an organization do not have to make every decision. Leaders have a responsibility to establish strategic goals, but a motivated, informed, and interested employee group is perfectly capable of making most, if not all, of the decisions dealing with the operation of the company. The more I allowed others to participate and make decisions, the more power I had to wield.

One activity at LifeUSA served as a wonderful example for employee empowerment. It was called "work simplification" and involved a group of employees representing different disciplines coming together to look for ways to improve the activity and productivity of the company. It could be anything from the processing of applications to the distribution of payroll. The idea was—as the company grew larger—to discover simpler or more efficient ways of running the company. Employees were not assigned to these committees—they volunteered. And we had them standing in line to participate. Why? Because they knew their recommendations would be taken seriously and that they had the power to impact the company. The power of these people working together made me—and other managers—all that more powerful.

One other small example in a long chain of actions designed to both functionally empower people and—equally important—make them feel powerful was the way charity giving was handled at LifeUSA. (And still is today at Allianz Life). When it came to charitable giving, the employees—not management or HR—decided where the funds should be allocated. The employees literally formed a committee to make recommendations and then voted for the charities they wanted to support. This is a minor point, but the more you can empower people to participate in activities that will impact their lives, the more they will be involved, care, and contribute.

Of course, the ultimate example of power sharing was the concept of employee ownership at LifeUSA. If wealth is power—if ownership is power—then sharing both is the ultimate empowering of people. How can anyone have more power—or feel more empowered— than to be a true owner of the enterprise?

The examples of empowering others demonstrate that it is possible to empower others—and increase your own power—but it does not have to be as dramatic as making all employees owners of the company. It might be the best way, but it may not be possible and it certainly is not the only way. The rules may say that power shared is power lost, but the reality is that power shared is power enhanced.

Wealth Is What You Make It

Not all of the founders of LifeUSA had a burning desire to be successful entrepreneurs. The fact is, of the group of five that left ITT Life and started the company, only Don Urban had any experience as an entrepreneur. (Surprisingly, the other founding members even wondered why Don should even be included. Of course, six months later all of them knew what a great idea they had to include him.) It's probably fair to say that most of the group were tricked into joining LifeUSA. At first I thought it was the promise of wealth and riches that motivated them to leave secure, stable positions to join in some wild idea about starting a new life insurance company.

I was dissuaded of that notion during a conversation with one of the founders—Pete Huffman—just before we left ITT Life. I asked Pete what he felt would be just reward to risk it all by leaving ITT Life and participate with the group starting LifeUSA. After pondering for a bit he responded with, "If my stock could be worth $500 thousand when all was said and done, I would be happy." This from a guy who in 1986 was making over $150,000 a year! (Of course, bear in mind that this guy is an actuary and their sense of reality is a bit warped, to say the least.) Risk everything—put in all on the pass line—wager your future, all in the hope of making just a little more than you have now? Maybe I was a better salesman than I thought! (This is the same guy who, when presented with his founder's stock certificate, looked at the number of shares and said, "The only thing I have had more of than this is Rice Krispies.") As I said before, wealth is relative.

I'll be honest with you here—no cheating—there were many reasons why I wanted to leave ITT Life to start LifeUSA, and gaining wealth was one of the reasons. Not the only one, but a strong one. (At least mine was a little stronger than Pete's.) For a long time I had studied the lives of those who had gone from nothing to something—it was certainly a path to follow, and I did have a leg up since I had the "nothing" part down pat. The question was, how to do it? What disappointed me about most of these rags-to-riches stories was that they all seemed to start with a leg up. Their rags had been gold-lined. They had either inherited money, were extremely bright, or had a marvelous new idea. All of which made me zero-for-three.

My parents were wonderful and the exact definition of hard-working, American middle class. We always had what we needed, but there was not much left over. After a quick peek at my scholastic record (not to mention your feelings after reading this far in the book), you would not be surprised to learn that my application for membership in the Mensa Society would be rejected out of hand. As far as a marvelous new idea – well, there has not been a new idea in life insurance since three days after the first Good Friday.

Certainly there were no riches—real riches—to be made working for companies like The Hartford. Besides, I was not sure how long I would even have a job with that company. I had the questions, but it was clear that different answers were needed for me to attain wealth. (As I defined wealth, not Pete!)

The traditional rule for attaining wealth is close to the rule dealing with power. Real wealth only grows through hoarding. The rule for building wealth is to get all you can and keep all you can till the end when you end up with a lot and then die! There is even a name for the rule—it's called the "time value of money."

The core of American economic philosophy is the "Puritan Ethic," which calls for hard work, saving money, and becoming wealthy. Who do you think made up those rules? None other than the guys who already had wealth and wanted us to work for them and save our money in their banks, that's who. How much of a chance do you think we have? By following these rules we may achieve some modicum of wealth and security, but by the time we do, we won't care because we will be too old to enjoy the benefits. I didn't have that kind of time, and besides, I wanted a bigger boat.

It occurred to me that the same cheating philosophy that worked with gaining power might work just as well in gaining wealth. If it were possible to create a way for others to become wealthy, would I become wealthy as well? There was also the concept of the "law of large numbers." I don't think it was meant to apply to the concept of making me wealthy, but maybe it was a law I could actually use, rather than cheat on.

The idea was simple enough. If I kept 100 percent of the ownership—and thus the wealth—how hard would the people work for me to become wealthy? On the other hand, if I only kept, say, 40 percent of the ownership and spread the other 60 percent among the people who would be asked to work hard to create the success of the company, how hard would those people work knowing that the more wealth they created for me, the more they would create for themselves? Seems pretty obvious, doesn't it? Yet the rules say to do it the other way!

Sure, there will be those ready to offer examples of entrepreneurs who started companies and kept 100 percent of the control for themselves and maybe a few close friends who became very wealthy. I recognize and respect those examples, but would simply suggest that maybe—just maybe—these entrepreneurs would have earned even more if they had shared even a small part of the wealth with those asked to create it.

My philosophy is that if you can do it alone, you can do it even better when others are motivated to help you do it. Do you think Bill Gates and Paul Allen are disappointed that they have a little less today because they allowed hundreds—even thousands—to become wealthy right along with the big boys? I think not!

That was the philosophy we followed at LifeUSA. Frankly, I had little choice. Not having access to capital of my own, not the brightest bean in the bucket, and with no revolutionary idea—except maybe to cheat on some rules—the only way I was going to become successful and, ultimately, wealthy was if others worked very hard to make that happen. And that's exactly what happened at LifeUSA.

Hundreds of employees worked hard to make the company successful because they knew that they, too, would benefit from this success. In so doing, they all benefited as individuals, and the residual of this effort was to make me quite wealthy. Much more so than if I had tried to do it on my own. I discovered that wealth was gained by sharing wealth.

LifeUSA was formed as an outsider in the life insurance industry. We were not part of the insurance club, and had only a small base of capital. The odds were against our success. The only chance to differentiate our company from all the others—and the best way to do that—was to share power, share information, and share wealth. Break all the rules and be different from all the others.

Keep Control by Keeping Less

It started with the initial organization of LifeUSA. It would have been natural—even logical—for me to keep the majority of stock. After all, LifeUSA was my idea and would not have seen the light of day without my efforts. No one would complain if I kept a majority of the stock. However, others—starting with the four other founders—were going to be the ones to make the company successful, so they should receive some stock. Still, I could have kept control.

Many people over the years have said to me, "Sure, I don't mind sharing some stock with employees, but I have to keep at least 51 percent so I have control." Of course, that is the normal way of doing things. Rules that suggest that to keep the power and wealth you have to have legal control. As expressed earlier in this chapter, my belief is that the way to real power is to share power.

When LifeUSA was organized, it was my conscious decision to distribute 60 percent of the initial organizational stock to the other four founders. The reasoning behind this idea was to set up a structure that would vest the other founders with the power, as a group, to outvote me and control the company. This was a signal to them that I was secure enough in my place and power that I didn't need the legal power of 51 percent to control the company. This structure also served as a way to keep me on my toes and challenged—knowing that I had to earn their continuing support, not just be able to demand it. I could not become lazy and use the 51 percent rule as a recliner to rest on while the others worked.

All the founders were in the effort together, but some more so than others. As the organization was being assembled, it became obvious that one of the founders was accepting a risk out of balance with the others. All of us were risking a great deal, but one of us had more to lose by moving his family from California to Minnesota, selling a profitable business, and putting a financial statement on the line that was greater than all the rest combined.

Following the philosophy that being equitable does not always mean equal (even though he never said a word to me), I determined that this founder deserved a higher allocation of the stock. The problem was that it would not have been equitable to take from the others, so the best solution was to carve out an additional block of shares (which came to be worth several million dollars) from my allocation and give them to him.

This action was neither foolishness nor charity on my part, but rather a sound business decision. It was obvious to me that this individual was critical to our future success and my giving up a few shares (remember, we had more shares than a case of Rice Krispies) would be a good investment—not only for the success of the company—but the future of my wealth. It was and then some! Not only did this founder commit his life to the success of the company (to be honest, many others did as well), but he helped spread that same philosophy of sharing wealth by telling anyone who would listen the story of my giving up additional stock to him.

If we felt the employees were critical to the success of the company, then they should be included in the pie as well, and they were. From the very beginning, employees were required to take 10 percent of their pretax gross income and buy stock in LifeUSA. As I said before, this was more of a sacrifice for a young mother making $18,000 per year than it was an investment.

Also, we did not make these stock options, stock grants, restricted stock, or the more traditional ESOP (employee stock ownership plan) where the employees own the stock as a group but not as individuals. No, it was important to "have their skin in the game" and we wanted them to pay for the stock.

Trust me, an individual who had to give up some new clothes or even a needed new car because of a requirement that the money go toward purchase of stock that had no current value and may or may not have value in the future, is a lot more interested in the success of the company than one who had the stock given to them. So, instead of just me working hard, or trying to convince others to work hard to make me wealthy, I ended up with hundreds of people totally committed to securing power and wealth for me because they understood that the more I gained, the more they would gain.

By the time LifeUSA was acquired by Allianz AG, my ownership of the company was down to 10 percent, but I am convinced that that 10 percent was worth significantly more than the 100 percent it would have been if I had followed the rules for wealth and power. By cheating on the rules, I became more powerful and wealthier than even I could have imagined.

Yet the irony is that if you were to ask the employees of LifeUSA about the stock ownership, they would tell you that I had not taken enough for myself. They would be wrong, of course, as they gave much more than was returned, but that is the essence of the benefit derived when we effectively cheat on the rules. That is the way LifeUSA worked and, as they say in fairy tales, "The rest is history and they lived happily ever after."

And the Moral of the Story Is …

Gaining power and wealth are among the most fundamental motivators of human interaction. With centuries of history as a base and generation upon generation of effort, there has developed an almost genetically inspired set of rules regarding the acquisition, use, and preservation of power and wealth. Like most rules, the basis of rules dealing with power and wealth were well intentioned at the time of enactment, but have been corrupted over time. Instead of being a path for others to follow to power and wealth, the rules have become institutionalized in an effort to protect the status quo and the status of those who "have," while keeping those who don't have from having.

The fundamental rule in the world today regarding power is that if you have it and want to maintain it, then you stockpile it, you do not share it; you keep it and control it. The same attitude is prevalent when dealing with wealth. All of the vestiges of power, communication, status, privilege—those you keep.

I can understand why people with power and wealth seek every way possible to squirrel it away and protect it. In the past, the strategy of those who did not have wealth and power was to take it from those who did. I advocate a different approach. The idea behind cheating on the power-wealth rules is not to take power and wealth away from others, but rather to create new power and wealth for all.

What's difficult for many people to understand is that if you take less, you will get more. And it works on all business levels and across the spectrum of wealth, information, and power. Amazing levels of power and wealth are acquired when we learn, believe, and implement techniques that empower others and enable them to share in wealth created. Like nuclear power, the chain reaction of atoms working together does not use power—it creates huge amounts of new power. This new form of power will actually dwarf the old power base. Cheating on the rules of power and wealth is like igniting a breeder reactor—more power is created than used.

The irony is that we are talking about stuff that is not rocket science. It is not hard to do if it is made a way of life. Recognize and understand exactly why you are doing this sharing—the bottom line is that you are doing it for your own benefit. The beauty of this approach is that by sharing the power, the wealth, and the success with other people you become immensely more successful than if you try to keep it all to yourself. That is cheating to win.

It is my hope that in this chapter, as in every chapter of this book, you come away with the mind-set that there is no simple, one, two, three explanation to living the cheat-to-win philosophy. There is no formula that says, "On Tuesday you do this and on Wednesday you do that." It is rather a mind-set of being willing to challenge the status quo, of refusing to join the ruling club. Gaining true power is a mental attitude, an *inherent inclination* to empower others so that you empower yourself. One of the most disarming facts about this book is that virtually all of the principles it contains are so easy to put in place. And it's the very ease of the effort that often makes them so difficult to establish.

Imagine that all you have to do to gain more power and wealth is simply share some of the power and wealth you already possess. Put your employees or team members on your side by inviting them to share in your company's (or your department's) power and wealth. It's a concept that's almost Biblical in its implications, a simple business Golden Rule: Give to others and they will give back to you tenfold

11

Cheating Women

*The most powerful power
is a pent-up power unleashed*

It is fair to say that women in the LifeUSA culture went all the
way. All the way to the top, that is. And it was noticeable. At
LifeUSA most of the management jobs that really meant
something to the success of the company were filled by women.

It was not at all unusual for outsiders visiting the company to
comment to me, "There really seem to be a lot of women in
management here at LifeUSA." These statements were received with
a slight wry smile (which could also have been taken for bored
irritation) in recognition that they represented both a broad
compliment and a social comment. It made me wonder how many
CEOs ever had a visitor come to their office and say, "Gee, you
really seem to have a lot of men in management here at your
company."

After LifeUSA had achieved some modicum of renown and
success, a number of other companies, both in the U.S. and abroad,
wanted to visit the company in order to learn our secret. Often their
reactions were a bit different—if not more insulting—when they
would comment, "It is amazing the success you have accomplished
with so many women in management."

Just when we are lulled into believing that real progress is being made to rid corporations of gender bias, something stupid happens to remind us that we're still groping, still learning to be fair, honest, and equitable. Such a situation emerged when two of our male employees filed a complaint with those "equal opportunity" folks at the Equal Employment Opportunity Commission (EEOC). Their complaint alleged that there was a "cement ceiling" at LifeUSA that prevented men from moving ahead. They further argued that the company had a specific practice of discriminating against males in favor of females. Can you imagine?

While that complaint was laughed at even by the EEOC, maybe those guys had a point. After all, at one time over 80 percent of the company's senior management—starting with the president—were women. Maybe LifeUSA did discriminate in favor of women. Then again, maybe LifeUSA was truly an equal opportunity employer and the best talent rose to the top.

The Missing Link

This is a chapter that almost didn't happen. Chuck (the "without" person) and I discussed the need and appropriateness of a chapter dealing specifically with women cheating on the rules. After all, my experiences go back forty years, and opportunities for women to have stress-induced strokes and heart attacks are approaching the level men have enjoyed for generations. (But still without the equal income to pay for treatment!)

One argument against this chapter was that it is chauvinistic to even distinguish between men and women cheating on the rules. But another point of view argues that, despite the advances, there are still many more rules designed to control the fortunes of women than men. If any group needs advice on cheating on rules that hold them back, it is women.

That's why this chapter is here. Back in 1987, when my equal employment education ostensibly began, LifeUSA clearly cheated on the gender rules of the day. It seemed like heresy at the time, and unfortunately, it's still heresy for many businesses and corporations today, but LifeUSA enabled—actually encouraged—women to assume positions of real power in management. The results of this effort to equalize the employment playing field were so breathtaking it's well worth adding this chapter to suggest how easy it is to cheat to win and make business a better place—for everybody.

Be Careful What You Don't Look For Because You Might Find It

One of the most fortuitous actions ever taken by LifeUSA was cheating on the rule that proclaimed that women (especially those lacking a college degree) were not the equal of men when it came to management. No one will ever be able to change my belief that cheating on the "women in power" rule was a decisive factor in LifeUSA's ability to achieve high levels of success so quickly.

It would be disingenuous to claim this outcome was due to a conscious, premeditated decision to shatter the rules that placed a glass ceiling on the upward mobility of women. The truth is, I blindly stumbled into this fortuitous bonanza.

You know the old theory of circumstances creating opportunity? It's like looking for gold but finding acres of diamonds instead. That's what happened at LifeUSA when it became apparent that we'd have to cheat on the rules regarding women.

Consider the problem: LifeUSA needed to build the management staff and do it from scratch, *right now*. But there was precious little capital in the bank and no income whatsoever. In the process of interviewing to fill senior positions it became obvious that being cash-poor created a problem, a huge one.

Everyone interviewed with any real experience in senior management was a man, but that was not the problem. The problem was that these guys were making far too much money—we couldn't afford to hire them. And if that was not bad enough, none of them were willing to either take less pay or take a risk. Added to this dilemma was our business plan to differentiate the appeal of LifeUSA on the basis of exceptional service and support. Not being able to attract and hire experienced senior management created a formidable challenge.

At this point the proverbial lightbulb incandesced over our collective heads. Almost out of desperation—with our backs to the wall—we turned to women! The initial group of candidates who applied at LifeUSA were a number of hard-working and talented women who had worked with me at ITT Life. The problem was, they had no bankable management experience.

Nevertheless, there were some distinct advantages to hiring women managers. For one, the women whose resumes we received already knew us. They knew firsthand the type of company we wanted to build. There would be no need to "educate" them about our objectives and goals for a well-run company based on a culture of parallel interests. They could hit the ground running.

Still, it would be a big risk. What would happen with women in senior management of a real company? Could women with little or no management experience and mostly high-school educations perform effectively in senior management positions? How would men react to the idea of working for women? Short on money and in dire need of a management team, we were too desperate to debate the question for long and took the risk. Circumstances forced us to cheat on the rule regarding women in senior management. It turned out to be a great decision, but I reiterate—it was just blind luck.

Open the Flood Gates

Being the typical insensitive male, I was amazed at the reaction of women when offered the chance to do what they never thought they would be allowed to do. Unlike our male applicants, they literally jumped at the opportunity to risk their entire future on the expectations that LifeUSA would succeed and prosper. Of course, I was too shallow to fully recognize the enormous consequences of this strategy, but I quickly learned the correctness of my ways. It's not an exaggeration to say that women stood in long lines in our hallways waiting for a crack at applying for jobs at LifeUSA (the offices were too small to hold everyone at one time). What I had heretofore failed to realize was that most of these women applicants had years of experience banging their heads up against the glass ceiling and flocked to our doors as if we were giving away tickets to an Oprah Winfrey give-away show.

The whole idea of being in powerful, high-paying positions on the senior management team of a company was way beyond the way these women had been conditioned as young girls growing up. The expectations for themselves and their future were continually stifled. But no longer. These women were willing to "work on the cheap" as an investment in the opportunity to do what other businesses would not allow them to do.

As one of the women said to me later, "My reaction and that of others to the opportunity at LifeUSA was not about title or money. Those things were nice, but the strongest motivator was the opportunity to actually *build* a company—to have a real impact on the success of a company. I never thought I would ever have a chance to be a player, not a pawn. That is what excited us. All the rest was gravy."

LifeUSA was fortunate to hire talented, experienced people (who just happened to be women) who had never before been given the opportunity to apply their talent and experience in a leadership role. Only two promises were offered to the first groups of women hired to fill out management positions with the company: 1) a letter stating that we had no money to pay them and no promise that we would have money to pay them in the future and, 2) the promise that if they took the risk to join LifeUSA and the company did become successful, they would have the opportunity to fill the role of senior managers in a large company. Equally important, the women were to be compensated on a par with men in similar positions. (Now there is real rule-cheating!) In other words, the women had a shot at breaking the glass ceiling in terms of both title and salary.

Only Encouraged by a Dream

There was a large lump of fear (not to mention a few negative comments from spouses and family) in the hearts of the women offered this opportunity, but there was no hesitation. One of the women said to me, "My husband and dad say I am crazy to think

LifeUSA is a good opportunity and even daffier to think that I can be in management, but I don't care. I am going to prove them wrong." (Can't you almost *see* her clenched teeth?)

They were presented with an opportunity that would never be available from their previous employer ITT Life, and probably not from any other company, either—and they jumped at it. That was a lucky break for LifeUSA, since these women ultimately gave the company an advantage—a secret weapon, if you will—over other companies. This silver bullet was the exceptional power, leadership, and contributions made by talented and gifted women who had not been given the same opportunities at other companies.

Benefits Multiply for All

An interesting, unanticipated benefit derived from cheating on the women-in-power rule was that these women became strong role models for other women who later joined LifeUSA, including women who had previously never envisioned themselves as moving up beyond the "administrative" level. And it was not because they didn't want it; it was because they were *conditioned* to believe that such achievement was beyond their reach. Once these women became successful in their new managerial roles, they demonstrated, in a most powerful way, that other women—with backgrounds just like theirs—can be just as successful in management.

In response to the opportunity offered, these women invested exceptional talent, unbelievable hard work, total commitment, and loyalty to the effort to build LifeUSA. While these women may have felt grateful for the opportunity to "show their stuff," LifeUSA benefited even more from their unbridled talent and effort. It was the classic win-win situation.

Of course, just like men, not all of the women were successful at the higher levels as the company grew more complicated and sophisticated, but all contributed significant value to the company. Today, many of these women remain in the senior levels of Allianz Life which, to its credit, continues to foster full gender equality.

The individual success of these women, welcome as it was, was not the definitive benefit that LifeUSA reaped by cheating on the rules. The ultimate reward was that, from the start—virtually the first day—the culture of LifeUSA was built on the basis of true equal opportunity, not obsequious lip service. Those women—who had yearned for, but had not been given opportunity at other companies—wanted to make sure that situation did not happen at their company. The culture unequivocally communicated the reality that LifeUSA offered opportunities that were—like justice— completely blind. Your gender, race, religion, or sexual preferences made absolutely no difference.

Success at LifeUSA was based totally on your talent, effort, and commitment. I know this may sound like lollipop, quiche, and custard pie kind of stuff, but in reality it was cold, hard, and utterly true. At LifeUSA you could be orange-topped, tattooed, Republican, dress like an actuary, commune with goats, and still be successful as long as you had talent and applied it to your work.

A Welcomed Ripple Effect

The open culture at LifeUSA produced yet another completely serendipitous result. This was a pervasive "domino effect" that caused the company to adopt other workplace-enhancing features. While appearing extreme (cheating) at the time, they heightened the attractiveness of the company and encouraged others to bring their talent and effort to the company. This created a strong family environment in the company that was quite atypical for companies at the time. (Or even now, for that matter now.) Flexible hours, family time, child care, maternity leave, casual dress, and full benefits—while seeming radical at the time—were structured to fit the new world of LifeUSA. It was not unusual for entire families to come to work at LifeUSA.

Contrary to what "fiscal conservatives" (a.k.a. "greedy bastards") have argued, we discovered that by cheating on the employee rules of the day, the company gained much more in loyalty and productivity than it cost to provide the benefits. In other words, the LifeUSA owners appreciated and respected the work environment and made sure the privilege was not abused. All of these ancillary benefits came about because LifeUSA cheated on the historical rules that insisted that the best place for women in business is the office typing pool.

Become a Nonqualified Employer

This happenstance of cheating to win with women also taught me another excellent management lesson—a welcome derivative from our culture of full equality in the workplace. It is a valuable lesson I would encourage you to learn.

The traditional rule tells us to hire the most qualified person. Look for a resume filled with copious amounts of experience in the open job. Seems logical: If you want to get the job done, hire the best people. It is an easy rule to follow, and people would often come into my office excited to have found the perfect resume for a spot they were looking to fill. The pitch was always the same, "I found this great guy. He has had the same job with three other companies." But, as was discovered building LifeUSA on what the women called "skirt-power," there is another side to the rule. The new rule became "don't necessarily hire the person most qualified to do the job today, but rather the one who has the most *potential* to do the job tomorrow." This is true for both internal and external hires.

What happens when we obey the rule that tells us to hire the most qualified person for a job? First of all, you have to pay top bucks for the experience. That's okay, I don't mind paying fair value, but it may not be the experience you really want. Sure, the person may have a lot of experience, but has that know-how been gained doing things the way you want them done? Being fully qualified for a job may limit room for future growth and create the potential for this person to become bored with the job. By cheating on the traditional hiring rule and seeking to identify potential rather than past experience, opportunity is given to candidates with high energy, high promise, and burning desire. My experience was that most employees selected on the basis of long-term potential worked exceptionally long and hard to prove the decision to give them an opportunity "before its time" was the right one.

Being forced to give women who were technically not qualified the opportunity to fill senior management jobs—and then seeing them grow into these jobs—convinced me that approach could work *even with men.* The objective in hiring became a search to find the person with the highest potential to grow into the job—man or woman—rather than someone already fully qualified to fill the position. The key was to find that person and then encourage, protect, and train them as their skills and experience blossomed to fill the job and achieve their full potential. This approach ignited people to the opportunity, since they were challenged by the position and grateful for the confidence shown in them. That kind of motivation worked wonders for the company, and our success.

In the process, we discovered that the antirule for hiring to an open position became finding the least obvious candidate, rather then one who others would consider the logical choice. It was amazing how many times this resulted in discovering the best person for the job.

Naturally, this strategy, like any corporate strategy, cannot work for all people in all situations. Sometimes, employees would apply for new positions in the company in areas completely outside their background of experience only to discover later that the new job was not a good fit. That happens. But we never punished employees for continually reaching beyond their grasp. They always had a job at LifeUSA, no matter the temporary missteps. And truthfully, they were few in number.

On the other hand, any number of examples can be given to illustrate the success of this approach to building futures and the success of the company. A woman in public relations with no top-level management experience earned the job of company president. A young (height-challenged) underwriter chucked the excitement of attending-physician statements to become a highly successful senior marketing officer. Then there was the fuzzy-headed accountant who became a field leader in the sales effort (and even took up golf!), and the head of underwriting who moved to human resources (owner services) to become a defender and builder of culture. And then there's Mark Zesbaugh. Thought by many to be "too young" at age thirty to become the CFO of a public company, he not only earned that responsibility with his potential, but eventually became the CEO of Allianz North America. (And delivered results that made people forget I was ever there!)

These are just a few of the *hundreds* of examples of cheating on the rules for hiring "qualified" people that benefited the company. We took a new road, a road less traveled, if you will, and it has made all the difference.

And the Moral of the Story Is ...

When it comes to cheating on the rules to win it seems a much easier challenge for women, yet in other ways much more difficult. How so? Well, when rules have been used against you all your life, they are much easier to identify. And the first step to overcoming a problem is to recognize that the problem exists—and then doing something about it. Likewise, you'd expect that women would have a greater desire to cheat on the rules, since they have so much to gain by breaking them.

Yet society makes it more difficult for women to cheat on rules. When a man cheats on a rule, others may not like it, but his peers will likely respect his aggressiveness, his innovation, and his "leadership." But just let a woman try that! She is more likely to be branded as "pushy" (is it okay to say bitchy?) and "out of line."

Today, the younger generations of women benefit from the cheating and rule-breaking of their predecessors over the past 30 years. The scales are not yet balanced, by any means. It is better than it was, but not as good as it can be if women will take up the gauntlet to cheat not only on the rules that seek to define the role of a woman but also on rules that impede all of us. The quirk of fate here is that by cheating on the rules regarding women in power, companies will actually benefit more than the women themselves will. This element of rule-cheating opens up a whole reservoir of talent that has been damned up and underutilized since Jesus decided all the apostles should be men. It's about time we go all the way and change that rule for good.

12

Hire and Hired We Go

There is more to a job than a job;
there is the job of making the job a career.

It was a tense time. I was being considered for a senior marketing
position that was just what the doctor had ordered to make
that big jump up the corporate ladder. One more step toward
the ultimate goal of leading a company. (Besides, all the excitement
and pressure of living in the wild and crazy town of Worcester,
Massachusetts, was beginning to wear on me. I kid you not—the
cultural and social highlight of Worcester life in 1976 was meeting
at a bulk-goods outlet store called Spags.) True, the initial meeting
with the headhunter had not gone all that well, but we had worked
our way through that and I was on my way to Minneapolis for the
all-important, face-to-face, make-it-or-break-it interview with the
president of the company.

The opening contact had come to me out of the blue from a
hired-gun recruiter who explained that he was charged with looking
for a top executive who could be "the number two guy" at a fast-
growing company. During the first phone call he let it slip that, "I
had been highly recommended to him." (This was exactly what he
said to every potential candidate, even if he got their name from the
phone book.) In any event, we agreed to meet at 4:00 P.M. on
Thursday, November 18, 1976, in the American Airlines flight

lounge at Boston's Logan International Airport. The date is indelibly seared in my memory because of the way the interview started.

Prancing into the meeting dressed in the finest suit I could afford at the time (a Sears-special, Buddy Hackett-endorsed line), I was ready to exhibit the air of a serious, polished marketing executive when this guy blurts out, "Let's get one thing straight from the start. This company doesn't want anyone who drinks a lot and whores around. So if you do that, we might as well stop the interview right now." I wasn't exactly sure how to respond to such an original opening for a job interview. (This guy must have been trying to really narrow down the field.) All prepped to talk about the subtleties of insurance marketing (which itself might be an oxymoron), I was thrown off balance by this frank and candid approach to determining a candidate's qualifying credentials. If not so convulsed with laughter, I would have ordered a double scotch to dump on the guy's head, kissed the hostess I'd been hitting on, and departed.

And yet, there was a certain amount of intrigue about a company that would send a headhunter out with such specific instructions. Of course, early on, companies are—for some reason—a little obtuse when it comes to the actual job requirements, but this approach was way off my radar. Later on, I discovered that the headhunter was right to lead with abstinence in drink and other things, but the logic was a bit convoluted. During the interview process it became clear that current company management sought to hire a "goody-two-shoes" because *they* were always out drinking and whoring around. At least they recognized the need for someone sober to drive the company.

In any event, it was now February in Minneapolis (where the only thing colder is the heart of a jilted second wife), and I was riding in a limo with the HR director on the way to a dinner meeting with the company president. In casual conversation along the way, the personnel guy mentioned that the company president had just celebrated his birthday (he was fifty-two), but he told me not to talk about it because the guy did not want people to know his age and was quite vain about his looks.

Early on at the restaurant it was obvious that this guy was checking out my drinking habits; but, forewarned by the headhunter (this wasn't difficult, since I don't drink). I was on my best behavior. In an effort to impress, the guy ordered a chardonnay, which it turned out was the only time I ever saw him drink anything less potent than grain alcohol. During the course of the conversation, I nudged him to tell me about his background. It didn't take much nudging. In fact, it was a little like asking Liz Taylor to talk about her husbands. He had a lot of experience to highlight. When the soliloquies of his accomplishments had spun their way out, I responded with a simple, "Gee, Jim, you have an amazing track record for someone in his early forties!"

Well, you can imagine the reaction!

His eyes lit up like fireworks on the Fourth of July as he blurted out, "No, no … I am in my early fifties." Shock showing on my face, I responded, "Really, Jim, you're kidding me. No way can you be anywhere near fifty! Not with what you have accomplished and the way you look." (See, I don't cheat on all the rules. This was a classic example of kissing both cheeks in one swift, wet move!) Okay, I admit it, such an approach may be lowbrow, stupid, and childish, but the guy bought it. (It is amazing what we are willing to buy, if we want it.) After that little exchange, I could do no wrong. Suddenly *he* had discovered the perfect candidate for the job.

From that point on, the leverage was all on my side. Not only did I have the power to decide if I wanted the job, but on what terms. (I did eventually accept the job and, three years later, replaced this chap as president of the company.)

This seems like such a simple, insignificant episode; why bring it up for discussion? Well, this was more than taking advantage of some guy's hypersensitive vanity. It is another example of how the reality of life is different from what those who write the rules would have us believe. If we really desire to be in control of the job-seeking and job-offering process, then this experience offers a wealth of rules to cheat on.

How Many Trees Died for You to Get That Job?

Of all the rules in business, none are more habitual than those controlling the process of being hired, promoted, or moving from one company to another. Shelves are filled with books outlining the finer points of resume preparation and job interviewing. In addition to being told how to shape the resume, we are instructed on what to wear, how to sit, answer questions, and present ourselves in the best light. But the books that promise to reveal the secrets of successful job interviewing fall far short of the goal. It's nice information, but useless in real life. At best, these books tender a collection of hackneyed ideas that succeed only in turning the readers into cardboard people. Yet the books are popular because we always seem to be searching for the job that will finally make us happy—and worse—we always feel like underdogs in the process.

A cottage industry thrives on teaching us how to have that home-run interview. Some even use the magic of video instant replay to point out flaws in technique. These are all fine. Getting the job we want is fairly important to a successful career; but the approach recommended is, for the most part, dead wrong, and the rules we are encouraged to follow do us no favors. This mating dance that passes for the recruiting process is an interesting, if convoluted, experience. Most of these "how to" rules are based on the premise that the person conducting the interview or doing the hiring should control the process. Cheat on that rule and you will win.

Such rules (most of which have been written by former personnel directors) are in place not to help us, but to make the interview easier for the person doing the hiring. That's ass-backward. You should be the one conducting and controlling the interview. You should be the one deciding if a particular job is best for you—not the other way around. Accomplish this role reversal, and you stand a good chance of being offered virtually every job for which you interview. And this is particularly true if you find yourself out of work and desperate for a job. When you cheat on the rules and lead the process—rather than be cowed by it—then you can be the one to pick and select.

The Pursued, Not the Pursuee

As much as you may want that promotion or new job, you have a higher chance of success by not showing your interest and having the job seek you out. The power is always on the side of the pursued. If you are chasing after a job, then the power belongs to the one who has the job to offer. If the one who needs to fill the job is chasing after you, the power shifts to you.

The trick is to pursue the job while appearing to be pursued. This stratagem is best accomplished by making yourself visible, while hiding your intentions. The classic rules tell us to read the want ads, contact headhunters, mass-mail resumes, network with contacts, register on Monster.com, and go to church and pray to God with the promise that if you get the job you will never ask for anything again. These steps may generate activity, but the results may not be all you want, because following these rules tells everyone you are out there, available, vulnerable and ready to be had.

Subliminal Advertising

There is a better way. If you know the type of job you want to have next, as opposed to the specific job, then you are better off to advertise yourself rather than advertise for the job. Here is what I mean. After a couple of years working at State Mutual Life I felt it was time to move up, but I was concerned about the long-term potential at the company. I was clear as to the type of job sought—chief marketing officer—but not to the actual job itself. The problem was how to find it.

Rarely is the job you really want openly advertised, because someone is still in the job. Moreover, if you are out looking for a new job—no matter how secret you think the search may be—there is a good chance your current employer will discover this activity. That makes for a rather difficult Monday morning staff meeting.

Doing Your Best to Get Better

At State Mutual, I had been charged with developing a new life insurance marketing strategy. We called this program TLC: Total

Life Concept. A highly visible advertising and public relations campaign was launched to introduce this program. Always eager for any material to fill the pages, industry publications hungrily accepted and published stories detailing the new marketing efforts. As the one responsible for development of the program, I was interviewed or highlighted in the media reports. In addition, bylined articles were submitted to various publications, and I was invited to be guest speaker at a number of industry organizations. This industry exposure ultimately triggered the call from the headhunter that led to the ITT Life opportunity.

You can see the method behind the madness. While the appearance and direct result of the activity were to promote the new marketing program of State Mutual, the reality was that Bob MacDonald (and his obvious talent) was promoted in parallel. Trust me, headhunters, or those looking to fill a key position, may not care about a marketing program introduced by another company, but they do notice and care about the person who is given credit for the program. There is no need to be disloyal to your current employer; but if you can also promote yourself, you are going to have more success finding the job you want than if you were to make the effort to identify and pursue a specific job. As that great oracle of attention-getters Anna Nicole Smith once confided to me, "Be visible and they will come!" (Or at least something to that effect.)

Once they come to you, then you are in control of the unfolding process. Following this philosophy of rule-cheating in my career meant that every job had come to me. Some, admittedly, took a little subtle cajoling, but not once did I find a job as the result of responding to an ad, mailing a resume, networking, or registering with a headhunter and you don't have to, either.

Setting the Hook

There is yet another job-searching rule that appears at first blush to be helpful, but under closer inspection is exposed as little more than a perfunctory activity. The rule is simple and straightforward: Learn as much as you can about the company you are to interview with.

The benefit is that you put yourself in a favorable position by making a serious effort to be knowledgeable about the company. Even more important is learning details about the background of the person who will be interviewing you. While it is a good idea to have information on any company you may be interviewing with, the key is the *type* of information you secure.

Sure, you can amass all sorts of mundane facts and figures from reading annual reports (although that's helpful to get an idea of how the company likes to BS) and reviewing Web sites. But the best information deals with the culture and the heart of the company, not just the facts and figures. Knowing what *drives* a company is much more important than where it has been driven.

A headhunter can be a good source of this information. If the job you're considering is offered by a company in your current field, it may also be possible to gain valuable information from personal contacts. Call links you may have with competitors or even customers of the company. Remember, the information you're seeking is not public, or published in superficial reports. You want to know what the insiders know. If you are successful in this effort, then you develop a strategy to take control of the interview. The more you know about the company, the better chance there is to make a favorable impression. If that's accomplished, it's an easy step to convince those in the new company that you're a "must-have" employee. This is part of the process of cheating on the basic rule of hiring—you want to be in control, not controlled. If that is accomplished, then you have the power to decide about the job.

As mentioned, a headhunter can be of value in this early process. Even though the headhunter is being paid by the prospective employer and most likely will view him as "the company," you can take advantage of this person's knowledge. The headhunter will give you tons of boilerplate information about the company, but work to get beyond that and get the headhunter to (unknowingly) help you cheat on the hiring rules.

Once the recruiter has secured all of the vital information needed from you, gently but firmly take over the interview and search for bits of information that you need. Of course, I'm not talking about salary or other subjects in that area. (I make a point never to be the first to discuss salary, perks, or benefits.) What you're looking for is unpublished, real information about the company. In a casual way, maybe over coffee after lunch, while you're waiting for the car, or in an airport lounge waiting for your flight, ask the recruiter the important questions.

Why did the position open up?
What happened to the person formerly in the job?
What are the people like?
Just what is the company *really* looking for?

The last question is very important. There is a distinct difference between what people may say they are looking for in a job description and what, in their own mind, they are really looking for. For example, the person doing the hiring may not like people who smoke a pipe. Of course he's not going to put that in a job description, but it would be very good information to have in your file—if you smoked a pipe. With a little bit of work you can gain some very important information.

Sometimes you don't even need to work very hard. Every little bit of information, if used properly, can be of value to you. When interviewing for the ITT Life job, the headhunter happened to mention the company was also looking for a new comptroller. When asked why, his response was, "The president likes the current comptroller, but wants someone who is a little stronger with the numbers." That reply seemed a little too standard, so I pushed a little further. Finally, the headhunter casually mentioned that "The president does not believe the guy works well with people." Of course, I knew that was no big deal. When have you ever met a comptroller who does work well with people? That small piece of information was filed away because it went to the heart of what the president was thinking.

During the interview process at ITT Life I met with this comptroller and later, when the president asked my impressions, I said, "He is a very nice guy, but it doesn't seem like he would work very well with people." Insincere? Shallow? Childish? Sure, but I could see from the guy's eyes he knew he was talking to someone who thought the same way he did.

Zeroing in on Numero Uno

The most important information you can gain before and during the interview process is information about the person who will make the hiring decision. Why? Because contrary to what rulebooks tell us, most hiring decisions are based more on personal than corporate needs. For you to control the process, personal needs must be understood. Many fully qualified people have lost the opportunity for jobs because they believed the company was actually looking for the type of person described in those lifeless job descriptions. They follow the rules that say you present your qualifications and sell yourself based on the specific job description. Forget those rules. Recognize that you are dealing with the hopes, fears, and desires of a human, not a corporation.

Once you learn exactly who will be making the hiring decision, take time to do a little homework and find out as much as you can about that person. But be careful; you don't need the bland stuff in a biography or the tasteless nuggets that you'll find in the *Who's Who* publications. What you need is the stuff people talk about at "happy hour." After reviewing the information, you can usually discover something that ties you together or something you should avoid.

The individual's office is another important source of information. It's the person's home away from home, and it can tell you a lot about the person who lives there eight or more hours a day. When I'm ushered into someone's office, the strategy is to look carefully for the personal effects on display because they tell you what the person thinks are important. A tennis trophy on the credenza means that if you are able to inject tennis into the conversation you will score some aces. Be subtle; you don't have to hit him over the head with the trophy, but get the subject into the conversation. A golf putter over in the corner of the office is like a free ticket to a good interview.

The Anti-Matter Matters

The rules encourage us to focus on the job we seek, concentrate on selling our experience, and impressing the decision maker with our ability to fulfill the job requirements. This is all well and good, but it is not the real stuff that establishes control of the process. You want to be the one to decide if the job is best for you, not have others decide if you are best for the job. To achieve this result, I have learned the ultimate anti-rule for the job hunt. And that anti-rule is: *The less time you spend talking about the job you are being interviewed for, the more likely you will be offered the job.*

In fact, the less time you spend talking and the more you can get the interviewer to talk, the more control you will have in the process. Talking about the company, the background, interests, and aspirations of the interviewer all reverse the process, cheat on the rules, and put you in control.

The Supposed Perils of Job-Hopping

One rule those in control like to impress upon young executives on the way up is this: *Don't be tagged with the reputation of a job hopper.* Why? Who benefits from this type of rule? The rule-makers don't want you to be a "job hopper" because it's part of the process of control. Those with the power want to control our future—to intimidate us—for their own benefit, not ours. If we follow the rule that says being a "job hopper" is by its very nature bad—who wins?

This rule is akin to the old days in professional sports: once a player signed a contract with a team he was bound to that team for life—no matter what! In baseball, this was referred to as the "reserve clause," and reserved the talents of the player to the team for life. Or at least till the team decided to trade or release the player. This "no team-hopping" clause of the contract meant that the player was at the mercy of his employer for the balance of his entire career.

There are many examples to illustrate the abuses of a rule like this (if you really do need such an example, stop reading the book now because it will be of no value to you), but maybe the best one involves two of baseball's greatest pitchers—Sandy Koufax and Don

Drysdale. Certainly, these two Dodger pitchers of the 1960s and 70s were the best of their era, if not all time.

After one particularly successful year in which the duo won over forty games, Koufax and Drysdale banded together to seek a higher contract from team owner Walter O'Malley. (They were not even looking to leave the team for the highest bidder.) After weeks of contentious "bargaining" (if it could be called that) the players capitulated and agreed to what the owner had offered to pay them. Why? For the players, they had no choice—it was their only option. They either accepted what their employer offered or they didn't play. Period. By contract they could not "job-hop" and had to rely on the benevolence of their employer—who happened to be making millions of dollars each year as a result of the players' talent. And exactly how much money were these money-grubbing, greedy (as they were described by O'Malley) players asking for? The outrageous sum of $100,000! (That's about a half-million in today's dollars). In some cultures that would be considered a less-than-subtle form of slavery. We can easily see by today's standards just how much money this rule cost hundreds—if not thousands—of players. And where did the money go? Into the pockets of the rule-makers!

The business "no job-hopping" rule may not seem quite as egregious as the sports example, but it could be argued that the cumulative impact on those who were intimidated into following such a rule over the years was even greater.

As with the inception of most rules, the idea of staying with one company for your entire career had some initial validity. In sports, the rule favored the team by employing the rationale that the team had given the player opportunity, and invested time and money to develop their talent: the player "owed" it to owners to remain with the team. Since business was not exempt from federal anti-trust laws as sports teams were, a contract could not be used to keep the employee tied to the company. The response was to come up with the, "do not be a job-jumper" rule. As stupid and one-sided as the rule is, it is amazing how well it has worked for years to benefit the company—and to the detriment of the employee. Sure, people made "progress" following this rule, but at what price?

In theory, the benefit of the rule for the worker was the stability offered by staying with a single company (of course there is stability in a dictatorship, too), and the idea that since the company knew your talents you would be moved up quickly. Most important—if you play by the rules and wait your turn then you will work your way to the top. Sure, just in time to retire!

Just remember, if you are going to make it to your vision in time to enjoy it—you *have* to job-hop. You can't make it standing still. The only way to make it to the top is to keep moving up. People who espouse the "no job-hopping zone" tell you that violating it makes you look like you can't hold a job. But those who follow the rule forfeit to others the decision as to when a change is best for their future. Those who cheat to win must be prepared to cheat on rules that place their future in the hands of others.

Whether you rise to your goal with the first company you join or with the fourth is irrelevant, just so long as each new job is a step up and not sideways or down. If you recall, back in chapter 4 – "Reminiscing about the Future," when you have a focused vision of what you seek, then determining the process to get there becomes much easier. This is especially true when considering changing jobs.

Moving on Up on the Inside

Making the right moves to move up within the company you work for may require some serious rule-breaking. (If you work for the right company the rules should work for you, but we know that is not always the case.) The first rule is to forget about all the rules for getting that promotion. The insider rules for internal promotion are still geared toward keeping control in the hands of the higher-ups, not yours. Forget about the obligatory job postings on the company Internet, casually mentioning to your boss your interest in a certain job, or engaging in the special ass-kissing through the company social circuit. What you need to do is force their hand.

In chapter 9—"Look Down to Move Up," it was suggested that the best path to promotion was from below, not from above. The key is to become a candidate for that move up the ladder based on what you control—not others. The point here is simple. Use your talents, experience, potential, commitment, and achievements as advertisements for your availability and readiness to move up. That is best accomplished by supporting, developing, rewarding, and motivating the people who work for you. Concentrate on getting them ahead so you can get ahead.

Frankly, if you are with a company that does not have the culture to recognize this form of talent, then "job-hop" your way out of that company just as soon as you can. You will know that you are with the right company only when you never have to seek that promotion or raise, where you are constantly challenged to do more and are fairly rewarded for what you do. Until you find that company—hop all you want.

Hire the Hired

Let's turn the tables here and talk about rules for doing the hiring. While I accept the rule that introducing some "fresh blood" into a culture can be good for the system, and prevent inbreeding or staleness, it is also important to recognize that introducing "Type A" blood (no matter how fresh it is) into a "Type B" body can cause rejection, infection, and even death. So you have to be careful when hiring from outside the culture.

A study of high-growth, winning companies will uncover a culture that consistently bred its own to be leaders. A winning team— a winning culture—always stands a better chance of continuing to grow if building on that winning record is accomplished by promoting people who developed in that culture. Cheat on the rule that offers an excuse for laziness by arguing that internal development of people cannot keep pace with rapid growth, requiring hiring experienced people from other companies to manage growth. (No matter that most of these "experienced people" probably come from companies that have stopped growing.)

History demonstrates that as the momentum of internal development and promotion began to recede in companies with a record of growth, future growth slows. A company lacking either the will or ability to grow its own leaders as it evolves is —at best— lazy and—at worst—on the road to self-destruction. As a leader you need to violate the rule that says a company can grow faster with outside people than it can with internally developed leaders.

The problem is that it is hard work cultivating a farm system of future leaders in your company, but the reward is worth the effort. The example of wild, free-agency spending in sports should be proof enough that throwing more and more money at experienced people is not always the path to winning. Often it is the prescription for disaster! For me it was always a red flag and sign of failure when— except for technical people like actuaries, who are manufactured not developed—we were forced to go outside the company to fill a need. Alarm bells went off when headhunter fees increased.

My rule was to always try to create a reservoir of talent within the company that could be drawn from whenever we had an opportunity to offer or a need to be filled. The rule says to look for time-in-grade and experience in a job seeker—I say to look for the potential. You can always instill knowledge and experience, but not potential or attitude. Give me a bright person with the right attitude and they can learn to do almost any job. People are inspired to do better when given the opportunity to learn more. Thus (as mentioned in the previous chapter), you should constantly violate the rule that says hire the most qualified and instead hire the most potential and give them the opportunity to become qualified.

There is another concrete benefit for embedding this approach in company culture. If people know they will be constantly exposed to opportunity and often the opportunity will actually seek them out, then there is very little incentive to look elsewhere and to "job-hop." My rule was that if—for some reason—we could not create or offer an opportunity that satisfied and challenged someone in our organization, then we should help them find that elsewhere. It wasn't that I wanted to lose a good person, but better for them (and us) to find another opportunity if we could not meet their expectations. It was simple logic—why try to keep someone in your culture when they are not happy?

Hiring Inside Outside

In any organization there will always come a time when it is both necessary and prudent to hire a senior person from the outside. For this process to be successful, the reasons for this action have to be right. Hiring from the outside will work if the person hired brings a value not present in the existing culture and has the potential to grow beyond the current open job. As mentioned before, the rule says to find an individual with experience and who is fully qualified for the job. This rule always made me uncomfortable. If the person possessed all the experience in the world and was fully qualified for the job, there was high potential for boredom and low potential for growth. Also, boatloads of experience – if it's the wrong kind—can sink the culture.

I created a few rules of my own to cheat on the traditional rules for outside hiring. If we were looking for experience—someone to train those moving up in the organization—then someone close to retirement or already retired was sought. The highly experienced person could add knowledge and stability to a young, growing company, but not be a threat to those working their way up in the organization.

Another rule was to avoid hiring someone looking for the job. If someone was out shopping the job market, too often it was for the wrong reasons. We were not looking for someone else's failures, but rather their future stars. Our rule was to try to identify not the number-one person in the department of another company, but the person with talent waiting in line.

The best reaction I could hope for from a candidate with this profile was to reject initial advances. The idea was not to find someone who needed the job, but rather someone who recognized and wanted an opportunity. For me, the need to fill a job was secondary to finding a person who had potential to do more than the job called for. I wanted them to buy the opportunity, not the job.

Give Up Control to Take Control

To find these traits in an individual it was important to see if they could take control of the interview process (to a point). What did they know about the company? Real knowledge—not facts and figures. Most important—what did they know about themselves? Did they know where they wanted to be? Why? Did they have a plan to achieve their goal? In short, they were tested to see if they had the inclination to cheat on rules. Did they understand what it meant to add value to a company in exchange for receiving opportunity and reward? The final test was critical. In short, was the candidate looking for a career rather than a job? Did they understand the difference?

The final exam was administered by never offering the candidate more income—in fact, usually even less—then they were receiving in their current job. It was a quick way to tell what the person understood about what was being offered and what they were looking for in a job. If a person came only for money, they would leave for money.

I wanted the person to recognize the opportunity and to make an investment in their future. It was important for them to demonstrate that the value for the job being offered was in the future, not the present. If they were only living for today, they would be of little value for us as we built for the future.

And the Morale of the Story Is ...

You can control your future to find the best job, secure rapid promotion, and take advantage of opportunity to achieve what you seek when you cheat on the traditional rules that put others in control of these elements.

Recognize that traditional rules dealing with hiring, firing, and promoting are—maybe more than any other set of rules—in place to control you and put you at the mercy of others. Not being in control of your career future is a little like being in an auto race and allowing competitors to set the rules for the type of car you can drive and how fast you can drive it. How many races would you win?

Your future is even more important, so why allow others to control it? Learn to recognize the rules that control your future in a company, and cheat on the ones that work against you.

13

Leadership Means
Being the Chief Cheater

Leadership is what you do when you empower others
to do what they never thought they could do.

If an organization is to create an environment in which cheating
to win flourishes, the leader must be the chief cheater. This calls
for someone who can recognize, understand, and act on the
reality that many of the accepted rules of leadership—especially in
business—have become (at best) self-serving and outmoded. At
worst, they are a corrosive element that both weakens and destroys
the ethics and function of an organization. For the good of all
concerned—especially the leader—these are rules to cheat on.

We've been raised and socialized on time-honored images of
leadership. Sifted through eons of history, we have come to recognize
the standard-bearer of leadership as one (a man, of course) who is
out front and visible. This vision urges us to believe that the best
leadership is provided when the leader is in the limelight, the focus
of attraction and attention. After all, followers can't follow if the
leader is not out front leading, can they?

Museums are chockablock with portraits that depict this
quintessential view of leadership. You know, the gallant Crusader
with flapping flag in hand astride the supersized charger—rising above
the chaos to lead his followers on to vanquish the evil marauding
mongrels. (Yes, all were men except for one woman, and she got

burned at the stake for her efforts, leading to the popular touring sitcom of the Middle Ages, "I Burned Joan." And also of note is that most of these portraits were commissioned by the subjects themselves to show what great leaders they were!)

The traditional images of the leader are often based on a single, dramatic event. The mention of Teddy Roosevelt invokes visions of his bravery while leading the Rough Riders in the charge up San Juan Hill. Think of Bonaparte atop his white steed on his way to glory through the St. Bernard Pass. George Washington is often depicted as (foolishly) standing up in a rowboat, leading his army across the Delaware River in the middle of winter. The movies show us the brave cavalry officer—saber waving—out front leading the charge against the Indian hordes made wicked for defending the land they had first. There is the World War II image of Douglas MacArthur wading ashore in the Philippines as if he were the first one to confront and frighten off the Japanese. I could go on and on with these time-honored examples of leadership, but why? The fact is, they are, at best, the old myths of leadership, not the reality of today—although the memory lingers on.

Over time, business executives have adopted similar military symbols in an apparent attempt to demonstrate their own illustrious leadership. How many portraits of the "great leader" hang in corporate offices? The only elements missing are the horse and flag. The massive corner office, private potty, exclusive dining room, staff of sycophants, stretched limo, corporate jet (and lately handcuffs for some), combined with obscene annual income and perks all take the place of the "flag and horse" for what some want us to believe are signs of leadership. But clearly these are more the corrupt trappings of position than a genuine demonstration of leadership.

The image of the leader out front heroically showing the way is a romantic idea, but that is not the essence of leadership in the modern world. No longer does the imperial, distant, aloof, infallible, and tyrannical approach to leadership work—if ever it really did. A truly effective leader will cheat on this rule and turn the old concepts upside down.

But how to do it? The best way to adopt a cheat-to-win leadership style is, first, to become aware of the current management fads that pass themselves off as the latest scientific breakthroughs. And, then, blend the best of them for yourself.

Leadership: Vision and Management

There are two distinct applications of leadership currently in vogue. One could be called "leadership vision." Here the leader demonstrates the ability to identify, establish, communicate, and support the "big-picture" vision of the organization's future, while at the same time motivating and inspiring others to commit to and make that vision a reality.

The second element of leadership could be called "leadership of management." This style encompasses the ability of the leader to understand, monitor, and direct the full scope of specific activity needed to accomplish the agreed-upon organizational vision. There is a difference between vision and management leadership, but the two are best inter-linked for the ultimate success of the organization.

Some are quite good at seeing, communicating, and inspiring others to the vision of the big picture, but could not manage their way to the check-out stand at a Wal-Mart. (Or, might be amazed to see the price of items registered on a scanner!) Some are quite good at guiding and implementing multiple tasks that combine to achieve the broader vision, but can't see any farther than the edges of their wing tips. Both of these types can be effective leaders in their domain, but the ultimate leader must be able to conquer both disciplines. Such a leader is truly multifaceted. The leader is a planner with a clear purpose who knows the details but deals with the big picture. The modern leader is not a benevolent despot (or for that matter any type of despot); but rather, he or she builds alliances while still controlling the agenda. The leader never, ever stops selling the vision and is a pragmatist who recognizes the reality of the environment.

Lead by the Numbers

Another traditional management scheme is called "leading by the numbers." This approach to management leaves little room for flexibility or creativity and is a rule that real leaders cheat on constantly. Remember the arts-and-crafts fad of the 1950s called "paint by numbers"? The idea was for people to buy a pallet predesigned to re-create a "masterpiece" of art by applying different colors of paint in prenumbered areas. For example, "1" was for red; "2" for green; "3" for blue, and so on.

If you followed the numbers and did as you were told, the company promised, "every man could become a Rembrandt." The completed masterpiece emerged and you could call yourself an artist. (After three successful paintings you received a certificate that allowed you to change your name to "Artist"—formerly known as David.) It is amazing how many millions of the paint-by-number packages were sold and are still being sold today. (Although today most sales are to nursing homes, mental institutions, and convents.)

What few realized (but I made an exhaustive study on this so I know) was that the inspiration for the paint-by-number craze came from traditional methods of leadership and management. It was an accepted rule that called for the leader to understand the big picture and for followers to do exactly as they were told to do "by the numbers." The theory behind this concept was that if the workers would simply follow the management-by-numbers rule, they would create a masterpiece of a corporate organization. There was no deviation, flexibility, or creativity allowed in the process. Workers were led by that wonderfully inspirational decree, "Do exactly as you are told and do it today!"

An advanced form of the "by-the-numbers" management style has emerged that is identified as "micromanagement." (The name was derived from the writings of a very anal management consultant from Micronesia.) Micromanagement differs somewhat from by-the-numbers management: employees not only have to operate by the numbers, but they also have to ask permission and direction for each numbered step to be executed.

The micromanagement approach to leadership is looked upon with some disdain today (for obvious reasons), but there are still a fair number of managers who continue to believe in the philosophy—

either out of disrespect for the capacity of the followers or out of fear of being discovered as lacking in true leadership qualities. Clearly, management by the numbers is a rule to be cheated on (unless, that is, you are in charge of managing a mental institution or convent).

The Adam Smith School of Management

At the other end of the spectrum is a management style espoused by many as an enlightened management philosophy, but its real purpose is to demonstrate deified leadership from above. The "invisible hand" will lead us, just as economist Smith said it guides the most efficient use of resources in a nation's economy.

The rule calls for the leader to pronounce from on high the great vista of vision that has been established, and then get back on the imperial throne, leaving the followers alone with the "freedom" to achieve the objective on their own.

This approach to leadership allows the leader to sound magnanimous and announce the "emancipation" of the people to "empower" themselves with the freedom to accomplish the objective based on their own wit. The message is, "What a wonderful leader I am to allow you to do it on your own." This "hands off" rule of leadership may be the most ineffective and devious of all, for it allows the "leader" to invoke the ultimate management cop-out: "When things go wrong—blame someone else!" It's also a great tool for ducking responsibility. Like the CEO saying, "Gee, I had no idea that stuff about cooking the books was going on. I just dealt with the big issues and left the details to others."

Which Style for You?

Which approach to management leadership should you use? Should you be "hands on" or "hands off"? In a modern world filled with sophisticated and well-educated followers (some more so than the leader), both of these extreme approaches to ruling should be rejected and replaced with an approach that seeks middle, yet solid, ground. Do neither. Instead, do both, but do them in a better way—the cheat-to-win way.

Manage from Below While Others Fly High

For modern management leadership to be effective, it must be reconfigured to fit into today's world of talented, well-educated, and sophisticated workers. This new approach to structured leadership could be compared to the air traffic control (ATC) system that allows airlines to safely transit the globe. This style enables the leader to be intimately involved in the process of achieving the vision, yet allows those charged with completing the process to have maximum flexibility and freedom to complete the task.

Think about how the ATC system works for the airline industry. Let's say we want to fly from Miami to Minneapolis. The vision is to transport a plane full of passengers safely from one city to the other. The first order of business is to complete a flight plan for the trip and file it with ATC. ATC then reviews the filed plan and either approves it as filed or (based on other information) suggests modifications to the plan. Once the flight plans have been approved, the pilots are free to decide what actions will best enable them to achieve their objective. As the trip evolves, the pilots report their progress to ATC. If problems are encountered, or if there is a need to change direction, this is also reported to and discussed with ATC.

At times during the trip, ATC may contact the pilots with important feedback and needed information such as changing weather conditions or other air traffic they are likely to encounter. If need be, ATC offers possible changes to the flight plan and how the final destination should be approached. This system is based on a high level of trust and confidence between ATC and the pilots flying the airplane. In order to complete the plan, both parties must have full faith and confidence in the performance of the other.

The pilots have confidence that the information they receive is accurate and reliable. ATC has faith that the pilots will take the course of action filed in their flight plan and report any change in direction should it be necessary. No, ATC doesn't fly the airplane or do the work of the pilots, but try to safely reach the destination without the help of ATC.

So who is in charge of the flight, ATC or the pilots? What would happen if ATC were to have vital information that was not shared with the pilots? What if the pilots decided to change direction, but not inform ATC? How confusing would it be for the pilots if in midflight ATC began to give directions to a different objective. Is this "by the numbers" or "micromanagement" by the ATC? Maybe it's some of both; maybe neither. The pilot is "in command" of the flight and physically directs the plane to the final destination. Do the pilots feel as though they are being micromanaged by ATC, or do they view ATC as a crucial partner supporting the effort to safely reach the destination? Who gets credit for the successful completion of the flight? Do the passengers go to the pilot, or ATC, and say, "Thanks for a great job"? Clearly, ATC was critical to the success of the flight and actually directed the process, but it's the pilots who get credit for the success achieved.

Just as ATC doesn't actually fly the airplane, a good leader doesn't actually sell widgets, keep the books, or run the marketing department. Instead, a good leader provides the information, support, and infrastructure that *enable* people to do their jobs. They encourage and support, allow others to do the job, and freely dole out the credit for a job well done.

Imagine a leader (ATC) who won't give you radar coverage or even provide radio communication. What would you like about an ATC who kept rough weather, conflicting traffic, or other severe problems to himself? What would happen if the ATC's attitude was to bully and berate the pilots? The working environment would be nothing but turbulence, disappointments, and disheartenment.

The successful management leader of today will cheat on the old rules and install this ATC-type management system for the organization. The leader and the department "pilots" can meet to discuss and agree on objectives. The department head files a "flight plan" with the leader, who suggests changes or approves. Once approved, the department head is free to do whatever is necessary— within the plan—to achieve the objective. Should the leader obtain new information that might impact the mission of the department, it can be effectively communicated to the department head. Should the department head discover issues or problems that impact the objective, they can be discussed with the leader.

This management leadership style is the best of all worlds. The leader is able to effectively manage and support the process of the entire organization (in coordination with other "flights" that might be in progress) while leaving the "pilots" the freedom to achieve the objective based on their own plans and actions.

Will the Real Leadership Please Stand Up?

As you can readily see, leadership is about showing others the way to be what they always wanted to be but never imagined they could be. Leadership is about helping others to help you be the leader they want you to be.

Genuine leadership has never been exhibited by a single, dramatic episode but rather an intricate series of actions and events that fuse the followers into a dynamic and focused force that is targeted to achieve the objectives of the leader—because they have been adopted as the objectives of the whole. In reality, *the best leaders lead best when they appear to follow.* While the most successful leaders have tended to be somewhat flamboyant in public, in private they have a propensity to be detailed, diligent, consistent, concerned, and sharing. (Some might add the word "insecure," but I am afraid to get into that right now.)

Not surprisingly, the most effective modern leaders are those who exhibit a penchant to consistently and calmly do those things that make the most of themselves, their team members, and the collective organization. And a frenetic, erratic, insecure, power-hungry air-traffic controller is just as unwanted as a stop-and-start, loop-the-loop pilot.

The most effective senior executives almost uniformly demonstrate a plethora (I am not sure that is the right word, but so many "smart" people use it, I thought that I should at least once) of similar personality traits that form the bedrock of my philosophy toward leadership and management. I have learned that executives who successfully cheat to win:

- Demonstrate consistency in all they do.
- Never demand obedience but always build trust.
- Communicate and consider but never equivocate.
- Spread power and information around like cold germs in a nursery school.
- Have the ability to simplify the complicated.
- Never rush but live by a sense of urgency.
- Live in the future but act in the present.
- Are great builders of consensus but control the agenda.

Modern Leadership—New Rules

Break the rule that puts the leader out front. Instead, put the mission and the people out front and make them the focus. Spotlight what is to be accomplished, not how accomplished the leader may be. As discussed in the chapter on reminiscing about the future, good leadership begins with a clear, focused, and staunch commitment to the big picture, the entire perspective of the corporate mission. The strong leader identifies, promotes, and communicates a mission to all that is not abandoned, qualified, or compromised until it is accomplished. This results in leadership with an unswerving purposefulness that does not allow the followers to be deflected from the ultimate objective.

A clear vision is important for both the leader and the constituency. You can't be a true leader unless you are willing to believe in your own vision. You may slide by for a while faking it, but—in the long run—if you don't have a deep-seated belief in what you're trying to do—if you aren't willing to stick with it under fire— you'll never bring the rank and file to wholehearted support of your efforts.

Real Leaders Are Consistently Consistent

Being an effective leader today requires accepting the fact that the mission is about the success of the organization, not personal aggrandizement. Leaders adopt the mission of the organization as the essence of their core beliefs and they refuse to be deterred from that no matter what happens.

217

Real leaders are *passionate about being consistent* in what they do. They may be flexible to changing conditions, but they do not easily change directions. They are not influenced by the nattering of outside influences; they recognize that there will always be those people who, for whatever reasons, will try to challenge, shake, and change the fortitude of a leader. Strong leaders may modify and adjust techniques, but the big picture remains consistent.

One of the chief benefits of this ultraconsistency is that those around the leader—employees, friends, family, even enemies—know they can rely on it. That is the essence of leadership. You *did* what you said you were going to do—again and again. People crave that type of consistency, that "stay-the-course" attitude, in their leaders. Followers require a clearly defined image of what the leader is trying to provide before they will buy into that picture. If the leader is not willing to demonstrate a consistent, complete commitment to the objective, it is unrealistic to ask the followers to give their full commitment to the leader.

Restless as a Willow in a Key West Hurricane . . .

The worst type of leader is one who is blown like a leaf in a hurricane. (President Jimmy Carter comes to mind here.) My criticism of many business leaders is that they are influenced by the last person to leave the office. Nothing is more bedeviling for employees than to have their team chief betray them with inconsistency. People want something to hang on to. They want something to focus on. They want to know they're on the correct ship of fate, not some tramp steamer meandering toward the business shoals.

Historians believe that Jimmy Carter—despite his high intelligence and meticulous management style—will become a "forgotten" president because of his inability to remain focused and committed to a pronounced objective. No matter what the cause, as soon as Carter encountered resistance, he folded and moved to a new flavor of vision.

Few would argue that Ronald Reagan was one of our brightest presidents. His idea of getting into the details was to be sure he knew what day it was, but he was clearly more effective than Carter and will be remembered well into history for his single-minded, focused battle to defeat the "evil empire!"

Do you remember when George H. W. Bush (the first one) stood before the Republican National Convention in 1988 and promised, "Read my lips—No new taxes!"? It was a defining moment in the campaign and may have won the election for Bush. But three years later Bush reneged on this statement and agreed, along with the Democrats, to raise taxes. Admittedly, valid arguments could have been made for the need to raise taxes, but that was not the issue. Despite Bush's high approval ratings from success in the first Gulf War, his retreat from what had been the cornerstone of his administration cost him his credibility and the confidence of the electorate. Certainly there were other reasons for Bush's loss to Clinton (being seen as an out-of-touch "dork" didn't help), but many cited this "change of direction" as an example of poor leadership and a key turning point in the election.

Leaders Build Trust

The traditional rules of leadership did not require the building of trust between the leader and the followers, because followers were supposed to follow and obey. People were being paid to do their job, and trust was not an element deemed critical to doing a job. Today, that philosophy needs to be cheated on. Being a trust-builder is essential to effective modern leadership because today most people will only follow someone who they can trust.

If a leader loses trust, then, no matter the objective, it's unlikely others will follow. Attempting to provide leadership while not simultaneously building trust from constituent followers is the prescription for a difficult time.

That contrast came home to me when Allianz acquired LifeUSA. After five or six months of careful negotiation, the one issue not discussed was the management structure of the merged company. Who would run the merged company? I had assumed that I would be reporting to the current president of Allianz Life; I was as surprised as anyone to learn that Allianz intended for me to be the CEO of the combined company—and that LifeUSA would provide virtually all of the surviving management.

(This result also served to confirm a rule-breaking policy I had followed during my career. I never sought a job, promotion, or raise, assuming that whatever talents I had would be properly identified and rewarded. In most mergers you will find that the existing managers worried about protecting themselves first, and only later thought about the rest. We cheated on this rule in the merger discussions with Allianz and won.)

Even more amazing to me was how the employees of each organization accepted this news. At Allianz Life, people were aghast. They were anxious, combative, and scared. They wanted answers that, unfortunately, I could not give them, because I didn't have them. I could only respond by saying, "I'm sorry, I don't have all the answers yet regarding what will happen as a result of the merger, and you'll have to trust me." I didn't realize at the time that I was asking the impossible of the Allianz Life employees, because over the years the only thing the management team had done well was to create an environment of complete employee distrust. By the time of the merger, nothing said by the Allianz Life management was taken at face value.

So when I talked to the people at Allianz, there was no connection. There was no tie-in because they did not trust me, nor had they ever trusted top management. It became immediately apparent that the toughest challenge to a successful merger of LifeUSA and Allianz Life would be the lack of trust for management on the part of the Allianz Life employees.

Immediately after meeting with the Allianz employees, a similar gathering was conducted at LifeUSA. There, the reception to the news was as different as night and day. Was there apprehension? Sure, and it was mixed with a good deal of anxiety. But after the meeting, a number of LifeUSA employees came up to me and said, "We are concerned about what is going to happen, but it is okay, Mac, because *we trust you.*" The almost childlike trust that had developed between the people and management of LifeUSA created an environment that enabled the merger to flow smoothly.

The same was true on an individual level. With the details still up in the air, Mark Zesbaugh, the CFO of LifeUSA, didn't know if he would have a job after the merger. In our first meeting after the announcement, I had to be honest and tell him that I didn't know what his role would be in the new company. My gut reaction was that since the leaders of Allianz in Germany didn't know Mark (or me, for that matter) they'd probably be more comfortable with the current Allianz Life CFO.

Despite this, I promised to find a role for him, even though I didn't know exactly what it would be. And his comment to me was, "Mac, I don't care what I do. I will do anything you ask me to do, because I trust you." Imagine the powerful flexibility a leader has when the followers are willing to put full faith and trust in what he is doing—even if their future for them is uncertain. (Mark's trust was rewarded a few weeks later when the executives in Germany informed me they wanted Mark to be the CFO. And, three years later, he replaced me as CEO of the company.)

Fortunately for Allianz Life, that spirit of mutual trust continues to flourish under Mark's leadership, as he has continued (actually improved upon) the cheat-to-win model of business management. (This, by the way, has enabled the company to triple in size since my retirement—an action for which I will never forgive Mark!)

Trust Does Not Develop Easily

The problem, however, is that you cannot command trust. Leaders must earn it. And like it or not, most employees have been led to believe that management is to be *distrusted* until proven worthy of full and complete support. Trust is hard to earn and easy to lose. Unfortunately, the old rules of management did not require building trust among the rank and file because the leader—as top dog—always knew what was best for the underlings. In addition, the old rules did not call for leaders to trust followers. In fact, systems were set up based on the belief that followers could not be trusted. How would you expect employees to trust management if management is constantly sending signals that they don't trust the employees? This is a rule you should cheat on.

Over time I discovered that the most effective way to build trust with people was the simple process of communication and transparency. By always being totally open (many said too open) with people regarding issues, challenges, objectives, and plans, I took the risk of trusting people with my future and the success of the company. In response, the people trusted me. As my leadership experience grew I discovered that the more I trusted people, the more they trusted me. It was simple but, then again, leadership is simple.

Communication Rules

An army may run on its stomach, but a winning organization runs on information: the data that pulses through the veins of your IT department, the plans for the expanded marketing program, the inside dope that fills the files of the CFO's office, your investor relations department, your PR department.

The old rules of leadership commanded that information should be hoarded like food in a fat farm. We all know the meaning of the phrase, "need-to-know-only basis." That concept comes from the traditional rule of leadership that equates information with power.

In our earlier chapter on power, the rules of power were extensively reviewed. If you recall, application of the rule measures power based on how much more information you are privy to than others. The old rule dictated that information be vested only in the leader, and that the leader uses the information to lead all others. It's a concept that worked for centuries on the following basis: If the leader alone knew where the organization was going, then all others had no choice but to "follow the leader."

To be a real leader of people today, you must not only cheat on this rule—but obliterate it. Institute a new rule that says your leadership and power are to be measured by how much information and power you *share* with those you seek to lead.

To motivate today's educated worker to play follow the leader and agree to work to achieve the vision of the organization, that vision—and progress achieved—must be constantly communicated. Relentless, steady, consistent communication becomes the navigational beacon that leads others in the direction the leader seeks to go as surely as the mnemonic phrase, "Red, Right, Returning Even" has for decades guided mariners home safely to port.

Without this commitment to communication, people will be unclear as to what path they need to follow and may wander off without accomplishing the objective. Establish a new rule to demonstrate strong leadership by being willing to share all information with those you want to lead.

Complicated Is as Simple Does

Traditional leadership rules called for imperial leadership, because issues faced by an organization were often presented as too complicated for the average person to understand. This rule was applied because those in charge argued that the "little people" just didn't understand the issues facing the organization, so they became the proper venue of the omnipotent leader. This attitude may have been acceptable when people were uneducated, but it has no place in today's world. Yet the idea hangs on.

A parallel rule used by wannabe leaders to prove they should be leaders has been to take a simple issue and make it complicated. This old rule of leadership sets up a "straw man" who suggests that only the leader can understand the complexity of the issues and is therefore the only one who could lead. If there is a rule to cheat on to improve your leadership skills, it is this one! Effective leadership calls for a leader who can take truly complex issues and make them simple. The fact is anyone can take a simple issue and make it complicated. (Just ask your IT guy how to turn on your computer!) It takes a talented leader to turn a complicated issue into a simple task. Demonstrate the ability to cut through the extraneous, identify the core issue and make it simple, and you have a talent that is fundamental to modern leadership.

A wonderful example of this ability was illustrated by Marlon Brando in *The Godfather.* Brando had instructed one of his lieutenants to secure a part in a movie for his friend "Johnny Fontane." The producer, you'll recall, had formally rejected the actor/singer and indicated he would never reconsider his decision. Fontane laments, "It's too late. All the contracts have been signed; they're almost ready to shoot."

We all remember Brando's response, "I'll make him an offer he can't refuse." Take a complicated process and make it simple; that is the secret to the success of the modern rule-breaking leader.

Plans fail when tasks or objectives are perceived as too complelx. Paralysis sets in when people have a difficult time getting their minds around the problem, spotting the solution, and putting it into place. Good leaders know that the best way to overcome the obstacle of a complicated task is to identify simple things to do and help the people simply do them.

Obfuscating the problem may appear to give you power; make you seem smarter, or better than all the rest, but that is rarely the best way. The true leader does just the opposite. Don't say "obfuscate" when you mean "confuse." And don't try to prove your manhood (peoplehood—to be politically correct) by making things more complicated. Prove what a great leader you are by making complicated things simple.

Closely related to the issue of simplifying problems is the ability to cut through the complications and quickly get to the heart of the problem. Good leaders have an instinct for getting to the core of the issue quickly, and they don't fool around. A recent TV commercial demonstrated this very well. Some software nerds are noshing in the company lunchroom and one guy begins choking on a piece of food. The others take note, and start considering the situation. One guy says the equivalent of, "Gee, look at what he did. He's choking on the meat." Then another geek says, "'Ya know, I think there is a way you can take care of that. Maybe we should do a little study." Then a guy gets up from another table and gives the poor bastard a Heimlich maneuver, and the guy spits the meat out. That's the difference between talking about the problem, the issue, and getting to the heart of the matter quickly. A good leader is decisive.

Leaders Live in the Future but Act in the Present

A true leader lives in the future, constantly trying to peer around the corner. However, while effective leaders may live in the future, they always act in the present. If leaders only live and act in the present, they can miss important opportunities and increase the likelihood of encountering problems. And certainly if the leader lives only in the past then members of the organization had better reserve their cots at the Little Sisters of the Poor.

It is possible to get a feel for this "live for today but think for tomorrow" philosophy by talking to an experienced public speaker. Most successful speakers will tell you that during a speech—even though they are talking in the present—they are concentrating on what they are going to say a minute or two from now.

As they are talking in the present, they are studying the audience to determine its reaction to what is being said in the present. This is done to see what will work in the future. Accordingly—adjusting to the reaction of the audience—the speaker is constantly mentally altering the script for changes minutes later. The audience has no idea the speaker is thinking about the future while dealing with them in the present. The same process works for good leaders. There is a constant focus on short-term goals to achieve the long-term objectives. The leader focuses on what has to be done today to be ready for tomorrow.

Quickly—Create a Sense of Urgency

As discussed in the chapter on bureaucracy, good leaders have a great sense of urgency that they vigorously communicate to others. They balance that urgency with both a challenge and reasonableness.

President John F. Kennedy demonstrated this style of leadership when, in 1962, he declared the United States would put a man on the moon and return him safely to Earth *before the decade is over.* He understood this sense of urgency in finding a way to overtake the Soviets in the space race. Despite skeptics who thought it could not be accomplished, Kennedy's dream became a reality when on July 20, 1969, *Apollo 11* commander Neil Armstrong took a small step for himself and a giant step for mankind, leaving a dusty trail of footprints on the lunar landscape.

Effective leaders create this same sense of urgency in their lives and in their organizations. Having a sense of urgency is having a feeling that you must get this done within a specific period of time and you are *absolutely committed to doing that.*

How many people have their highest peaks of productivity in the last two days before their vacation? Why? Because they have a sense of urgency, a need to get their work done so they can go on vacation. A simple rule of modern leadership: Leaders set the example by always operating as if they were two days from vacation. (Of course, some seem to think the true rule of leadership is to operate as if one were always out to lunch.)

Leader Creates Consensus

Under the old rules of leadership, the idea of building a consensus for action was considered to be time-consuming and soft. Consensus was "nice," but it was not something that needed to be achieved. The assumption was that by the definition of leadership, leaders needed to make all the important decisions. Many feared: If the leader was not needed to make all the decisions then why do we need a leader? This attitude was a variation of the theory that the only way to be powerful is to hold all the power for oneself.

In reality, this is a sign of failed leadership. It is one thing to have the power to make all the recommendations and decisions. It is quite another to use it. Harry Truman believed that the surest way to lose power is to use power. Every time you say, "Do it this (my) way," you are reducing both your own power and the free flow of information that may assist in making the best decisions. You are becoming a problem solver, not a solution facilitator. You are not being a leader. You are acting like a dictator. That might have worked in the past, but times are different. The world moves faster, competition is fierce, and followers are well educated and experienced. It is neither efficient nor effective for the leader to make all the decisions regarding the actions of an organization.

We need to cheat on this old rule and make a new one. When it comes to dealing with issues—at any level of leadership—the most effective leaders *appear* to make few specific decisions. Leaders create long-term objectives and concepts of the organization's core beliefs, but a strong leader creates a consensus that facilitates solutions to setting these objectives and concepts into action.

Traditionally, leaders come into a meeting and show how dominant they are—demand answers or give answers to questions that have not been raised and then leave—thinking that the meeting was successful. Modern leaders view their role in meetings as the point guard—a catalyst who starts the play in motion—not as the one who makes the decisions. They bring people together—diverse elements of different chemistries—to solve a problem. Going into the meeting, however, the leader knows what decisions will likely be made and the direction of the meeting will take as well. In the world of today, it is a failure of leadership if—at the end of the meeting—the leader has to say, "No. We are going to do it this way."

A great leader inspires and motivates others to recommend to the leader very specific actions to accomplish the desired objectives—exactly what the leader would have directed had a consensus not been sought.

Being Wrong the Right Way

There is an additional benefit gained when a leader works to create consensus: the opportunity to be proven wrong without admitting it. A traditional meeting may start with the leader saying, "Okay, we are going to do this and we are going to do it this way, now tell me how we will get it done." When that happens, open discussion shuts down and there is little opportunity for someone to say, "Doing this is the wrong thing to do. We should take a different approach."

The leader, as a catalyst building a consensus creates, the opportunity to hear viewpoints unfettered by preconceived notions or decisions. Most of the time—if it is done right—the decisions will go in exactly the direction the leader intended; but there are times when ideas offered will provide insight that had not been considered. Old management rules became inflexible and inefficient because they required the leader to always be right. Real leaders can be wrong but always seem to be right. Leading by building a consensus allows the leader to benefit from more flexibility and efficiency in decision making.

A true leader builds consensus like a chief gardener tends to a fertile plot. The gardener as CEO determines the type of "seeds" to be planted, but allows others to tend the garden. If the leader wants to grow pumpkins, he supplies the others with pumpkin seeds to plant, but allows the team to make the decisions about how the garden is tended, watered and fertilized. But make no mistake: if you plant pumpkin seeds, you're going to get pumpkins. Give others the credit for the fact that they grew the biggest pumpkins in the world. You don't care. You wanted to have pumpkins.

An excellent example of this principle is the working relationship that existed between President Ronald Reagan and Dan Rostenkowski, Democrat from Illinois and chairman of the House Ways and Means Committee. These two were not the closest of philosophical buddies. When Reagan became president, one of his first objectives was to push Congress to pass a huge tax cut. Amazingly, even though the Democrats controlled both branches of Congress, Reagan got his tax bill passed.

Later, someone asked Rostenkowski how Reagan was able to get so much of his agenda passed when he and others in Congress did not agree with the president philosophically. The response was a simple one. He said Reagan was successful for one uncomplicated reason: Reagan didn't care who got credit for the victory. And because Dutch did not care who got the credit, he was able to create a consensus. He was able to accomplish what very few other people could, because they wanted the credit for the success.

When you get right down to it, the most effective leaders are solution facilitators rather than problem solvers. This viewpoint may differ from the old rule of leadership that positioned the leader as an all-knowing deity who rules with an intimidating iron hand. You will be more successful if, as a leader, you develop a style of management that provides the tools to others, allowing them to solve the problems and receive the credit for doing so.

And the Moral of the Story Is ...

The leader as a "demigod" out front and hell-bent-for-leather may have been an effective image in the past, but leadership in today's world calls for a different approach. Leadership in the modern world is defined by the appearance of leaders following the followers to achieve the objectives the leader led the followers to believe were the objectives the followers had established for themselves. (See how I said leaders take complicated things and make them simple?)

The traditional concepts defining leadership have been in place for centuries, but many of them have outlived their time and should be replaced. Those who seek to offer leadership to will gain their following, power, and success when they cheat on the old rules and develop a different set of rules. Their power will come from understanding that:

- When the rule says be out front; allow others to ride the horse.
- When the rule says be the hero; let the others carry the flag.
- When the rule says retain power; make sure power is shared.
- When the rule says know it all; make sure others learn more.
- When the rule says be above it all; be accessible and in the trenches.
- When the rule says tell people what to do; teach people how to do it.
- When the rule says have all the answers; look for answers from others.
- When the rule says put the portrait on the wall: Put others up first.
- When the rule says take all the credit; give all the credit away.

Putting it all together, to be a leader today means being a visionary who can reminisce about the future in a way that allows others to see the future they can make. The leader "lives the vision" but motivates others to adopt it as their own and commit to achieving the vision in order to please the leader. The leader is followed when he or she is flexible enough to adjust to the environment but is consistent to the vision itself. The leader is a decisive, multifaceted person who lives in the future but acts in the present; is a planner with a clearly communicated purpose who builds alliances that allow others to achieve the vision. The leader is recognized by the followers as ethical, decisive, consistent, communicative, and willing to share the accomplishments with all. Most of all, the leader is one who can be trusted. When the real leader finishes, the pictures on the wall are of the others who made the vision a reality and proved that the leader truly was a leader.

14

Hothouse for Humanity

Building an Entrepreneurial Culture in a Bureaucratic World

An entrepreneurial leader has the talent to clearly, simply, and consistently communicate corporate objective to others, involve them in the process, and motivate them to achieve a success that is shared by all.

Miracle management methods methodically move in cycles. As companies grow larger, management methods become increasingly systematized and complicated. The end result? The bigger the company, the bigger the rulebook.

Favored systems have moved from the brutality of the work boss during the American Industrial Revolution, to the even more insidious calculations of Frank Gilbreth who, in the 1920s and '30s, pioneered the famous time and motion studies, on to the organizational man of the 1950s and, '60s and, finally, the late twentieth century Japanese theory of invisible individuals working anonymously for an unknown goal. At one time or another, all of these approaches were thought of as the nirvana of management systems.

Yet these techniques failed to deliver as promised because they universally contained a fatal flaw. That defect was the rule that assumed as companies grew larger and more complicated, so too, should the management systems used to control the people working for the company. In reality, the successful management system will cheat on that rule and function in exactly the opposite way. As the organization grows larger and more complicated, the management system should become increasingly fundamental and simple.

Frustrated with management systems that don't seem to work, and with employees who lack motivation, corporate leaders continue to seek the magic bullet. The most recent theory—and the current hot buzz-phrase among management gurus—is the "entrepreneurial organization" or "entrepreneurial culture." These managers marvel at and covet the success of those companies that have been christened with the tag "entrepreneurial."

It seems everyone talks about, promotes, and espouses seeking the Holy Grail of the entrepreneurial organization. (One of the reasons the French have such a poor work ethic among employees is because they don't have a word for entrepreneurial.) Searching for improved performance, companies high and low rummage around the management kitchen for the supernatural potion that will deliver an "entrepreneurial culture." That's all well and good, but my fear is that the concept of "entrepreneurialism" will become the sizzling management fad of the early twenty-first century, only to fade away like Bill Clinton's girlfriends when the results don't seem to measure up to the promises.

I say this despite believing (knowing) that creating an entrepreneurial culture is *the* definitive management system. It's an excellent paradigm; we need only to implement and improve it.

The issues and ideas discussed in this chapter revolve around the advantages of operating under the influence of an entrepreneurial culture. While the emphasis centers on actions leaders can take to either build or imbue an organization with entrepreneurial spirit, those same ideas will apply equally well to us as individual managers. There is no need to be the head of a large company to use and benefit from entrepreneurial management techniques. Understanding, implementing, and following many of these ideas will make us better and more effective managers. This is true regardless of whether we are managing a three-person department, a small dress shop, or O.J. Simpson's private detectives looking for Nicole Simpson's "real killer."

Developing and maintaining an honest entrepreneurial culture is ultimately the only way for a company—large or small—to remain responsive to consumer needs, and maintain competitiveness, growth, and profitability. Systems manage down—entrepreneurial cultures push up! Nurturing an entrepreneurial culture allows management to become simpler as the company grows complicated.

Getting to There from Here

The chief obstacle standing between the old way and the entrepreneurial way is a fundamental lack of understanding as to what it means to be an entrepreneurial company. In addition, there is a need to recognize that developing and implementing a true entrepreneurial culture requires deep commitment, persistency, consistency, and hard work from management leaders. (Unfortunately, that eliminates most managers looking for an easy way out of their problems, unless the entrepreneurial spirit could be infused in them in the form of a suppository.)

The general misconception that emerges when people think of entrepreneurialism is that of a swashbuckling, devil-may-care, risk-taking, win-at-all-costs, money-grubbing, egotistical Capitalist pig. (Someone like Donald Trump might come to mind!) In short, most people equate the entrepreneur with an obsession for money. It is assumed the only motivation for the entrepreneur is selfish greed. (If Ted Kennedy had ever worked for his money instead of inheriting it, he would get off this idea.) This perception could not be more wrong. Entrepreneurialism is not about financial economics; it's about human ergonomics. The true entrepreneurial organization creates the natural habitat for humanity. (No, I am not referring to the exceptional international humanitarian outfit by that name, but something just as compelling.) A true entrepreneurial culture brings out the best in people, encourages effort to add value, and rewards honest achievement. Money is not the cause, but rather the residue, of an effective entrepreneurial system.

Building an entrepreneurial culture does not come easily—nothing really good ever does. This is not silkscreen, topsoil stuff here. True entrepreneurial spirit has to be woven deep into the very fabric of the culture. And that is not easy, especially if you are trying to move a company away from the traditional bureaucratic approach. But the rewards are worth it.

Think of it this way: Fixed management systems, rules, and structure become increasingly burdensome and brittle as the company grows. It takes more and more effort to accomplish less. Soon, the whole momentum that pushed the company to achieve and grow slows down and ultimately reverses course.

Just try wending your way through government rules and regulations, especially to accomplish something new. If you do, you'll know the frustration inherent in the effort to get the system to work properly. The same lack of inertia applies in spades to companies as they become larger and encrusted with heavy barnacles of management rules and systems.

On the other hand, an entrepreneurial culture, by its very essence, increases in simplicity and remains pliable as the company grows. But it would be a mistake to assume that entrepreneurial companies do not have controls and that laissez-faire anarchy prevails. Nothing is farther from the truth. In fact, true entrepreneurial companies are much more effectively managed and controlled than other types of endeavors. This becomes evident when we come to understand the difference between rules and principles. Bureaucratic companies are required to mandate the right thing to do. Entrepreneurial cultures know the right thing to do.

Critics may cite Enron, WorldCom, Tyco, Adelphia, and any number of rogue companies as examples of pure entrepreneurialism run amok, but I disagree. Rather, they are examples of out-of-control, bloated bureaucratic organizations with cultures that both tolerate and foster lack of accountability, unadulterated greed, and fraud at many levels. Ken Lay, the disgraced former Enron CEO, argues that he did not know what was going on below him and that he was lied to about what was being cooked in the accounting department. That may be true (though I doubt it), but, it still does not absolve him of responsibility. He is the one who allowed a bureaucratic culture that countenanced the illegal and fraudulent activity to develop at Enron. The true entrepreneurial culture will always identify and reject such deadly infections.

The same is true with Richard Scrushy at HealthSouth who, like all bureaucratic managers (especially dishonest ones) always fell back on, "I didn't know that activity was happening." Or, "We have rules in place to stop that activity." It's not what you *knew* was happening in the company that's important—it's what the culture you built will *allow* to happen. In a true entrepreneurial organization, the culture—not the managers—controls and resists inappropriate actions.

Defining an Entrepreneurial Organization

If an entrepreneurial organization is not what we think it to be—then what is it? An entrepreneurial organization is one with a strict adherence to a core set of values, a constant focus on clearly defined objectives, and free-flowing communication to support the efforts of the members of the organization. In an entrepreneurial organization accountability is demanded of all, while risk is encouraged and accomplishment rewarded. A sense of urgency (there is that phrase again—must be important!) is an operating lifestyle in an entrepreneurial environment that views change as an opportunity, not a threat. An entrepreneurial culture attracts those who have the ability to add value to the organization and encourages them to do so by allowing all members to participate in the value added.

Of course, entrepreneurial cultures just don't appear; they have to be created. That calls for a strong entrepreneurial leader. Such a leader has the experience to recognize opportunity, the instinct to visualize its fulfillment, and the courage to reach for it. An entrepreneurial leader is one who, by nature, has the talent to clearly, simply, consistently, and relentlessly communicate the objective to others, involve them in the process, and motivate them to achieve a success that is shared by all.

Growing Entrepreneurialism for Fun and Profit

Building new or converting an existing bureaucratic organization into an entrepreneurial culture is easy, but it is also hard. An entrepreneurial culture will emerge in any company—old or new, big or small—when it is driven in a single, simple focus to commit, concentrate and drive passionately to be a unique place where success will thrive and survive over time. And that place is a place I call a *Hothouse for Humanity*. What is a hothouse for humanity? Simple— it's a place where people can go to grow to be great!

If—as you go forward—you are passionately focused on fostering, building, and maintaining a hothouse for humanity, then you will have no problem nurturing and building an entrepreneurial culture. Remember, the objective is to create and maintain an environment that encourages people to become great. And how do we do that?

- We constantly reminisce about the future with our people so they know where we are going.
- We establish and maintain certain inviolate principles of ethics and rules of engagement so people have support, stability, and consistency as they grow.
- We constantly communicate and participate but never equivocate.
- We never lose sight of parallel interests so that success is shared equitably.
- We encourage people to do simple things, and to simply do them.
- We encourage risk and teach from failure.
- We recognize that the way we gain power is to empower others.

- We recognize that the way to build wealth is to share wealth.
- We are consistent, available, open, and honest.
- Most of all, we never lose sight of the fact that the most powerful and critical assets of our organization or company are the people.

When we focus all our strength and effort to create a culture with transparent, free-flowing communication that encourages all members to participate in and benefit from the success achieved; if risk is encouraged and accomplishment rewarded; if ethics are solid, objectives are clear, priorities are maintained, and support is constant—then you will build a hothouse for humanity that will encourage people to grow to be great.

Simple, But Not Easy

As you read the definition of an entrepreneurial culture and leader, you may have found little to disagree with—maybe even nothing new. It seems so simple and fundamental. You would be right. None of the attributes of an entrepreneurial leader or culture should be new to us. They are elementary, clear and reasonable. Scores of management books have preached the acceptance of these concepts.

So, if that's the case, why are there so many more underachieving (or dishonest) corporate bureaucratic cultures than entrepreneurial ones? The answer lies in the fact that it's easier to be complicated than to be simple. Anyone can make things complicated (have you ever read an army manual on how to walk?), but it takes a very talented person to make things simple.

Entrepreneurial cultures are by their nature simple. That's what makes them so effective and that's also what makes them so difficult to achieve and maintain. To build an entrepreneurial culture, one must be willing to cheat on virtually all the rules of management that have been established through the old system—rules that say big needs to be complicated, the powerful get perks, and the employees should know their place.

People love to talk about the values of an entrepreneurial culture, but, unfortunately, most managers are more at ease with the old ways. They may talk a good game, but they are uncomfortable because true entrepreneurial management goes against the grain of established rules. In entrepreneurial cultures information, power, and reward are all shared on an equitable basis. Not so with the old ways where information is used as power, power is to be accumulated, and rewards are hoarded.

Good for the Little Guy but Not for the Big Guy

The common cop-out used by those looking for a reason not to build an entrepreneurial culture is, "Sure, entrepreneurial spirit is fine for a small company, but it just can't work for the large company with thousands of employees." If traditional rules are followed, those people are right; but they are wrong if you are willing to break the rules and cheat to win. It's not the size of the company that determines the success of a company—it is how good it is at what it does.

With all its rules and regulations, a government entity would seem the least likely to benefit from entrepreneurial concepts. Well, think again. At the start of World War II, there was a pressing need for transport ships to carry all manner of supplies to the war front. At the time, few if any such ships existed, and thousands were needed. The rules of the time said it would take months to build one ship. By the time Henry Kaiser got the "Liberty Ship" program sailing at full steam, five ships a *day* were being launched. The Manhattan Project created the first atomic bomb in only nineteen months. Something that had never been done before was done quickly, efficiently, and effectively by a massive government organization using entrepreneurial actions. If these shining examples of huge organizations that can—under the right conditions—achieve amazing entrepreneurial results, then any organization should be able to do the same.

Sure, some will argue that these successes are due more to gobs of government money thrown at the project than any magical management system, but I don't agree. These are good examples of entrepreneurial concepts applied in a big way. In each case there were strong leaders, a clearly defined purpose, consistent focus, constant communication to reinforce the objectives, and a shared reward for the accomplishment. Certainly, having enough capital is important for any enterprise, but if money were the only answer then bureaucrats could solve all our problems. It's not the amount of money you have, it's how the money you have is used.

Why Make the Effort?

There are two good reasons to make the effort to build entrepreneurial cultures: It's the right thing to do and it is the only way companies and individuals can achieve lasting success. This is the case because the employees of today have become the new capitalists of the twenty-first century. What do I mean? Well, in the late nineteenth century the Industrial Revolution in the United States was stimulated by the advance of technology but fueled by the risk-taking leadership, ideas, and capital of legendary American capitalists such as Rockefeller, Carnegie, Bessemer, Ford, Mellon, and scores of others. Advances in technology are marvels, but they are worthless without the capability to apply them in a practical fashion.

The capitalists of the time provided this capability by risking capital to build the needed infrastructure of machines, factories, and transportation facilities to take advantage of the emerging industrial technologies. Without capitalists who were willing to take risks, apply their talent and contribute their capital, America would not have become the world's economic and industrial colossus of the 20th century.

The early capitalists were richly rewarded for such risk-taking and application of pioneering talent. (Some would say too richly rewarded, but that's another debate.) The point is that the challenges, incentives, and rewards of entrepreneurialism stimulate progress, growth, and success that could never have been accomplished by other types of organizations.

Today, America is experiencing another revolution—a pure

revolution of technology—that offers as much potential for the future as industrial technology did in the past. The implementation has given rise to a new class of capitalists. These modern capitalists are as important and critical to the technological revolution as the capitalists of the past were to the Industrial Revolution.

There is one difference, however. The primary contribution of the capitalists of old was the power of the capital they risked, while the primary contribution of new millennium capitalists is the power of the education, experience, and the influence of intellect that they apply. Thus today's employee is as critical to the long-term success of the modern information organization as the industrial capitalists were to the successful development of the manufacturing infrastructure. Just as the industrial capitalists of the last century needed an entrepreneurial culture to encourage and reward their participation, so, too, do today's employees need an entrepreneurial culture to encourage and reward their participation.

So why should we make the effort to cheat on the traditional rules of bureaucratic management to create the entrepreneurial culture? Because cheating on these rules is the only way to build a true hothouse for humanity that will inspire a winning organization.

Building the Entrepreneurial Habitat

Building an entrepreneurial organization is not confined or limited to a certain-size organization. It can be new or old, small or large. While it may be easier to build an entrepreneurial organization from the get-go, sometimes the late conversions are even more effective. The key point to understand—and the point that most miss—is that an entrepreneurial culture is as much a state of mind as it is an operational structure.

Everything an entrepreneurial organization does flows first from the mindset of the culture, not the legal structure of the company. Peter Drucker, the guru of management consultants, has long argued that an (intended) not-for-profit organization can be just as entrepreneurial—if not more so—than many companies just out to make a fast buck.

If you as a leader are willing to cheat on enough of the traditional rules of management, then any organization is capable of becoming truly entrepreneurial. People will respond to strong entrepreneurial leadership no matter the size of the organization; it's the leadership in large organizations that tend not to be entrepreneurial—not the people.

Leading with Leadership

Building an entrepreneurial organization starts with great leadership. Entrepreneurial organizations function from the bottom up, but need to initiate activity with the leader at the top. The leader of an entrepreneurial organization must exhibit a unique form of managerial talent. Traditional corporate rules say that leaders tell— but entrepreneurial leaders must show. The entrepreneurial leader is by nature different from the conventional manager; instead of boundaries, they see opportunities. While there are many who can see opportunity, few have the instinct to visualize its fulfillment and even fewer the courage to reach for it. All entrepreneurial leaders seem to exhibit certain consistent, if unique, characteristics.

The cliché everyone applies to the entrepreneurial leader is the "river boat gambler." Many believe the entrepreneurial leader is someone who is always out on the ledge doing novel, if not crazy, things. (For many, even thinking about starting a company is a risk!) The rules say that to be an entrepreneur means gambling the future. The reality is that entrepreneurs are—taken as a group—more conservative in their actions than those viewed as "mainstream." Entrepreneurs are risk-takers, but they are not gamblers.

There is a difference between a risk and a gamble. A risk is an event in which one has some control over the outcome. A gamble is an event over which one has no control over the outcome. It may be a risk to start your own business, but it is a gamble to try to win the lottery. A risk can be managed and measured; a gamble can only be experienced—never controlled. A person addicted to gambling will always lose and lose big. A person conditioned to clear, reasoned risk taking will win more often than lose, and the wins will always be bigger than the losses.

241

For me, those people who "BASE jump" (leap off Buildings, Antennas, Spans (as in bridges), and other rarefied Earth edifices like mountain cliffs in a single bound) are crazy coots who gamble with their lives to fulfill a death wish. (Kinda what people thought about me when I started LifeUSA.) The BASE jumpers don't see their activity as a gamble, but rather, a measured and mitigated risk. The good ones have trained, studied, and prepared for what they do. (We don't know what the bad ones did, because they are dead.) Sure, sometimes even the best BASE jumper is injured, but not often and it was a risk for a reward.

When I left ITT Life to start LifeUSA most people wondered, "Why take such a gamble?" They would point to a young family, a good job as president of a large company, a nice income with good benefits, and a pension plan. They'd question how I could give all that up for the risk of starting a new company. (If they worked for a company like The Hartford, they probably would not have asked that question!) What they didn't understand was that it may have been a risk to start LifeUSA, but it was a gamble to stay with ITT Life.

With LifeUSA, I had the power to influence my future; with ITT Life, my future was controlled by others. In my mind, the decision to leave ITT Life and start LifeUSA was not at all difficult. (Of course, when the phone company wanted cash up front before installing phones in our offices and we had to go down to the lobby of the building with a handful of quarters to use the pay phone to make recruiting calls, some doubt might have crept into my mind.)

Entrepreneurial leaders shy away from gambles, but they embrace risk. They understand that risk is an opportunity to earn a reward and that there can be no reward without risk. But entrepreneurs have another secret. They recognize that risk—by its nature—can be managed and is not as uncertain as it may seem.

Entrepreneurs have learned another secret. The rewards for successful risk taking far outweigh the penalty for failure. The rule-writers want us to believe that if we fail attempting an entrepreneurial risk, then all manner of curses and plagues will descend upon us.

That's just not true. So what if we fail? Remember the words of Teddy Roosevelt:

"Far better it is to dare mighty things, to win glorious triumphs, even though checkered by failure, than to take rank with those poor spirits who neither enjoy much nor suffer much, because they live in the gray twilight that knows not victory nor defeat." Would you rather fail while trying or feel the failure of not trying?

When You Wish Upon a Star

Talk of the successful entrepreneur usually evokes the image of two strong attributes: being a dreamer and a visionary. It's like entrepreneurs are successful because they have some gifts or magical powers the rest of us don't have. We all can dream; why can't we be entrepreneurial leaders? Entrepreneurial leaders may dream at night, but they don't have time for such activity during the day. Entrepreneurs don't dream—they do.

There is the assumption that the successful entrepreneur is some sort of visionary, as if entrepreneurs have a gift that allows them to predict the future. The future can't be predicted—especially by us—so it's a good excuse for us not to be an entrepreneur. Well, entrepreneurs don't have the power to predict the future, either, but they do take actions that allow them to *make* the future. And it's always better to make the future than predict it, because if you can accurately predict the future, it means you can't control it.

Using the term "visionary" to describe an entrepreneur can be misleading. If you recall, in chapter 4 on "Reminiscing about the Future,"successful entrepreneurs have the ability to actually reminisce about the future. We all reminisce about the past—winning entrepreneurs condition their thinking in order to reminisce about the future—as if it were the past! Armed with this power, they take actions and make decisions that will allow the future to be made, almost as if it were predicted.

Once the "vision" has been established, it is not kept a secret. The leader works hard to make sure that all people—at all levels of the company—can see and share the visions. Nor are they allowed

243

to forget it. The entrepreneurial manager always keeps the vision up front and visible. A little like a "heads-up" display for a pilot, who can always keep an eye on the destination while keeping his head up to fly the airplane. And there is no going back. The leader is flexible to adjust to a changing environment, but not to the vision itself.

The Straight and Narrow

One entrepreneurial trait rarely mentioned—but probably the most important of all—is that of being an ethical leader. A true entrepreneurial leader exhibits highly ethical core beliefs that are never compromised, qualified, or abandoned. The leader is not sidetracked from these core beliefs, nor is there tolerance for any ethical lapses from any level of the company.

The combination of reminiscing about the future to create a vision and the ethical core of the company allows the leader to establish—and the followers to understand—a series of "rules of engagement." Rules of engagement are not specific rules, but rather, guiding principles. They are the boundaries, the banks of the river that allow the company to navigate safely to its objective.

Traits of an Entrepreneurial Culture

What distinguishes an entrepreneurial organization from a bureaucratic one is a sense of ownership among all members: a feeling of participation by all, a common mission, an environment that encourages risk and where all who contribute share in the rewards of success. To achieve such an organization, many of the established corporate management rules have to be cheated on. For example, in bureaucratic organizations information is viewed as power. If I know something you don't, then I must be more important and more powerful than you. In a bureaucratic organization, information is used to limit and control. In an entrepreneurial organization, information is used to empower.

Learning the Easy Way

Shortly after becoming president of ITT Life, I set up a series of company-wide quarterly meetings called "Report from Management." The meeting was conducted in a large theater and, while all employees were invited, attendance was not required. As the employees entered the theater, management was positioned to greet them and offer a Coke, a bag of popcorn, and a synopsis of the company's latest financial results.

The meeting would start with a welcome from the young, vibrant company president (at least that's the way I know he saw himself), followed by a presentation from the chief marketing officer. (This guy's Irish brogue was so thick you couldn't tell if he was giving a marketing report or saying mass—in Latin!) Next, the financial and administrative people gave their reports on the progress of the company. (I would never allow the HR person to talk because that would put a total damper on the meeting. The actuaries did not get to speak, either—because they couldn't.) After the presentations were completed, the meeting was opened up to an off-the-cuff, no-holds-barred question-and-answer period. The entire session usually took no more than forty-five minutes.

For me, the meetings seemed somewhat mundane. Not that they weren't interesting, but that they seemed so natural and logical. We were asking the employees of the company to work hard and apply their talent to help turn ITT Life around and build it into a successful and profitable company. It seemed so natural to keep the people being asked to build the company fully abreast of their progress to achieve it. Of course, that had not been the attitude of previous management, so these meetings were new and most did not know what to expect.

Initially, the employees were a little skeptical. Was this another boring propaganda meeting for management to spout off? Was this just another meeting to tell the employees they are not going to downsize just before they do? Sure, the meeting gets the employees out of work for a while, but maybe getting paper cuts from sorting dead-letter files would be more fun.

As a result, some of the early meetings were—shall we say—sparsely attended. However, as time went on more and more employees would sign up to attend the meetings. Pretty soon these meetings became quite the event. The theater filled up and virtually everyone in the company wanted to attend the meetings. There was solid feedback that the employees enjoyed and appreciated the meetings.

For me, these meetings had a dual purpose. (Not counting the fact that I did like to get up in front of a captive audience!) The message we sought to deliver to the people of the company was that they were important, respected, and appreciated. By taking the time to report to the employees, showing trust by sharing vital information about the company, detailing future plans, and allowing free-flowing questions, my hope was to engage all employees in a *unified* effort to build the company.

All this went fine, and I thought nothing of it till one day, in Hartford for a series of meetings, my boss, Fred Richardson, asked if I could meet with him and the HR director after lunch. After we sat down, the focus of the conversation was these employee meetings. Fred said, "We understand you are conducting quarterly meetings with employees during which you discuss the performance and plans of the company."

"Yes," I responded.

The HR guy then jumped in (I don't recall his name because they all look the same. You know, that blank, pasty, jaundiced look that reminds you of a prison guard at Attica) and said, "We can't have you conducting those types of meetings. You have to stop right now."

"Why?" I asked.

Fred responded with, "Well, those people don't need to know that information. They won't understand it and their job is just to do their job." This was not an issue of insider information or concern that someone would learn some great trade secret (there are none in the insurance business) at the ITT Life meetings.

No, this was just another step in the management education of Bob MacDonald. What seemed to me to be a simple process of involvement for employees—to encourage them to care—was a violation of some management rule that I could not understand.

No amount of discussion or argument on my part could dissuade these two guys from laying down the rules of the game. No more meetings!

Of course, the ITT Life meetings continued—bigger and better—till the day I left the company. Interesting, but never again did I hear another word about the meetings from Hartford. But that's the way bureaucrats are.

The point to be made is that—contrary to traditional rules—communication flowing through a successful organization is like blood flowing in a healthy body. The more efficient the blood flow, the healthier the body. Cut blood off from part of the body and soon it atrophies and dies. The same can be said regarding communication in an organization. Communication is the life blood of an organization. It helps people understand what is expected, why an objective is important, what the plans are, and progress to date. Information is power. Keep it and lose it. Share it and multiply it. The choice is yours to make.

All I Want Is a Little Respect

Nonentrepreneurial cultures profess to care about the people in the organization, but their actions say something else. These cultures view employees as a resource to be used, not as capitalists who are critical to the success of the company. More than a few corporate managers follow the old rule that says, "Employees should be happy to have a job." Human resource departments are more likely to view employees as prisoners who can't be trusted, who need to be guarded and goaded to do work. (Sometimes it seems as though HR departments use the 1957 movie *The Bridge on the River Kwai* as their primary training film.)

A good way to check the culture of the organization is to determine the attitude of the HR department. In a nonentrepreneurial organization, the HR department believes it works for the management of the company, helping to keep employees in check. In an entrepreneurial organization, you will find that the HR department views its mission as that of supporting the employees of the group.

To build a winning culture, we need to cheat on these attitudes. Managers need to understand, believe, and act in ways that show employees they are the most important assets of the company. The employees must be treated as though they are investors in the organization—stakeholders—because they are.

The very first action I took as CEO of Allianz Life was to change the name of the HR department to Employee Support Services. Right on the heels of that action, we closed the Allianz Life executive lunchroom. (At LifeUSA the personnel department was called Owner Support Services, because all employees were shareholders and there was no executive lunchroom.) These actions were designed to begin the process of converting Allianz Life culture from bureaucratic to entrepreneurial.

The difficulty of making this change was brought home to me during one early budget-planning session when an Allianz Life employee challenged me, "Why are you so worried about these expenses? After all, this is Allianz money, not ours!" That's what you get when you have a traditional bureaucratic culture. It's not that the people of Allianz Life were bad people and didn't care, it was just that they had never been given any reason to care.

In direct violation of the traditional rule, in an entrepreneurial culture there is the philosophy that management works for employees. The LifeUSA organizational chart was constructed upside down from the traditional format. The chairman of the board and the CEO were at the bottom of the chart, and it worked its way up so that administration and services were at the top—the traditional signal of importance—of the chart. It was always a good feeling when someone would say to me, "You know, Mac, I worked for this other company for nine years and I rarely even saw the CEO, let alone meet or talk to him. I can't believe I can just talk to you."

In My Own Little Corner in My Own Little World

I thought nothing could top the insular attitude of the "core" offices at State Mutual (see chapter 7), but my arrival at Allianz Life changed that. For a period of time after the acquisition of LifeUSA, both

LifeUSA and Allianz Life continued to operate as separate companies, with me as CEO of both companies. Until a new combined corporate headquarters could be constructed, both companies operated from separate offices.

This required that I split my time between the two companies, particularly needed to support the Allianz Life employees who were initially in a state of shock. It was not clear to them why, when Allianz Life bought LifeUSA, that LifeUSA management ended up in charge. Especially someone they had heard was as wild and crazy as MacDonald.

Anyway, when I walked into the Allianz Life executive offices— on the top floor of the building, of course—I could not believe how difficult it was just to get into my office. First, I had to get to the corner of the top floor, then I had to get by the first administrative assistant. That accomplished, I had to enter a small office occupied by my secretary. Once past her desk, there was a small anteroom (actually an antiroom) and finally, my office. (At least I felt secure. Not even Al-Qaeda could have found me in that office, let alone any employees.) The CEO office itself reminded me of an official crying room in a rundown funeral home. The style would have been out of date in 1946. I think prisoners being interrogated in Iraq's Abu Ghraib prison were more comfortable than employees would be coming into this office. On top of that, there was another piece to this office suite: a formal conference room. The Kremlin was friendlier than this place.

After a few weeks of isolation in this office, I had to make a change. First, I moved out of the official office and into the conference room. It had a door that opened directly to the hall, so people could see me and maybe come in. I moved the desk up against the wall, so no one had to sit across it, and brought in a small table to use for meetings. The old CEO prison office was converted into a "public conference room" that was made available for anyone to schedule meetings. I am sure that 95 percent of the people who attended meetings in that office had never before seen it, much less been in it.

The House Upside Down

As I experienced at State Mutual and Allianz Life, traditional office layout has been used to display the "important" people in an organization. As Allianz Life was merged with LifeUSA, it was decided to recognize the power of this rule but to send out a different message by cheating on it. To bring the two companies together, a new ten-story corporate headquarters building was constructed. It was a typical projection for a strong financial institution—high quality, substantive, imposing, and large. But the inside was completely different. The time-honored internal design rule of a corporate headquarters was turned upside down. Instead of housing the corporate bigwigs on the expansive top floor with the beautiful vistas of the city skyline, the largest processing unit (the ones who did the work) was placed in that space. The senior executives of the company—including the chairman and CEO—occupied offices on the first floor, right off the lobby and next to Employee Support Services. (The new name for the HR department.) We had people processing new applications sitting in the corner space on the tenth floor, while the chairman of the company looked out on the on-ramp to the freeway.

When employees enter the building each day, they do not walk past the usual expensive corporate art, but by large pictures of the true corporate heroes—the employees of the company. This upside-down structure and office decoration was intended to send the signal that it was the management who supported the employees of the company—not the other way around. Also, it was a sign as to just who were the most important people in the company.

No Free Lunch

Another way entrepreneurial organizations show respect for employees is to hold them accountable for their actions. Traditional organizations equate accountability with blame. Because of this approach employees have developed an immune system that allows them to both hide from accountability and have no concern for it. This manifests itself in the form of well-developed "cover your ass" strategies and the "If I can't be seen, I can't be blamed" behavior. (See chapter 8.) People will shy away from accountability—and therefore concern about doing a good job—if they have no power to do the job and are not rewarded for their efforts.

Accountability is a sign of power and respect. If there is no accountability in a culture, then there can be no basis for learning, or setting consistent standards of performance or reward. The reason the people at Allianz Life did not care about the budgeting process was the lack of accountability within the existing culture. People did not care about expenses because spending or saving money had no impact on them. They were neither rewarded for saving money nor penalized for spending it. It does not take much exposure to that type of culture to slip into a feeling of, "I don't care because they don't."

This attitude of nonaccountability was pervasive across the entire Allianz Life organization. It's not that the people of Allianz Life didn't want to care, it was that no one cared if they cared. As a result, divisions were hemorrhaging red-ink losses in the millions. After a series of increasing distressing financial revelations from our Group Marketing division, with each one promising a "light at the end of the tunnel" to the losses, with the next report always bleaker (I thought for a while I was back in the Viet Nam War days reading the "Pentagon Papers" report), I called the head of the division into a meeting.

I asked him for two things: The absolute worst possible numbers that could come out of his division and his letter of resignation—to be effective only if those numbers were exceeded. I placed no limitations on this guy, other than to provide me with the worst possible loss numbers he could imagine. Two months later his division exceeded the worst-case scenario he had given me. To this day, I doubt he understands (or believes I had any reason to do so) why he was fired. His letter of resignation was made effective, not because of the losses in his division, but because he had no idea what caused those losses. He was not in control of his division.

The mercy killing of this executive was an important signal to everyone else in the company. Accountability was to play a critical role in the future of the company. Failure to enforce accountability is one of the inherent vulnerabilities of a bureaucratic culture and it weakens the entire organization. Without accountability, no measurements can be made and no standards enforced. However, to enforce accountability, people must have the power to make decisions—and they must be rewarded for success to the same extent they are penalized for failure. These are two actions that are unnatural to a bureaucratic organization.

Holding someone accountable for their dealings within an organization is a strong signal that you recognize and respect the talent they posses. Accountability, when used as part of a learning process, helps people benefit from failure and encourages them to seek better solutions.

Parallel ... Parallel ... Parallel

The concept of "parallel interest" is so important that an entire chapter is dedicated to it (chapter 5), but it's such a critical element to any discussion of an entrepreneurial organization that a few words here are justified.

Being in parallel means that the interests of all company stakeholders—shareholders, employees, customers, and vendors—are in line with each other. No action is consciously taken to place one group at an advantage. Actions that benefit shareholders should also benefit employees and customers. Entrepreneurial organizations all strive to "be in parallel" in order to maintain the integrity of the philosophy. Being in parallel is what keeps an entrepreneurial organization in balance. When an organization loses the balance of being in parallel, it is on its way to becoming a bureaucratic organization.

A Penny for Your Thoughts

Probably the most important, inviolate, necessary, and critical element in building an entrepreneurial organization is the concept of shared value and reward. You can't build a successful organization if financial reward is the only objective; but if **a** group has all the other attributes of a winning association except shared value and reward, then it will fail to achieve its potential.

The single, clearly identifiable mark of an entrepreneurial culture is that it operates 24/7 under the philosophy that people with the ability to add value to the organization will be encouraged to do so, if they are allowed to share in the value created.

That's it—simple—done! Believe, implement, and live by this philosophy, and any organization you lead—large or small—will be on its way to becoming the entrepreneurial culture so valued by so many. This does not guarantee the organization will be successful, but it does guarantee that you will attract the type of talented employee who will die trying to make it successful.

When word got out about LifeUSA, we had people standing in line to come to work with the company. Not because we were a big company offering stability and security (a misnomer for most big companies nowdays) or that one didn't have to work hard and the money was good. No, people came to LifeUSA for the exact opposite reasons. People knew that if they brought their talent to LifeUSA and contributed to the growth and success of the company, they would benefit directly.

For that attitude, we had people showing up to work in the dark and going home in the dark. (To be honest, during the winter in Minnesota there's only three hours of daylight—that's not too hard to do!) When the offices got crowded, people brought their own card table and chairs so they would have someplace to work. Work was taken home and completed while watching the kids' soccer games or after they had gone to bed. In short, it is amazing how involved people will be if you allow them to become involved in the success of the organization.

And this wasn't just about money. For the first time in their lives, people felt they were involved in something where they made a difference—and the difference they made was respected and rewarded.

LifeUSA sent the message of shared value through the ownership of stock, but that is not the only way to get the message across.

Employees do not have to be shareholders to share in the value they contribute.

There are many ways of sharing value added. It can take the form of expanded opportunity and increased responsibility. Rewards take many forms, large and small, and the specific reward is not the point. It is the signal that is important. Shared success encourages consistent activity and signals that people are moving in the right direction. Compensation based on the value of the person, rather than the value of the job, creates entrepreneurs.

Bonus compensation that is bottom up and not top down is another effective way to communicate the importance of the people in the organization. At LifeUSA my bonus and the bonus of other executives was a factor of the bonuses paid to others in the company. We were the last—not the first—to receive a bonus. Bonuses for employees were based on measured and agreed-upon tasks that added specific value to the organization.

The reaction received from the Allianz Life employees the first year we instituted the "bottom-up" bonus system was amazing. (To the credit of Allianz AG in Germany, we were allowed to implement this LifeUSA plan, even though it cheated on all the existing rules for Allianz bonus plans worldwide.) At first, the Allianz Life employees were skeptical and did not understand the concept of the plan. How could they? They only knew the old bureaucratic world. At the end of the year, when the bonuses were distributed (though small because the company was just starting to turn around), more than a few employees came to me with the comment, "I have been with the company eighteen years and this is the first time I have ever received a bonus."

They had worked for years and watched as the executives drove in their company cars, ate in the executive dinning room, and shared big bonuses—while they were told to be happy with a paycheck. Is it any wonder they didn't care? Of course, after the first year it was different. The compensation plan was real. It worked. It did not take long for the Allianz employees to acknowledge to the LifeUSA group, "Aha, now I know what you were saying. I thought it was Kool-Aid, but this is just cool." From that moment on, there has been a new attitude from the Allianz Life employees as they recognize that they are important, respected, and will be rewarded when they use their talent and effort to add value to the company. Suddenly, it became "their money" not just Allianz money! (As a result, both had more of it!)

And the Moral of the Story Is ...

It's a new world. The old management rules of the twentieth century no longer apply in this century. The highly educated and talented employee of today is the modern capitalist. The capital they have to contribute is not the same as the capitalists of the nineteenth century, but it may be even more valuable. The organization that builds a culture designed to recognize, acknowledge, respect, challenge, stimulate, and reward these modern capitalists will be the success story of this century. We may give them the name of "entrepreneurial cultures," but in reality they are organizations that cheat to win by building a true hothouse for humanity that teaches, encourages, allows—and most important—motivates people to grow to be great.

15

Be Peerless in the Face of Peer Pressure

You win not by being on a par with the competition but by being the competition.

Maybe the most sinister of all the rules we encounter is the bodybag full of social mores that translate into what is called "peer pressure." No set of control sticks are more imbedded in the pantheon of rules that are intended to assume power over our potential and performance than "peer group pressure" rules. You know the rule—you've been dealing with it all your life. If you have to choose one rule to cheat on—pick this one!

You will never ever achieve your full potential if peer group pressure rules are allowed to restrict your performance. The only pressure worthy of your attention is the pressure inside yourself to be the best that you can be. Satisfaction, achievement, success, and fulfillment will come to you when you respond to "personal" rather than "peer" pressure.

Of course, cheating on peer pressure rules is easier said than done, but the rewards for doing so are immense and, as you'll see, well worth the risk. When you cheat on the peer group rule, you may feel like the proverbial salmon swimming upstream blindfolded with your hands tied behind your back (no small task!). But it's the degree of difficulty required to break the rule that makes it so worthwhile when successful. Just be prepared for the fact that you will have to cheat on the rule on your own. You won't get a lot of help from your peers!

Peer Pressure Starts Early

The homogenizing pressure to be like others starts almost as soon as we are able to recognize that we have peers in this world. Parents warn us against falling prey to peer group pressure (Lord knows they have enough experience doing what they tell you not to do). Children are largely heedless to that advice because parents are not peers and there are more peers than parents. You see kids who dress alike, talk alike, eat the same food, and smoke the same (whatever) because there's peer pressure to be "part of the crowd."

You'd think that we'd outgrow such childish "monkey-see, monkey-do" attitudes, but we don't. Peer group pressure becomes even more menacing as we grow older. And wherever it spreads, it serves to limit our opportunity to stand out, to make a mark, and achieve success as individuals, employees, and even as business managers.

"Society everywhere is in conspiracy against the manhood of every one of its members," says Emerson. "The virtue in most request is conformity."

Many of the rules this book suggests should be broken were put in place with at least some modicum of logic for their existence. But, but for the life of me, I can't find a single good reason for peer group pressure rules. Clearly there is no "socially redeeming value" for rules designed to enforce the herd mentality of mediocrity. Think about it! The only value that can come from peer pressure is to achieve a complete leveling effect for those who fall prey to the rules. I guess peer group pressure rules can prevent people from going off the deep end—that is, unless everyone else does. Imposing peer group pressure simply makes everyone act, talk, think, and be the same—as if we were the dwarfed semi-moron Epsilons of Aldous Huxley's *Brave New World*.

In a peer group, success is defined by mediocrity. By following peer pressure rules, the lowest common denominator, rather than the highest measure of achievement, becomes the benchmark for performance since (as the quote goes) "mediocre minds usually dismiss anything which reaches beyond their own understanding."

You might think that all the silliness, inefficiency, and repression caused by peer pressure rules would stop at the corporate doorstep— but think again. The influence of peer pressure becomes even more entrenched as we take our first job and work our way up the corporate ladder. Surprisingly, in the corporate world the concept of peer group pressure goes beyond the individual and even applies to the company itself.

Peer group pressure doesn't just exist in the corporate world; for many it has become the thread that weaves through the entire fabric of business management, planning, and measurement. This management mentality could be referred to as "suicide by imitation." You will find this philosophy taught at Harvard Business School, Stanford, Wharton, and many other "leading" business colleges. In fact, the fastest-growing segment of the consulting industry promulgates peer group comparison as a leading management tool to measure and judge how well you are doing in business. (A recent study illustrated that 68 percent of all fees charged by the largest dingleberry consulting firms related to an off-the-shelf study of peer group companies. And you thought you hired them to study your company!). Peer pressure and peer comparisons become our soothing "Soma."

It amazes me to see this attitude so prevalent in business today. Companies and management are obsessed with comparing themselves to others. Computer manufacturer Dell is compared with Hewlett-Packard, IBM, Sony, and a slew of others. Northwest Airlines is compared to peers like Delta and American Airlines. The result of such endless and idiotic comparisons is to foster a despicable uniformity within the marketplace that often leads to the death of many businesses. Everyone looks the same, acts the same, and does the same. Businesses become a "herd of crowds" and no one knows whether the herd, or the crowd, is doing the right thing or the wrong thing because everyone is doing the same thing.

Management Falls Prey, Too

Interindustry peer pressure is what irks me the most. Peer pressure comparisons are now more prevalent than poppy fields in Afghanistan. Pick an industry—any industry. You'll find some trade group or analyst that has generated reams of comparative data to make peer comparisons. The trouble is, most of the time you're comparing apples and oranges, and comparing your company or department to what others are doing is a futile exercise. Why? Because peer group comparison is useful only if your company is as good or better than others in your industry. That means most of the information gathered is meaningless.

Imagine the futility of saying, "Our company has been rated the fastest-growing widget manufacturer in America," when sales *doubled* from 100 widgets to 200—but, at the same time, the competitor increased sales a "lousy" *25 percent*—from 1,000,000 to 1,250,000 widgets. See what I mean?

Be Your One and Only Peer

It's always good to know what your competition may be doing, but that's so you can beat their brains out—not for judging the effectiveness of your performance. Trying to determine what you should be doing by shadowing what other companies are doing is a bad idea. Instead, measure yourself based upon your own accomplishments and those of your company. Winners create their own peer pressure! Are you constantly improving? Are you getting better at what you do each year? Are you increasing productivity, selling more goods, answering more of your customers' product needs with fairly priced goods and services they can use?

Forget what others are doing. Cheat on the peer group rules by asking this question: Am I better off today than I was last year? Am I closer to achieving my objectives at the end of the year than at the beginning of the year? Does this seem too simple or too easy? It's not. It's the type of peer pressure that can't be manipulated and is just the right kind of peer pressure to motivate you. It's you against you!

Not even once during my twenty-two years of managing a company from the CEO chair was I concerned about or swayed by the performance of a peer group company. My concern was for my personal performance and the accomplishments of our company. Yes, I received peer group comparisons, but the only peer being compared was the specific performance of our company this year, last year, and the year before.

I understand the argument made by the "management gurus" that it is foolish to be blind to the competition. I am not suggesting that we operate in a vacuum—but close to it. Understand that you have to make decisions and take actions based on your resources, capabilities, and experiences—not those of your competitors.

Although not a perfect analogy, managing your golf game in competition offers some compelling comparisons to the effects of peer group pressure. Golf may be the most individual of games. In professional tournaments 144 individuals compete against each other on the same playing field under identical conditions. Most of the top players will tell you that they never watch the scoreboard. Why? Because there is nothing they can do about the other players. They can only control their own game. If the golfer does his best and still gets beat by another player, that is the rub of the green. If another player is having a great day, then watching that player or trying to duplicate what he is doing will accomplish nothing.

If you play golf, think about participating in a match-play tournament at the club. The chances are great that if you concentrate on your opponent's game and try to respond to his actions, rather than just playing your own game, most of the time you are going to lose. You get the same dismal results when you follow the peer group management rules. The more you concentrate on and chase what the competition is doing—at the expense of concentrating on your own talent—the more likely you are to lose.

My management reports consisted of only a few pages. The purpose of the reports was to compare the critical items measuring the current performance of the company with previous levels. (This information related to the insurance business, but it works just as well with any industry.) For example: How many applications per employee (owner) did we receive and process this year compared to last year? What was the trend in revenue per employee? What were expenses per policy? How many forty-eight hour challenges were paid per application compared to last year?

So long as we were making our best efforts, and the numbers were constantly improving, I could give a twit what other companies were doing. My objective in cheating on the peer pressure rules that called for chasing the performance of other companies was to put pressure on chasing *our* performance and making it constantly better. In other words, make your own performance the peer benchmark by which your progress is measured.

I am willing to make a bet that you cannot attend a business plan meeting or read a company performance report without at least one section of the presentation based on peer group comparison. For the most part, it is a waste of time. Recognize that you can control your own performance and that of your company. You have no impact, control, or—for that matter—any real understanding of the performance of the other companies, so why try to chase or worry about them?

During my career I discovered that if other companies were consistently outperforming my company, they were either much better than us (and I never wanted to know that) or they were doing something stupid that could not be sustained over a long period of time. In any event, why should I compare my performance and company to something I can't control? Or, more to the point, why should I compare myself to failure? (The truth. as it turned out, was that most of these other companies—or individuals—that looked too good were, in fact doing, stupid things!)

Think *Kaizen*

Cheating to win against peer group rules calls for your greatest competitive effort, deepest complex comparison, and the most

261

challenging motivation possible to improve. When you are always improving yourself you never have to worry about peer comparisons.

The Japanese have a word for that. It's *kaizen*. And it means "continuous, incremental improvements," and that's what you should be aiming for. Each day, each week, each quarter, each year, you should strive to be better than you have been, and comparisons against the peer group competition will take care of themselves. Try to do your job, whether line employee or manager, a little better. Slow and steady wins the day. If you stay focused on making your company better, or making yourself better, and don't worry about what other companies are doing, you will be better off.

Peer Group Pressure Can be Dangerous to Your Health

There was an article in the *Wall Street Journal* a few years back that chronicled just the sort of nonsense that happens when people get sucked into dim-witted peer group comparisons. And if the story didn't have such tragic consequences, it would have been funny. The subject of the piece was a marketing executive who worked for AT&T. Even though AT&T's numbers were growing briskly, he was fired because AT&T had fallen behind the growth numbers of their primary peer group competitor.

The irony is that this hapless soul kept writing memos to his bosses arguing, that his marketing efforts should not be compared with the big competitor because their numbers just didn't make any sense. The way they are doing things just could not work. "Something is wrong," he pleaded.

But each quarter the flashy competitor would report dazzling new numbers. With the marketing efforts at AT&T unable to keep up with the competitor's "reported" voracious growth, peer pressure mounted and eventually convinced the powers in charge that the marketing chief had to be replaced. It was a terrible mistake.

The company with whom AT&T was fruitlessly comparing itself was, of course, WorldCom. And WorldCom was faking the numbers by disguising its true operating performance using undisclosed and improper accounting methods.

In short, it was a saga of income that never happened, a well-orchestrated ploy of deceit and corporate betrayal. When WorldCom filed for bankruptcy, one of the darkest chapters in business history was written: an ignominious testament to the value of peer pressure comparisons. The marketing guy at AT&T was vindicated, but that is akin to being found not guilty just after the execution. "Oops, we made a mistake" just doesn't cut it.

Recently, a potentially destructive peer-group pressure incident struck very close to my home. After Allianz AG acquired LifeUSA, I was asked to serve on the company's International Executive Committee (IEC) that met quarterly in Munich. (Just what I needed—quarterly trips to Germany!) This group was composed of the Board of Management (board of directors) of Allianz AG and the CEOs of the company's largest subsidiaries. Their meetings were a free-flowing discussion of the issues facing Allianz on a worldwide basis. Invariably, a standard part of these discussions was peer-group activity.

While Allianz tracked a number of peer-group companies, none was higher on the list than American International Group Inc., (AIG) led by Hank Greenberg. It frustrated the leaders of Allianz to find that no matter how well Allianz performed—by any measurement—the Allianz results always looked anemic in peer-comparison to AIG. It reached the point that sometimes the concern about peer-group comparison to AIG seemed more important than the actual performance of Allianz.

To their credit, the ethics and integrity of the Allianz AG executives led by Michael Diekmann were strong enough to keep the company from straying off the path and changing the corporate fundamentals. But the temptation was there in spades, because the AIG numbers and performance looked almost too good to be true. And, now we know why—they *were* too good to be true! By the spring of 2005, Hank Greenberg had been unceremoniously fired and *The Wall Street Journal* was reporting that as a result of "improper accounting and possible errors" the shareholder equity of AIG could be slashed by $1.7 billion. Things could get even worse!

Allianz leadership fell into the trap of peer-group comparison, but fortunately, they were strong enough to remain patient and continue to do the right thing in the face of difficult and unyielding pressure. Unfortunately, other companies are not so strong and fall prey to allowing peer pressure to undermine corporate self-determination.

Technology companies, insurance companies, airlines, banks, and corporations of every stripe and hue can get sucked into this vain pursuit of peer group comparisons. Those who religiously obey the peer group rules spend at lot of time chasing everyone else, without knowledge of what it is they are really chasing. Rather than becoming the competition to be chased, they fall in behind the herd trying to chase the competition. It is difficult for most to cheat on this fatal flaw in management because all their peers are doing the same thing, and the highly paid consultants praise its value.

The way to cheat on the peer pressure rule is not to chase the competition, but rather, to create the competition. Make other people compete against you, as opposed to you competing against them.

Be Peerless Instead of a Peer

Peer pressure rules almost ruined LifeUSA even before the company got off the ground. Those "smart people" in lockstep with peer group comparisons figured there was no way a new company like LifeUSA could ever compete or survive against giant peer competitors such as Prudential, Metropolitan, or New York Life. Blinded by these odious rules, LifeUSA was dismissed by investment firms, bankers, and other insurance companies. Of course, they were right. Under the existing peer group thinking, a new company would not have the size, experience, or financial muscle to go head-to-head with these giants. And here's the kicker: If LifeUSA had not cheated on the peer group rules, if we had not moved in an entirely novel corporate direction, the big companies would have "peered" us to death!

This example is the very core of the cheat-to-win philosophy. Traditional rules tell us to learn from the leader. Learning from the

264

leader means you always follow the leader. These peer group rules are in place—at all levels of application—to keep the leaders leading and the followers following. To survive and have any chance at success, LifeUSA had to acquire the audacity to cheat on the peer group rules and be as different from these companies as they were trying to be like each other. In effect, we had to make these companies compete *against* us. This approach is the key to anyone's success when attempting to resist peer group pressure.

In our case, we recognized our chief advantages. From our perspective, the big guys were doing the wrong thing the wrong way. By refusing to adopt the "me-too" attitude of peer group pressure, and moving in an entirely new direction, we didn't copy the old competition and instead became the new competition. The same approach will work for you as you battle peer group pressure.

What Happens When You Chase the Market?

At a recent business seminar I was discussing the dynamics of competition, and the issue of peer group marketing came up. (It just amazes me just how many executives carry over what they learned as children and plan their actions based on peer group actions.) My presentation argued that chasing, or responding to, the actions of peer group companies—especially in a soft or declining market—was a particularly disastrous action.

The "accepted" rule is that maintaining "market share" is essential in a declining market. The "accepted" way to maintain market share is by following the competition in a fast race to reduce the price of the product, even if the price fell below profitable levels. My position was that this was a peer group rule based on a fallacy and should be broken. No sooner had I hoisted the "cheat to win" flag to see who would salute it when one participant (the president of a bank, so he could be excused) launched into a spirited defense of the "lemming-to-the-sea" argument.

"If the rest of the industry is cutting price, then you have to cut price, too," he insisted, "otherwise you are going to lose market share. You'll be forced out of the market." While acknowledging that his comments were a perfect recitation of the traditional rule, it was nevertheless a rule to be broken. Unlike used car salespeople who seem able to get away with the claim that they are selling each car at a loss but making up for it with volume, it's always dumb to sell your product—be it insurance or anything else—at a price that is not profitable. "Your peer group companies are cutting the price to maintain market share," I declared, "and they are not going to be profitable. You're moving with the herd and then everybody suffers. That kind of stupidity will bring down whole industries."

Well, since this guy was German, I was not able to convince him to cheat on some of the traditional peer group rules, but we did have a lively discussion. This business circumstance—a declining market with peers cutting prices to save market share—is a classic example of how you should look at a bad situation and make it better by cheating on the rule. Simply put, it is this: Ignore peer pressure and look for a better way. In this instance, the way to maintain market share and sales volume in a declining market is simple: Don't cut prices—expand distribution capabilities. That may sound too simple, but it's not. Most cheating to win is obvious and doable—it just takes an attitude and willingness to win.

A LifeUSA Example

LifeUSA suffered and survived just such a sucker market condition. In the mid-1990s, when the stock market was soaring and dot-com had yet to become dot-bomb, interest rates were declining. This market environment created the perfect storm for a decline in sales of (conservative and boring) fixed annuities. Companies responded by artificially increasing interest rates credited to annuities, increasing commissions in order to buy business, and reducing expense charges. (Even I was smart enough to recognize that paying out 5 percent interest on money when only earning 4 percent was not a good path!) Still, industry sales declined and profits vanished, causing some companies to either fail or exit the market completely.

Yet, all during this difficult period, LifeUSA sales remained steady and market share increased. The reason was simple: LifeUSA did not follow the peer group copycats of the marketplace who were cutting prices and reducing profitability in order to maintain market.

(If we couldn't keep a product profitable, it was taken off the market.) When faced with a soft and declining market, our response was to double the recruiting efforts. I am not going to tell you that what we did was the easiest thing to do. It's never always easy to do the right thing, but it is the right thing to do.

Instead of applying an expensive artificial Band-Aid to cover the wounds of unprofitable business, LifeUSA focused on increasing and expanding distribution. The result was that while each agent may have sold less individual business, we had *more agents* in the market so market share went up (at the expense of the competition, not profits) while other companies were either forced out of the business or could not figure out why they were not making any money in the business.

Another benefit from cheating on the peer group rule emerged when the stock market crashed and day-traders became day-die'rs, causing the boring annuity product to be more attractive. LifeUSA was positioned with the strongest distribution in the market and sales increased multifold—suddenly, other companies were following and trying to copy LifeUSA.

Buy Market and Pay the Price

The same concept of cheating on peer group pressure rules applies to "buying market share" for your business. My antirule here is simple: If you attempt to buy market share, you will pay for it. If you earn market share, you will be paid for it. Instead of attempting to buy market share with price—a strategy that ultimately loses—market share is better earned and rewarded with value and service.

The airline industry is the poster child of the peer pressure mentality. If United Airlines were to cut fares by $20 a ticket, within an hour, every other airline in the universe will cut fares by $20. Conversely, if Northwest Airlines decides to stick travel agents with a $7.50 service charge and the other airlines decide NOT to follow suit, Northwest will rescind the surcharge faster than John Kerry can flip-flop on any given political issue.

Be Aware—But Don't Be a Copycat

Earlier in this chapter, I noted that ignoring group pressure does not mean ignoring the competition completely. Let me reiterate. It's important to be aware of what your competition is doing, if for no other reason than to avoid some of their stupid mistakes. Just make sure to observe your competition with a jaundiced eye so as not to be pressured into doing the wrong thing simply because others are doing it. The first effect of following peer pressure is to inhibit your ability to exceed the group performance. This can lead to an even greater disaster—and that is to follow the group into disaster.

So What if You Are Better?

There is another danger when comparison with peer group companies is taken too seriously. You could actually be better than your peers! So what's wrong with that? Wouldn't you want to know if you are the best in your field? Doesn't that confirm that you are doing the right things to be successful?

Yes, of course; but there is a danger. The greatest risk to getting better is to think you are already the best. Just as peer group comparisons breed disinformation when you seem to be "falling behind," so too can it lull you into complacency if peer comparisons are favorable. So what if you are twice as good as all the rest, but you are only half as good as you should be? Again, peer group pressure is quicksand for suckers. Get lured into that quagmire and you'll get sucked down. Be your own peer pressure and measure your performance against your potential.

The Home-Field Advantage

One of my first decisions after taking the helm of Allianz Life was to significantly expand the amount of variable annuity business being written by the company. The goal was simple. I challenged the variable management of Allianz Life to become Top Five in Five! This meant that Allianz Life would be one of the top five variable annuity producers in the industry within five years. (Not an insignificant accomplishment considering that Allianz ranked about seventy-fifth at the time.)

When this objective was first presented to the management of Allianz Life, their reaction was traditional and typical. After we got by the "Oh, God, we can't do that!" they recommended we "Go see what the leaders at Hartford, Scandia, and Safeco were doing. Then, we know what we have to do."

My retort was firm. "No, forget about what the other companies are doing." Cheat on the rule that says we should research the leaders to find out what they are doing. Instead, try to discover what the competition is NOT doing, and do that. You will never catch a leader by following the leader. By the time you learn what the leader is doing and try to do it, they are gone. The smart businesses are long gone before you can catch them—they're off doing something new, brighter, and more creative. Besides, the leader may be doing something you can't or don't want to do. Don't worry about what the other guy is doing. You will always have a losing record if you play all your games on the other team's home field. No matter how big you are, you can create your own home field advantage. Build your own stadium and make the others play on your home-field.

The Allianz variable annuity management guys were (grudgingly) sent off to find a new path. Find product benefits not being offered by the leaders; explore different forms of distribution and approaches to the market. Go where they are not, establish a post, and make them chase after you. Trust me, traditional competitors (in any industry) are so encrusted with the old rules of peer group competition they will fail to notice you on the way up and will, by knee-jerk reaction, follow you when you show them a new way. And that is the key—they will follow you! Three years later, Allianz Life had become the fastest-growing—almost the only growing—company in the variable annuity market, producing multibillions in production and assuming a leadership role in the market. Those companies the management wanted to copy had either fallen back or exited the market completely.

Closer to Home

The biggest peer group challenge faced by LifeUSA was not of our own making, but rather, came from the actions of others who were firm believers in peer group comparisons. These individuals—analysts and institutional investors—wanted to make peer comparisons between LifeUSA and another insurance company that came into the market just a few years before LifeUSA. This company was called Conseco and their business plan was diametrically different from the LifeUSA business model that called for building by writing new business. Conseco's business plan was to grow by acquiring blocks of existing business.

Since the stock of both companies became publicly traded at roughly the same time—and Conseco stock price had run up to north of $50 while LifeUSA stock never got higher than $22—we were under constant pressure from many directions to do what Conseco was doing. Conseco became the darling of the market and its executives the hotshots of the industry. Senior management couldn't show their faces without somebody—analysts, agents, lenders, and even a few employees—suggesting that we do things the Conseco way. (It wasn't fun, either, to watch the Conseco executives take literally hundreds of millions out of the company while we still flew coach and stayed in El Cheapo Manor.)

Each quarter, Conseco reported numbers that continued to rise like yeast in a hothouse. Naturally, this only increased the peer pressure to copy what they were doing. It did no good for me to explain to analysts and shareholders (including one large producer who was using commissions from LifeUSA to purchase Conseco stock) that the Conseco model was a short-term plan (get in quick and get out quick with as much as you can) as opposed to the LifeUSA plan to build value over time. Resisting the peer group rule to be like Conseco was not easy, but, fortunately, we did.

Eventually, in 1998, intoxicated by the drug of peer group leadership that converted into an inflated market capitalization (defined as being able to borrow enough money to leverage the company to the hilt), Conseco acquired the subprime lender Green Tree Financial Corporation for $6 billion. I mean, not one hour after the announcement of that deal I began to field anxious calls asking when we were going to follow the "creative leadership" of Conseco in the market. It didn't take long for the calls to stop.

Greed Tree, I mean Green Tree, was a big lender in the mobile home business, and their loan portfolio soon suffered massive reversals. Mobile home repossessions skyrocketed. Mortgage defaults ballooned to stratospheric heights. Conseco stock subsequently cratered to less than $2, and soon thereafter the company went Chapter 11, marking the third-largest bankruptcy in U.S. history. (It's interesting to note that—unless you wanted to sell a ton of credit insurance—mobile home lending had nothing to do with Conseco's core business of insurance. The problem for Conseco was that they also experienced peer group pressure—and since other big financial companies were expanding beyond their home turf, Conseco felt they had to follow.)

It takes a certain amount of courage (or arrogance) to say, "I do not care what the rest of the companies are doing. I know we are doing the right thing and we are going to keep doing the right thing." In the end, you have to believe that doing the right thing is going to work. You have to have the courage to cheat on and ignore peer group pressure and do what you do best.

Ultimate winning is not being intimidated or pressured; it's knowing the right thing to do, being willing to do the right thing, and sticking with it even when you are getting beat up as other companies seem to be growing faster than you. Be strong enough to recognize that the best path for you is to do what you do best; if you try to copy what others do—especially when they are not doing the right thing—you will end up losing anyway. If you are going to lose, lose doing what you know is the right thing to do. Every time we were challenged by peer pressure to follow others, we said, "No!" We focused on what we were doing and in doing it better than we did before. In the end, most of the companies we had been pressured to follow had lost their momentum or had even failed completely. We, however, were still there doing our thing.

Imitation is the Sincerest Form of Flattery

C. C. Colton, the fellow who coined that familiar saying above, got it halfright. If someone is doing something that is successful, everybody runs in and copies it. I'm all for imitation, as long as the other guy is the one doing the imitating. In other words, the key to sustained winning is not to run in and copy the products of others, or to chase them in the marketplace, but to create a new and different marketplace.

Take being copied as a medal of accomplishment and enjoy it. To be copied confirms that you must be doing something right. Each time LifeUSA developed a new type of product, we would announce it from the rooftops. The products were heavily promoted and we would talk up a storm (yes, we were even willing to boast) about our creative innovation. This bothered some of the marketing people at LifeUSA, because they were concerned that other companies would copy the products. They feared that we would lose our competitive edge if big guys like Prudential got wind of what we were doing and "knock off" our products.

My thinking not surprisingly, was just the opposite. When larger peer group companies copied our products, their action not only established our competitive edge but gave us greater credibility in the market. When a maverick company like LifeUSA jumped out ahead of the pack, leading the way as the only company to offer a unique product, then people were going to question its true value. But let Prudential or another large peer group company copy that product, and suddenly LifeUSA had all the credibility in the world—because we were there first. Again, the key is not to be seduced by the acceptance of peer group pressure, but to turn it around against the peers so that you are the one creating the pressure.

I am reminded here of Robert C. Atkins, MD, the guy who dreamed up the so-called "Atkins Diet." The Atkins Diet is considered a leader among peers today, but when this "low-carbohydrates" approach to eating hit the streets back in the 1970s it was a unique approach that snubbed its tummy at all the other diet plans of the time. Initially, the Atkins Diet was uniformly savaged by just about every living dietitian in the universe. It seemed that everyone railed against it, claiming that it short-changed users of precious nutrients, and promoted high cholesterol, heart attacks, and every other imaginable medical ill.

Now, I am not here to defend or denigrate the Atkins Diet. I only want to point out that when the *New York Times* published a lengthy article suggesting that the Atkins low-carb approach was truly effective in weight-reduction programs, the world did a flip-flop. Suddenly everybody was jumping aboard the Atkins bandwagon. Researchers, dietitians, nutritionists, GPs, food manufacturers—the whole bloody lot had to get on board and follow along. Soon, the Atkins Diet became the benchmark of diets, forcing other diet plans, restaurants, and food processors to respond to the peer pressure.

Avoid Peer Group Comparisons

It is possible to avoid falling prey to per group pressure. Let's review some of the rule-cheating principles written about in this book. It starts with reminiscing about the future. If you know what you are about, if you are committed to achieving that vision, and if you develop a culture of true parallel interests, then the need to follow peer group pressure is greatly diminished—and it's much easier to make the right decision.

I firmly believe that had LifeUSA fallen prey to peer group pressure, and had we followed the rules as we were supposed to, then we would have been like every other company that suffered peer group failure. Fortunately, LifeUSA had developed a culture that was willing to cheat on those rules. The result was success. Could LifeUSA have achieved more? Should we have achieved more? Who knows? What I do know is that those companies that were supposed to be our "peers" are not around today. Sometimes we get so caught up following the rules of peer group pressure that we get trapped into doing what other people do, right or wrong. As mentioned before, the way to avoid this is simple: Don't chase peer group competition; make the competition chase you.

And the Moral of the Story Is . . .

When you're in business, any business, the easiest and yet the hardest thing is to do the right thing. And that means keeping your own counsel. Be a congenitally bad listener when it comes to comparing your business to others. If you have studied your market, considered what is right and what is wrong, if you have put all the major players in your business scenario on a parallel course, the easiest thing is to do the right thing – not the same thing.

That's the spirit of this book. If you can create an environment that seeks to do the right thing, and then consistently do the right thing, you will be successful. Success may not mean the same amount of dollars that other people have; it just means that you will have achieved the vision of your reminisce, whatever it might have been.

But you have to have patience and believe in yourself. A lot of people do not know what the right thing is; the right thing sometimes takes time to play out. Compare the progress you make with your potential and effort. If you do so, soon you will be the comparison by which others compare themselves. You will have defeated peer pressure by creating peer pressure for others.

16

Outsourcing to Oblivion

*If it sounds too easy, looks too easy, feels too easy,
and the promises are easy to come by, it is not easy.*

Speaking of peer group pressure to follow the crowd, nowhere is that nasty force being felt more strongly than in the new management craze of outsourcing. This management dogma entices businesses to believe there is a magic bullet to reduce costs, increase productivity, stimulate dynamic growth and increased profitability, all the while freeing up time for us to concentrate on the "important issues"—not to mention the golf course. In reality, it's a house of cards like the slick doctrines of failed presidential campaigns.

The current candidate for this intriguing solution to management challenges is called "outsourcing." Playing on short memories and the human desire to find the perfect epiphany of management via the shortcut, the proponents of outsourcing mask one important fact. While there is always the promise of discovering something new in management techniques, there is never anything new in management techniques. As with most political campaign promises, the only reality is a rehash of old ideas in new packages.

It is difficult to pick up a business magazine or attend a meeting and not have people talk about, propose, or implement outsourcing. Indeed, "outsourcing" has become the Atkins Diet of management reduction. In simple terms, the proponents of outsourcing want us to believe that if we hire "experts" (them) to do our job, then our job will be easier. Of course, any job is easier if we don't have to do it. But you need to cheat on the allure of the outsourcing promise, because the job of management is to manage.

Nothing is sacrosanct when it comes to potential outsourcing. Managers are reminded they are not in the computer-processing business. Therefore, they should outsource that process to those who are. There is also the hue and cry to outsource "human resources" because government regulations are complicated, while payroll and employee benefits are distractions from the "real job" of the company. Consider the last time this outsourcing mania reared its head: there were those who recommended totally outsourcing employees and "leasing" them from another company that specialized in employee relations.

Other perceived candidates for the promises of outsourcing are customer service (have you read about the call centers in India?), product fulfillment, distribution, marketing, and manufacturing. If taken to its extreme, it would be possible to outsource each and every activity of a company. Then, executives would be left to do what many of them do best: nothing. But even that activity can be outsourced by hiring management consultants to do the thinking and planning. The irony of outsourcing is the number of companies that have become large and profitable by offering to do the jobs companies should be doing for themselves.

We Should All Be Doubting Thomases

While you may conclude a writer's bias against outsourcing, in fact there is a time and place for outsourcing. The point is, cheat on any notion that suggests one simple solution to management challenges. Outsourcing can be an effective tool, but it is hardly nirvana. As a veteran corporate chieftain, I've been on the receiving end of numerous outsourcing pitches. The promise is always to make my life easier by doing the job better and cheaper than my company can. Can you think of a more direct insult to an executive?

After years of dealing with this issue, I developed a personal litmus test for outsourcing: If you don't care if the process gets mucked up—outsource!

As perspective on this conclusion, consider the following postulates. The fundamental rule for successful corporate management requires that the management ten of a company always be in control of those functions that are critical to its success or failure. An executive should never consciously allow someone or something not under his direct control to be in a position to impact the future of the company. In the insurance business, this was called avoiding "antiselection." Meaning that if you give someone else the power to "antiselect" against the best interests of your company, eventually they will.

Essential to the effective control of a company's future is to never give up control of three critical functions: product development, distribution, and customer service. It's all right to outsource janitorial services, parking lot management, and printing. If these functions go bad, you may be irritated, but you are not out of business. Outsource customer service or distribution—if they go bad, you go down.

The ripe plum for outsourcing has always been IT—information technology processing. After all, IT is expensive, confusing, mystifying, and frustrating. IT activities chew up an inordinate chunk of the operating budget, require large numbers of employees (none of whom you can communicate with), and have an insatiable appetite for continuing capital investment.

Don't Surrender Control

There can be no more tempting entreaty than one that goes like this: "Let us *relieve* you of the IT function. We are the leading experts in the field. We can reduce your costs, improve output, manage the geeks, eliminate the need for capital investment, and—best of all— you don't even need to be involved." The logic is wonderful—since they specialize in IT processing, they have more expertise than you ever could afford, and since they have ten clients instead of one, their expenses can be lower and the technology available is always state of the art.

This may be true, but it comes with a different kind of cost. When you give up control of IT functions (as frustrating as they can be to deal with), you give up control of what is the oxygen system of the modern company. Can you think of any company today that can function effectively *without* some form of computer technology support? Your IT function may be expensive and difficult to manage, but the point is that it's yours to manage. When you outsource IT, you may reduce short-term costs and aspirin use, but the real cost is loss of control over a function that can make or break your company.

Yes, the outsource resource will emphasize that they have ten clients, so they can do the job better. But how good is it to be one of ten as opposed to one of one? If you need to quickly change a function, how long will the line be? What happens if you outsource IT, get rid of all your machines and employees, and then the outsource company goes out of business, is sold, or simply does not perform as promised? Does it do much good to sue them while you are in the process of going out of business?

This is not to suggest that these calamities will happen. That is not the point. But they *could* happen, and you have no control over the impact. A few years ago when I became CEO of Allianz Life, the company had significant performance problems. The culprit was a management group that had violated not just one, but all three of the underpinnings regarding control of product, distribution, and administration. The company was, in essence, the epitome of outsourcing. Yet they kept parking lot management and printing in-house. (Explain that to me!)

Pluses and Minuses

By offering products developed by other companies, distribution controlled by another group, and administration and customer service provided by yet other companies, Allianz initially was able to reduce costs and increase production—and appeared to be profitable. However, when the products provided by others turned bad, the distribution was diverted away and those providing customer service failed to deliver. The company nearly failed and would have if it had not been a subsidiary of Allianz AG.

It was not that the company lacked the potential for success. In fact, there was the potential for extraordinary growth. The problem was that by outsourcing activities that were critical to the success of the company, management had effectively given up control of the company's future. When outsourcing failed to deliver on the promises made, the result was disaster for the shareholders, the company, the employees, and management.

Once Allianz Life began developing products internally, established a distribution system controlled by the company, and recovered the ability to issue and administer our business (which we did by acquiring the outsource company) performance turned around and the company became a star performer.

The decision whether or not to cheat on the outsource rules can be a simple one to make. The key is to look long term, not short term, and to calculate the impact on the company if something goes wrong, because it will. If the function is not critical to the long-term success of the company, and you can survive the worst (not the best) that can happen with outsourcing, then it should be given strong consideration. If that is not the case, then walk away.

And the Moral of the Story Is ...

Outsourcing carries an illusion of less work, improved productivity, and reduced costs, but at a very high price. The problem is that the pitch to outsource activity is usually targeted at your most important activities—where the fees are—and this creates the most risk. The real risk with outsourcing is that once you have made the move to the outside resource, you are at their mercy. No longer do you control costs, quality, or priority of service. Once dependent on the outsource provider, you can be held hostage—even with your own business. Moreover, there is the potential for the provider to experience financial or management problems, go out of business, or even be acquired. It's easy to say you can find another provider or bring the service back in-house. But there may not be another source available and the ability to most likely perform the service in-house has atrophied. Even if the service could be recovered or moved, by the time that's accomplished, your company may have hit the skids.

Outsourcing rhetoric, to a large degree, mirrors most recent presidential campaigns, where you can listen to all the glowing promises you care to. But you need to remember that, postelection, the promises offered have little weight and you have to live in the real world.

And no matter how much we may want to outsource that, we can't.

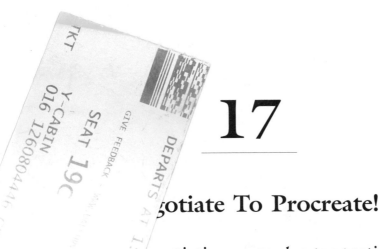

17

...gotiate To Procreate!

...negotiation occurs when two parties reach
...nt and each believes the other got screwed.

Have you ever experienced one of those wacky, out-of-body experiences that made it seem like you were living a real-life *Twilight Zone*? You know, like when you're having a vivid, surreal nightmare—no, not the kind where you leave the house naked because you forgot to get dressed—where you see yourself being led up to the gallows for a painful execution in front of thousands. Instead, just as you are about to say good-bye, the president comes up the steps, apologizes to you, and awards you $10 million and the Presidential Medal of Freedom. You know that kind? Well, I have. (In fact, quite a few really strange ones, but most I will never tell you—or anyone—about!)

However, Hartford Insurance firing me from my job as president of ITT Life was one such strange occurrence I will share. I choose this example to illustrate a wonderful lesson in the art of successful negotiation. Let me explain.

It happened in Hartford, Connecticut. (God created Hartford to make Biloxi, Mississippi, seem like a good place to live.) It was February—it was cold in the city—the insurance capital of America. I work here—I'm an insurance guy. I was visiting the city—not for the jocularity and frivolity offered by Hartford—but to quit my job as president of ITT Life, a subsidiary of The Hartford Insurance Group. By resigning from ITT Life, I would be free to start my own company—LifeUSA—and, with any luck, would never have to set eyes on Hartford again.

Discussions regarding a possible management buyout of ITT Life had been under way for several months, but those negotiations (if they could even be called that considering the bumbling bureaucracy of The Hartford) had broken off for good, *really* good, at the end of the year. Activity related to the start-up of LifeUSA had reached the point that in January our lawyer suggested—in no uncertain terms—that we either had to stop meeting about LifeUSA or quit working for Hartford. (We knew drastic action was required when a lawyer, of all people, started talking to us about ethics.) We had gone too far to go back; quitting was the only option. (Besides, starting a new company—even if it led to failure, abject poverty, and homelessness—was a better option than continuing to work for a company like The Hartford.)

When I called Fred Richardson, my boss at The Hartford, and asked for a meeting, he agreed, but, for some reason, put me off for several weeks. That was fine with me because, requesting the meeting gave us the cover to "legally" work on plans for LifeUSA (the lawyer's ethics did not stretch that far), while still employed with Harford. (Of course, we did so only after business hours and on our own time!)

When the fateful day arrived, I flew to Hartford full of anxiety, but ready to negotiate my departure from ITT Life. "Negotiate" was probably a misnomer, since I was walking into the meeting with absolutely zero leverage. Despite having no financing in place to support the new company and even less money in the bank, I was in Hartford to quit my job. My best hope was to secure a couple of weeks' severance pay.

We met in The Hartford cafeteria—a place where you had to wash your hands *after* you ate—to have breakfast. As I was there to quit my job and walk out the door with no source of income, I prudently delayed broaching the subject for as long as possible. (At least till I was sure Richardson was going to pay for breakfast.) Finally, after we had exhausted the obligatory small talk, I tiptoed to the subject of the day by suggesting that it might be time for me to leave ITT Life.

Much to my chagrin (not to mention injury to my ego), Richardson instantly agreed. What? No argument at all? You mean you would let the guy who turned the company around and put ITT Life on the insurance map just leave without even so much as feigning concern for the loss? I didn't expect him to beg me to stay (well, maybe a little), but at least he could have faked being taken aback and gone through the motions of reflecting on the issue for more than a nanosecond.

As it turned out, he *had* thought about it—more than I ever would have believed. Turns out Richardson had his own legal reasons for delaying the meeting. When I called, it seems he had already decided to *fire me* and needed the time to clear the action with the Hartford board and find a replacement.

In the recovery mode, and trying not to appear to be too deflated by his eagerness to dump me, I stumbled out with the simple offer, "Fred, I would be happy to stay for a while and assist in any transition at the company."

Another dagger quickly pierced the eye of my ego when his retort was, "I don't think you should go back to the company."

Are you kidding me? Here I had just resigned after almost ten years of leading the company to prominence and profitability, and this guy not only didn't offer any resistance—he seemed downright giddy about the situation.

Now all my air was really gone. Sure, I came to Hartford to resign, but he didn't have to agree to it so easily. It was a little like meeting your wife for lunch at a restaurant and saying, "Honey, things have not been going so well for us, and I was thinking that maybe—well, maybe—if you want to, we should think about a divorce" —only to have your wife respond with, "Honey, you are right. In fact, I filed the papers this morning; your clothes are being packed now, so don't bother returning to the house."

Needless to say, I was stunned. Seeking to salvage some shred of victory – however trifling it may have been—I suggested that I stay till March first, my ten anniversary with the company, so I could be vested in the pension plan. Richardson responded with, "That won't be necessary. You will be vested in your pension plan as part of your severance package approved by the board."

Wait! Whoa! What? Before I could take a breath and respond to the hot coal just dropped in my lap, he followed up with a comment that literally burned in my soul. "You have crossed the line from being a manager to being an entrepreneur," Richardson said, "and The Hartford does not want entrepreneurs running their companies!"

Only then did I realize that both of us had come to the meeting with the same objective, but with an entirely different motivation. My objective for the meeting was to quit so I could become an entrepreneur, and he came to fire me because I exhibited the telltale traits of an entrepreneur! One man's resignation is another's execution! As I sat there, dazed with disbelief, Richardson explained to me that, even though I had "crossed the line" with my impure entrepreneurial thoughts and was to be terminated, I would be paid one year's salary and bonus, full medical benefits, and complete vesting of my pension plan.

As I look back on the moment, it should have been clear that possessing an entrepreneurial spirit was a "thought crime" deemed to be illegal and immoral only in Hartford, Connecticut. (Which is not all that far from Salem, Massachusetts.) I am sure that Richardson's offer was only a starting point. Had I been swifter and smarter, he probably would have gone much higher to prevent a public disclosure that entrepreneurs might actually have been lurking within the halls of The Hartford. Then again, he might have wanted to make an example of me to prevent any possible vestige of entrepreneurial spirit from germinating at Hartford.

Richardson was probably more relieved that his initial proposal was accepted than I was giddy to receive it. The irony is that we both walked away from the meeting getting exactly what we wanted (maybe even more than we expected). We also felt that we had each gotten the best of the other person. Well, all's well that ends well.

Richardson walked away from the meeting rid of an evil entrepreneur, a new president in his pocket, and no threat of a lawsuit. At the same time, I walked out of the meeting ready to start a new company, with $200,000 in my pocket instead of the two cents that would have been there, had he simply allowed me to quit. (This is just one, but not the last, example of how Hartford's corporate ego caused them to do stupid things in an effort to prevent the success of LifeUSA.)

Making Matters Worse

As happy as I was with this deal, Richardson could not let sleeping dogs lie. He had to make it even better for us! Immediately after our meeting, he got on a plane and flew out to Minneapolis to meet with the executives of ITT Life to determine which of them were joining me in the great LifeUSA adventure. (He knew how fast I would try to escape from Hartford and wanted to beat me back. However, he did seem to forget that phones actually do work in Hartford.) Upon arriving in Minneapolis, Richardson challenged each ITT Life executive with, "Are you with MacDonald or us?" The four who gave what he felt was the wrong answer, "MacDonald," were terminated on the spot and given the same type of severance package.

So our world became surreal. We started the morning thinking that by nightfall we would be jobless, penniless, and maybe even homeless (our wives certainly were worried about that), and we ended the day with several hundred thousand dollars of Hartford money in our collective pockets. It was money we could (and did) use to fund the start up and early financing of LifeUSA. It is no hyperbole to suggest that if Hartford had not taken this negotiating position, LifeUSA might have become an unfulfilled reminiscence, a dream that never came true. It is striking irony that the company with the strongest desire to prevent us from starting LifeUSA had, in fact, funded our humble beginnings.

Lesson Learned—Lesson Followed

What did I learn about negotiation from this experience? Well, for starters, for the first time, I learned the value of shutting up in a meeting and letting the other person talk. This encounter taught me that when in negotiations, there is a better chance for success if you don't shoot from the lip. Listening to what others want to gain increases the likelihood of getting what you want. More important, I became convinced that *any deal worth doing could be done*, so long as you are willing to cheat on the normal rules of negotiation.

All Life Is Negotiation

Negotiation, like intimidation, is something we have to deal with all of our lives—whether we like it or not. It permeates practically all our relationships, and almost every act of life is the result of some type of negotiation. One way or the other we are always at the "bargaining table" discussing small deals that seem as natural as a breath, all the way up to interactions that could change our lives forever. Therefore, if deal-doing will have such a significant impact of our lives, then the more skilled we are at bringing negotiation to a favorable conclusion, the better off we are going be.

Having grown old during the lifelong process of negotiating, I have learned a good deal about the art of successful "deal-doing." The most important lesson learned was similar to other lessons learned—and that is, don't follow the traditional rules—be willing to cheat if you really want to win! (Hey, reading this book, would you be surprised with anything else?)

Entering the business world as an inexperienced young man, I found a bucket of hard-and-fast negotiating rules that had been in place so long you'd think they'd been handed down on tablets of stone. You know what most of these rules are—you've seen them too. The rules are that to "win" when negotiating we must . . .

- Be strong
- Be rigid
- Be aggressive

- Be intimidating
- Take as much out of the deal as possible and leave only crumbs for the vanquished.

And above all, we are admonished to look out only for ourselves and let the other guy worry about covering his butt.

The fundamental rule of traditional negotiations is this: "What's mine is mine and what's yours should be mine." This is the rule that people are conditioned to follow, and those who don't are wimps! Accordingly, when it comes to negotiating a deal, most will try to gain the upper hand, to get as much as they can, take advantage of you—in short—screw you! But don't think badly of people who take this approach, because it is what they are taught to do.

Negotiating has been positioned as a form of a mental jujitsu contest with an "every man for himself" type approach. For many males, deprived by modern life of the opportunity to hunt and kill, negotiating becomes a game that allows us to tack scalps to the wall. For women, conditioned as the "weaker sex," negotiating comes with instructions for the use of guile and cunning to achieve desired results. Both approaches are wrong!

I suppose there are times when you can be successful by following the hard line of negotiating. You know, like Donald Trump á la *The Art of the Deal.* In the long run, though, the old rules will produce more bane than benefit.

If you want to be a consistent winner at the process of negotiating, then be ready to break all the fixed and stereotypical rules that make the process of negotiating more like a battle or a war. Instead, you can make it more like a picnic with friends.

Precepts to Power Negotiating

There are three critical precepts, or principles, involved in a successful negotiating process. These principles are:

- Never be so in love with a deal that you can't walk away.

- Understand the difference between bartering and negotiation.
- Always make it appear as though you gave up more than you received.

If you never lose sight of these points you will usually be a winner in the negotiating dance, and you are guaranteed never to be a loser. You will always be a winner if you can make sure that all parties walk away from the table not only believing that they have just won, but are totally convinced that they have absolutely gotten the best of the other party.

Love Means Never Having to Get Screwed

Most people get the short end of the negotiating stick poked in their eye when they fall too deep into the romance of the deal (which is a prescription for getting screwed rather than making love). When one party gets so intoxicated by the deal that they lose their senses, they become prime candidates for the negotiating equivalent of "date rape." You may not always want to say "no," but the key is to never lose the ability to say "no" and to have it stick. People can become so enamored with the deal that it becomes a quicksand of the mind that pulls them in deeper and deeper until they lose control over the ability to walk away from a bad deal.

Yes, I know that walking away can be difficult. Oftentimes we fall in love with a certain acquisition or get our hearts primed for a particular negotiating result. My advice is simple: Don't be beguiled. If you fall in love with a house or a job that you simply "can't live without," you're begging for trouble if you pay too dearly to obtain it. Always have a point at which you'll walk away from the deal. Simply put, "Know when to hold 'em, and know when to 'fold 'em."

The Line in the Sand

When we give away too much in negotiation because we need the deal too much, we will ultimately become disenchanted with the deal. When we fail to recognize and honor our limits—and those of our counterparts—we have sown the seeds of future discontent, which makes for a multiplicity of problems later on. Customers will say, "You screwed me once but I learned my lesson, I'm not coming back for more." Anyone else you seek to shaft through negotiation will feel the same way. And the same goes for you. If someone takes advantage of your negotiating naiveté because you didn't do your homework or fell in love with the object of the negotiation, you will feel bad about yourself and even worse about the other party.

If you always retain the ability to walk away from any deal—no matter how romantic it may appear to be—you will never be taken advantage of and—in reality—will win many more deals than you ever lose.

Learn Your Limits

There is an effective way to protect against falling prey to your romantic feelings for a deal being turned against you: know your limits. Prior to entering into any negotiation, draw your bottom line. That means knowing what you will not do or relinquish in order to make the deal. This has to be a hard-and-fast base-rock of beliefs not to be violated – no matter what happens. Just like you can't be half pregnant, you can't go halfway with your deal limits. Either you understand there is a point beyond which it is not worth it to make a deal and have the courage to walk away, or you don't, and run the risk of being made a loser by someone applying all the old rules.

Virtually every time I have walked away from a deal, the opposite side came scampering back again more fawningly attentive than before. I had, in a sense, called their bluff. And when that happens, all the leverage is on your side of the table.

Doing Your Homework

The best way to position an exit strategy from a bad deal is to solicit input from everyone who will be impacted by the proposed deal before negotiations start. To do this, I'd go to each individual—be they marketing person, lawyer, or actuary—and ask them one simple question, "What is the minimum you would accept to agree to this deal?" Once their input was combined with my own feelings about the minimums of a deal, it was like having a very good GPS system in my pocket at the negotiating table. It told me where I wanted to go and warned me if I strayed off the path. With this guideline, I could concentrate on trying to make the deal happen. This approach offers a good deal of latitude in negotiating because when you know when to walk away from a deal, anything achieved north of the minimums can be considered a victory.

Fortunately, I learned this technique early in the development of LifeUSA. We had been in business for a little over a year when our CFO, Joe Carlson, came whining to me about the need to raise more capital simply because our money had just about run out. (Joe was a bean counter but had a special way of motivating people.) He suggested that unless we quickly replenished our capital base, we would soon to go out of business, be put in debtors' prison, and be forgotten by all except those Harvard business professors who would use us as a textbook example of failure. (Till the day he retired, Joe always cried, "We needed more money!")

With our lives and future dependent upon the company staying in business, we set out to raise $2 million. As an indication of just how dire the situation had become, some of the groups we approached were venture capitalists. (More on venture capitalists in chapter 18—"Finding and Financing the American Dream.") You should know that it is easier to negotiate a fair deal with a wife who has the tapes and pictures than with venture capitalists. They are used to having more things on their side than a herd of cows at a tipping contest. The main advantage venture capitalists have over you is that they have the money and you don't! Plus, if they don't give you the money, you might go out of business. They know that you love your business like a mother loves a child, and will do almost anything to keep it alive. They have all the leverage in the negotiation and you have none.

After weeks and weeks of back-and-forth, in-and-out, up-and-down frustrating negotiations that sometimes made me wonder why I had ever complained about my mother-in-law, I was ready to give up. It was like trying to reason with bankers, except these venture capitalist guys were actually intelligent. It seemed that every time I would concede one more point, they would ask for two more. Yet I was locked into the discussions because we needed their money—under almost any terms—to survive.

As the offering was drawing to a close, things were getting really desperate. We still had no deal. (It didn't help my confidence to one day walk into Joe's office to see him filling out an application for food stamps.) While it seemed close, a deal was yet done.

Then, late one Sunday evening, a call came in at home from the vulture . . . er, venture guys asking for just one more little advantage in the deal. That was it! The end! I didn't care how much we needed the money, I told them the deal was off—and I meant it.

Much to my surprise, early the next morning, as I was trying to explain to Joe why I had turned down the deal, there came a call from our contact with the venture group. He wanted to confirm that I had actually lost my mind and was stupid enough to turn down good money from the venture group. From his viewpoint, I was like the ungrateful condemned man who had turned down the governor's pardon because he wanted me to promise to pay my taxes. But I held firm and told him, "No deal!" We would take our chances without them. Confirming that I was serious, he made one last request for us to meet one more time with the venture boys. I agreed, but reiterated that nothing would change. We set the date, and I walked back into Joe's office to tell him of the meeting, just in time to convince him to take the rope from around his neck and get down off his desk.

The atmosphere at the meeting with the venture boys was decidedly different from all previous meetings. They made me feel like the beautiful bride rather than the ugly goat suggested in earlier meetings. Instead of demanding, they pleaded. Rather than require controls, they promised to comply. They offered reasons to let them invest in LifeUSA, rather than excuses for needing more to give

291

less. These guys were so compliant that I began to wonder if we were part of the reality show *Extreme Makeover*. Anyway, the deal was done—on equitable terms.

It turned out to be a great transaction for both sides. The venture boys ultimately received "techlike" returns on their investment (when techlike returns were good), and LifeUSA gained the support and involvement of some very talented financial people. It was win-win for all of us. (In fact, it was such a good deal that it was almost a full month before Joe was back in my office telling, me we needed more capital.) But even more than that, I learned a wonderful lesson in negotiation.

If you know the right time to say "no" in the negotiation process, you earn the respect of the other party and go from the hunted to the hunter. Dealing with the venture capitalists taught me that strength in negotiation comes from cheating on the traditional rules that make negotiating more like a duel to the death than an opportunity for both sides to win. By cheating on the negotiation rules, you discover that often the best deals are struck when you focus first on what you won't do instead of what you want to do. And to do that, you've got to know the difference between bartering and negotiation.

Bargain, But Don't Barter

A big mistake many of us make is to confuse "barter" with "negotiate." To barter is to haggle—not negotiate. In the process of bartering—simple buying and selling—both parties struggle to gain the upper hand over the *same* issues and the *same* objectives. On one side, a person owns something of value they want to dispose of (including services that may be an illegal renewable source of income), for the highest possible exchange of value. The buyer wants to acquire the value for the lowest possible exchange of value. The exchange is not negotiated; only the *price* is bartered. Trying to negotiate a barter will fail, just as trying to barter a negotiation will be unsuccessful. What can be confusing is that there is virtually no negotiating involved in bartering and virtually no bartering in negotiation.

Don't get me wrong, bartering really can be a fun sport. In fact, God invented Persian rugs so we would have something to barter over. Barter is to negotiation as graffiti is to the frescoes. Bartering is a game—negotiation is an art. Most people misspell the places where the art of bartering is practiced. They call them a "Flea Circus" when the original spelling was "Fleece Circus," because that is what happens when you barter. You barter for price and negotiate for value. If there is a true exchange of value, then price will never be the issue. I hate to barter unless it is a game, but I love to negotiate for something meaningful. In fact, bartering is most fun when it is a game.

A great place to learn to barter is Mexico. The national sport of Mexico is bartering. Few are better barterers than native Mexicans. In fact, many Mexicans believe God created gringos so there would always be someone to lose at bartering. Knowing that I can't out-barter the natives when in Mexico, I have adopted the defensive strategy—if you can't compete—then confuse!

When approached at a beach bazaar with the pitch, "Hey amigo, pure hand-woven blanket here for you, only $20." My response is to pause … feign interest, and counter with, "No, no—I will only pay $22 for the blanket." The merchant blinks, pauses, and responds with "No, you don't understand amigo. This is wonderful blanket you can have for $18 US." My quick response is, "OK, OK, I'll go $25!" There usually follows a series of bounce-back exchanges, with the seller trying to explain the rules of barter by constantly lowering the price of the blanket and me seeming confused—but just as persistent—as I counter each lowered bid with a higher one. Eventually, the interaction ends with my comment, "OK, I'll offer $35 dollars for the blanket, but not a dollar less!" If I am persistent enough, the guy finally gives up, takes my money in exchange for the blanket and wanders off, convinced that he has just met the dumbest of all gringos.

What's the point here?

The point is that bartering can be fun. But you should never get trapped into bartering about important things. Barter for the secondhand Persian rug or the pink yard flamingos at a garage sale, but not for anything that makes a real difference. Spend your time learning to be a winner at negotiation and don't be diverted by the apparent activity of barter. The rules in place are structured so that bartering can easily be confused with negotiating. If that happens, you might seem to win the battle (barter), but will definitely lose the war (negotiation) on the big issues.

Build a Career That Pays—Not A Job

Traditional rules call for us to focus on the salary to be paid when we interview for a job. Since we are pressured to take care of things like food, clothes, and lodging, it is easy for those writing the rules to make us believe that starting salary is the pivotal point to win. In reality, if we focus on the potential and power of the job, the rest should take care of itself.

Throughout my entire career, never did I ask about salary or bonus when interviewing for a new job. Despite the rules and books purportedly written to help us get that raise, never ever did I approach my boss to ask for a pay increase. Recently, after being asked to join the board of directors of a growing young company, I had multiple meetings with the existing board members, management, and employees, all for the purpose of researching the company. Over a period of two or three months of discussion, not once did I inquire as to the compensation for the board, but I did focus on what was expected from board members and involvement desired by management.

We should always cheat on the barter rules for compensation and instead negotiate for the responsibility, involvement, potential, and future of the job. Negotiate for the position, but never barter the salary. My belief was that bartering for a salary or a raise was demeaning to the job I was doing. It is one thing to barter for the cost of a blanket, and quite another to barter your value to an organization. If you are working for an organization that does not recognize, appreciate, and reward the value you are contributing and you are required to barter for your pay, then you are working for the wrong organization.

The same tune was sung when hiring, retaining, or rewarding those who worked for me. Nothing turned me off more than the individual who was more interested in salary than opportunity. I recognized that most were only playing by the rules they had learned when they tried to barter for pay, but it was not a game I wanted to play.

When we did have to go outside our organization (which I hated to do) to fill a need, it would always disappoint and irritate me when someone would come in and say that they had found the right person for the job but that we had to pay more to get them. I was even more put out when told that we had to make up for a lost bonus or even pay a "signing bonus" to encourage the candidate to join the company. It was a ransom I refused to pay. In fact, when someone tried to barter compensation, I would take the Mexican beach approach and go in the opposite direction. Instead of caving in to the barter request, the amount offered would be reduced.

Those individuals who joined LifeUSA in the early years taught me a lesson we all should remember. When someone "buys into" a job they are much more valuable than those you have to "buy" to do a job. My strategy was to cheat on the rules of attracting new hires and negotiate for the talent the individual had to offer in exchange for the opportunity and future our organization could present. Not to do so would be disloyal to those early "LifeUSA owners" who took the risk to join the company in the beginning and—at the same time—invest 10 percent of their salary in company stock.

The harsh reality is that if the person joins a company as a result of a bartered compensation arrangement, then they will leave the company for the same reason. However, when they make an investment in the company, it is more likely they will stay around for a return on the investment. Likewise, when people join the company for the right reason—for opportunity—then when the next company comes calling, the employee would focus on the opportunity instead of just being bought. I felt we could always negotiate when it came to opportunity and never wanted to compete on the basis of the dollar.

Implementing the No-Barter Zone

A good example of this type of antibartering hiring took place at Allianz shortly after the merger with LifeUSA. An Allianz division leader was in desperate need of a senior marketing person and came to me with a request to begin a search. It became obvious during the selection process that the executive did not share my approach to hiring.

One day, after several months of searching (during which time he became increasingly concerned about finding someone), the guy bounded excitedly into my office to announce that he had found the "perfect candidate."

The prospect lived in our town, offered years of experience, was with a direct competitor, and was willing to make a change. There was one problem—he was looking for us to "buy" him away from his existing employer. In short, the candidate not only wanted to barter for a higher salary, but also a bonus that he would be leaving at his former company. (This happened despite the fact that the individual had been "found" because he was registered with a search firm.) The division head assured me that if we didn't comply with the request, "There is no way we would ever get this guy!"

I didn't blame the candidate for his position—he was following the rules of barter and doing quite a good job. However, I was upset with my guy for trying to barter his way out of a problem. In my usual respect-in-the-workplace candor I replied, "Bullshit! We do not have to give this guy a raise to come here, and no friggin' way are we going to pay some other company's bonus. If he is not willing to come here at what we want to pay (remember, always identify your drop-dead position) then we will pass. In short, our company represents a better long-term *opportunity* than his old job, regardless of his bonus. And, besides, we don't barter!"

Seeing the look of confused resignation in the eyes of my guy (the look of those who don't understand why the rules don't work), I offered to meet with the candidate. When we met, our discussions quickly moved off the short-term issues and focused on the long-term potential for career advancement and compensation. I was clear that we would pay no more than he was making now and that there was "no way" we were going to pay a bonus for another company. My focus and objective was to negotiate the future, not barter the present. Either he would recognize the opportunity to join Allianz was much more than short-term pay, or he would stay where he was.

I knew that if we succumbed to his barter tactics and paid him more today, he would lose sight of our opportunity and be willing to move to another company if they would pay him more tomorrow. (Of course, I also knew that his current company was thinking of exiting the market he was in and that with a young family he had no desire to leave the area. But that is another part of negotiation.)

What I wanted this guy to do was make an *investment* in his future with the company. If he was willing to take less to join our company, then he would work hard to reap a return on his investment. This aligns his and the company's interests in parallel— the best way to be.

I give the guy credit, he pushed hard to follow the barter rules. But in the end—to have a good deal – good negotiation will always beat hard bartering. A few days later he called me at home. He started by cursing me for putting him through the process of recognizing that short-term salary was not important—and accepted the offer. Now, I knew we had a winner and someone taking the job for the right reason.

The next morning I went to our division head and told him to make the formal offer with a starting salary 10 percent higher than the candidate had been earning at his previous employer, and agree to pay 50 percent of the bonus he was giving up to join Allianz. The signal sent by this approach was twofold. One, I wanted the guy to know that our discussions were not about money, but about *opportunity*. Second, I wanted to reinforce and reward his decision to take less to join Allianz by giving him a quick return on his investment as a taste of what his future dedication and hard work could produce.

Pot At End of Rainbow Crap

I had the same attitude regarding people who threatened to leave the company for higher pay. Every time someone would come to me with, "John Jones is going to leave us because Night Life of Las Vegas has offered him more money," my response would be to wish him well and let him go. We prided our culture on paying people equitably for the value they added to the organization. If we were convinced that was being done, then we would not be held hostage by someone who wanted to offer higher pay just to take the person away. By the same token, I did not want to have people with us who would leave only for bartered money.

On the other hand, if we could not challenge an individual with opportunity to fit their perceived talents, or if another company was offering a true enhanced opportunity—that we could not match— then I would not only wish them well, but also help them secure the opportunity.

The Real Fun—Negotiate To Procreate

Once you have armed yourself with the knowledge of what you won't do, and recognize bartering for what it is, you are ready to get on with the enjoyable sport and art of negotiation. As mentioned earlier, most of the rules for negotiation suggest preparation as if going to war. My experience says to cheat on those rules and approach negotiation as if seducing a new lover. You may be surprised to learn that the famous phrase, "Make love, not war" didn't come out of hippie frustration over the Vietnam War, but was actually first coined in the classic but long-forgotten business book *Barters Are From Bulgaria And Negotiators are from Neptune*. Really!

Let's start with some perspective for real negotiating. Imagine that you are trying to secure a financing agreement or an important acquisition. Let's assume that you are almost as good as you think you are, and "fair and square" (that's how we view it when we get the better of someone else), you clearly come out on top in the deal. In other words, you connive, bluster, and use your rapierlike mind to walk away from the table with the other party's scalp. What happens? As soon as the other person realizes that you have tomahawked them (is that a politically correct term?) into a deal, anger and frustration will emerge in the form of a call to the mutated species that actually wrote the negotiation rules—the lawyers. That will start the inevitable process of making one or several of them rich by trying to sort things out.

Now reverse the process. What if, after the romance of the deal has worn off, you discover that the other person "lied and cheated" (that's how we view it when someone gets the better of us!) in order to hoodwink you into a deal that would embarrass even Bill Clinton. What do we do? Well (for justice's sake only), we call a lawyer and start the same process. (Have you ever noticed that any time the lawyers get involved they are the only winners? God must have created lawyers so he could have his own situation comedy reality show.)

But what if, after the deal is signed, sealed, and closed, *both* sides are totally convinced they have the cleaned out the opponent— taken all his chips and the box he brought them in? You know what would happen? I'll tell you: It would be the lawyers' worst nightmare and cause them to become homeless beggars on the street. Wouldn't that be fun to see? When a deal is signed and all involved parties see themselves as pure demigods of negotiation, ready to accept the accolades and deification from their friends, everyone is happy but the lawyers. Seriously, believe it or not, this type of outcome to negotiation is possible. In fact, it is fairly easy to accomplish on a consistent basis. And here's how.

Winning By Losing

There is a simple method to achieve successful negotiation. I promise that if you seek it as your objective in any negotiation, you will become a true artist, painting great deals. Ready? Here it is: *If both sides walk away from the negotiation believing that they have totally screwed the other side— it will be a great deal!*

The traditional rules of negotiation instruct us to focus on the "top line" and not the "bottom line" of a deal. Conflicts are created (just what the lawyers love) because both sides fight (sometimes literally) for how much they can take, and consider it a weakness if they appear to give anything. You should cheat and do just the opposite. If you are willing to work openly and honestly with the other side, to help them achieve their goals, it is possible to procreate a deal without prostituting your position.

The trick to successful negotiation is to obtain all you need or want, while creating the perception in the mind of the other party that they took you like a Mafia don making a deal you could not refuse. In other words, they way to have a successful negotiation is to learn how to win while appearing to lose.

A good negotiation is a little like running a game on the old carnival midway. You know the player wants to "win" and look good for his girlfriend, so you "lose" a $3 stuffed bear for $20 worth of chances. The money exchanged may not have been equal, but if it allows the player to look good for his girlfriend and "get a little," then both sides are happy with the value exchanged.

Then again, successful negotiation reminds me of the scene at the end of the old movie, *The Sting,* when Paul Newman turns to Robert Redford and says, "The essence of a good con is for the mark never to know he has been conned." If you can master the concept of winning while appearing to lose, you will become a master at negotiation. Success will come easily in deal-making; especially when compared to following the old rules that call for each party to beat the other over the head till one quits.

The Real Art of the Deal

When you get down to it, there are two basic concepts to successful negotiation, and both have their underpinnings in the overall concept of this book, which, if you haven't guessed by now, is simple: Respect and reaffirm the dignity of others and they'll help you create the success you deserve.

Practicing the art of negotiation is a lot like playing seven-card stud. As the cards are dealt to the players, some are face down—so only the player can see them—and other cards are dealt face up, one at a time. By looking at the "up" cards, you get some idea as to the strength of hand the other players have, and they get a feel for yours.

But what if you knew what the other players' hole cards were? How good a card player would you be? How much could you win if you could convince the other players to *TELL* you what cards they held and were looking to draw? When you engage in cheating on the negotiating process in the proper way, it's like playing cards and knowing what the other players have—because they tell you!

The only way you can accomplish this trick is to "get on the other side of the table" and convince the other participant that "you are on their side." Of course, in order to accomplish this objective, you are going to have to meet without lawyers present. Lawyers will poison any early discussion with cynicism because they know that what they do justifies distrust. We kid about lawyers, but we shouldn't because it is true. The reality is that all early negotiations I conducted were one-on-one with the other person. I would only allow others into the discussions after the basic agreement had been struck and the details needed to be ironed out. (Remember, I already knew what the others would agree to prior to entering into negotiation.)

You get on the other side of the table by asking the person you are negotiating with a simple question like, "For you, what would be the very best results you could hope to achieve from our discussions? What exactly would make you happy?"

Some will open up right away and tell you everything you ever wanted to know and more. (It's sometimes a little uncomfortable when they tell you that they need the deal so that they have enough money to run off to Bolivia with the girl they met polishing the pole at a local strip club. But at least you'll know what it will take to make the deal.) However, most will be a little more reserved and constrained. After all, they are coming from the traditional approach for negotiating that says to keep everything close to the vest and disclose nothing. It's been my experience that a little patience and soft cajoling will get most participants to open up. You are catching them off guard—no one has been concerned with what they wanted from a deal. It was always what others were trying to get. When you gently and persistently push for what it is people really want, they usually will tell you.

This approach does not need to be insincere. In fact, it shouldn't be. Remember, this is a negotiation, not a barter. You are not haggling over something they have and you want, or visa versa. In pure negotiations both parties have something of value they are willing (or should be) to exchange for something of different but equal value. The objective of true negotiation is to accommodate this equal value-exchange. You can be perfectly sincere in trying to determine and achieve the needs and desires of the other party because—by their nature—they are not in conflict with yours. Of course, if the other party asks what you seek from the discussions—which they usually don't do because it is not normal negotiating—you have to be willing to tell them. Confused yet?

Putting It All Together

If you enter the negotiations armed with the knowledge of the bottom line you will accept to accomplish the transaction, and then gain an understanding of what it is the other party seeks to achieve, you are ready to begin the fun part and put the deal together. This puts you in a position to give everything away without giving anything away. What do I mean by that?

Well, by knowing what you need to keep or gain to make the deal work for you, you know exactly what you can give up without sacrifice. If you have been successful in cataloging the list of things the other party seeks to achieve, then points that are not in conflict with your interests can easily be given away. The objective of your discussions should be to determine just how much you can give to the other person, while seeming to take little for yourself. In other words, you want the deal to be *equitable,* but it does not have to be *equal.* These two points are a clear violation of classic negotiation rules, but you will be more successful when you cheat on them.

When You Give, Others Give

Humans have an almost compulsive need to reciprocate in kind to another human. (That is, except for Donald Trump.) Ever notice that when you compliment a person, a very short time later they'll return a compliment? When you tell someone a joke, they will try to respond with one. Ever been in a situation where someone has given you a gift that you did not expect? You were embarrassed (or peeved) because you did not have a reciprocal gift in hand.

The same human reaction works in negotiation. If you "gift" the other party with several points they want but are unimportant to you, then they will have a very strong inclination to respond favorably when you ask for something that is important to you. (If they don't, it's time to follow rule number one and walk away from the deal.) The art is to appear to always give up more than you are asking for, and put subliminal pressure on the other party to give the few things you need. It's really very simple.

Test-Drive This Concept Yourself

Let's say, for example, that you are negotiating the acquisition of a business. There are good reasons to acquire the business. A definite value can be placed on the business and you know how it will be run after the acquisition. You also know that the current owner (because he told you) is tired of working eighty hours weeks, is worried about succession, and wants to be able to retire in a few years. With this information you can be his friend and set about—working with him—structuring the deal so that he can achieve exactly what he is looking to accomplish. Knowing what the other party wants means that you can work honestly and diligently to accomplish those goals—just so long as they do not violate the basic minimums you have established to complete the deal.

The critical action is to deposit your ego at the door. Think of yourself more in the image of Mother Teresa than Rasputin. To win big, cheat on the traditional rules that say get as much as you can—regardless of what you actually need.

Now, don't get me wrong. I am not suggesting a Michael Dukakis "milquetoast" strategy here. (Five bonus points if you remember which character is fictional—Rasputin or Dukakis.) On the contrary, strength is your ally when you know what you will not do to do a deal and understanding what it is the other party will do to do a deal. Forget the old negotiating rule that says, "What is yours is yours, and what is his should be yours." You will be eminently more successful adopting a new rule that says, "What I don't want you can have, and what you have that I don't need you can keep." Don't try to get it all, just all that matters. Most of the time what matters to you will not matter to the other party, and what is important to them is not to you. And that is the basis of perfect negotiation.

Negotiating for Capital Funding

When it came to securing the initial funding of LifeUSA, we had the option of working with either Transamerica or Lincoln Financial. Both are outstanding companies and either would have been a good partner. However, following the different rules of negotiating we ended up working with Transamerica. It's not that Transamerica was easy—they were very demanding negotiators—but they had a different objective than Lincoln and only asked for things we were willing to give up.

Neither company was in the banking or venture capital business, but they were major players in the reinsurance market. Transamerica's primary objective was to increase the business for their reinsurance division. (Reinsurance companies receive a fee for sharing in the risk of policies written by another company.) Since LifeUSA needed reinsurance to support the business we planned to write (even with the proposed start-up financial), there was no conflict with Transamerica's objective. We could "get on the same side of the table" and do what we could to help Transamerica secure what they sought from the deal—which was a ton of reinsurance business, not really a specific return on their investment. This situation is really the magic of pure negotiation. While Transamerica didn't really care what rate of return they received on the investment, we did, because the cost of financing was critical to us. As a result, we ended up securing inexpensive financing in exchange for giving up something (reinsurance) that we needed anyway. Voilà! Magic!

It may seem like a big deal for a company to give up flexibility over how it does business, but here is a case where LifeUSA needed the reinsurance—we were giving away what we would have, anyway. While LifeUSA offered Transamerica 100 percent of the reinsurance business, the contract required that Transamerica match any other offer for reinsurance that we might receive from another company. LifeUSA gave the appearance of giving up significant control over our business (in exchange for $10 million of much-needed financing at prime bank rates), but the reality is that very little control was lost.

Not that Transamerica got a bad deal. Deals won't work unless both sides feel they took advantage of the other. Transamerica did not put up a dime of cash to do this deal. Instead they simply offered their corporate statement as a guarantee. Sure, they took a risk, but they mitigated that risk by taking control of the LifeUSA board and acquiring a proxy on controlling shares, while the loan was outstanding. If things got bad, Transamerica could step in to protect against a call on their guarantee.

Again, even though it appeared that LifeUSA gave up too much by allowing Transamerica to control the board of directors and proxy over a majority of stock, the reality is that this action gave LifeUSA credibility. We could point to being a credible company *because* a large company like Transamerica had senior executives on the board and was reinsuring 100 percent of our business.

Critics of Transamerica could say they gave up too much to do business with an unproven company like LifeUSA. Others could argue that LifeUSA gave up too much freedom and flexibility to receive the financing. Both sides were winners, because both sides looked like losers. Amazing, but that's what happens when the traditional rules of negotiation are broken.

And what of Lincoln Financial? They were also a major player in the reinsurance business (a competitor of Transamerica) and were willing to finance LifeUSA in exchange for using Lincoln as the primary reinsurer. The only difference was that Lincoln took the traditional approach to negotiating that called for them to get as much as they could—not as much as they needed.

Initially, we favored doing business with Lincoln. (I think we were impressed to be flown to their headquarters in a private jet.) We had come so close to a deal with Lincoln that they sent some of their people to our offices for final due diligence. I was out of the office and missed these meetings, but I certainly heard about them. I received a number of desperate calls from the LifeUSA owners who had met with the Lincoln people. They pleaded with me not to do the Lincoln deal because Lincoln not only wanted to reinsure the business we wrote, they wanted to tell us how to design, write, process, and service the business. We were looking for someone to support our business, not control our business. Even though Lincoln was offering more financing on better terms than Transamerica, they had crossed the line to ask for things we simply would not give up— so we walked!

All sorts of fur began to fly after I called the president of Lincoln and told him that while we appreciated their offer to support LifeUSA, we had decided to pass. As I had learned from other such situations, as soon as Lincoln understood that we were serious about passing on a deal with them, they changed completely and became open to almost anything we would propose. I received daily calls, promises, and invitations to visit again—anything—just so long as we would reconsider. But it was too late. If they could not do the deal the right way when they had the chance, how could they be trusted in the future?

Getting Good at Negotiation

Learning the art of negotiation requires understanding the reality of the process. In true negotiating, both parties enter into the discussions with different values to offer and different objectives. Probably the best example of how this worked in the real world was a series of negotiations and transactions entered into by LifeUSA to become a minority owner of independent insurance marketing companies. A good deal of true negotiating was required to complete these deals. Sometimes the owner of the marketing company didn't even know he wanted to sell a piece of his company.

Just for background, independent insurance marketing companies have become the way that most insurance companies now distribute their products. Unlike twenty-five years ago, when most agents were "captive" to the big companies, today most of the business sold is by independent agents not tied to any one insurance company. To fill the training and support void left by the insurance companies, entrepreneurs stepped in and formed companies that recruited, trained, and supported the insurance agent.

Over the years, these companies became very large and profitable for their owners. They, in effect, became "choke points" through which companies had to go to make contact with agents. If a marketing company did not want to support a particular insurance company, that company was effectively blocked from access to the independent agent contracted with the marketing company.

All of the business written by LifeUSA was through the independent marketing company system. While this is an efficient and low-cost way to distribute a product, the company bears an inherent risk. The company does not control the distribution system and is at the mercy of the independent marketing company to continue supporting the company's products. If the marketing company decided to discontinue its relationship with LifeUSA, we would lose an important distribution channel. Obviously, this was a concern to me and was brought to my attention by any number of analysts following our stock. We needed a solution to the problem.

At the same time, marketing companies had their risks and challenges. It was all well and good for the marketing company to be independent, but it did not control the structure or flow of the product, so it was really not in control of its destiny. The marketing company could recruit hundreds of agents and build up an important stream of income from the sale of a particular company's product, only to have the company change or pull the product from the market. The marketing company—and its investment in marketing for the product—could be left high and dry. They would be forced to quickly find another company or product to replace the stream of income, or face losing all the agents they had recruited.

In addition, while the owner of the marketing company was generating very high current income, all of the value being built was in the form of intangible good will that could evaporate overnight. This made it difficult for the owner of the marketing company to have a viable exit strategy or retirement plan.

This scenario provided a perfect opportunity to test our cheat-to-win negotiating strategy.

Usually, the owner of the marketing organization wanted to retain control of his company, create some immediate liquidity, and establish an exit strategy to take effect when he wanted to retire. At LifeUSA we sought to expand our distribution system, create guaranteed "shelf space" for our products, and be assured that no other company would ever take control of the marketing company, without our approval.

When it came down to negotiation, these deals were easy to complete. I knew from the LifeUSA side (the actuaries and bean counters told me) exactly how much liquidity we could offer to the owner of the marketing company, the value of having guaranteed shelf space for our products, and assurances that no other company could ever gain control of the marketing company. (The true value of the company, combined with the intrinsic value of shelf space and control, allowed us to offer a price for the liquidity that was always more than even the owner thought it was worth.)

With that on my side, it was easy to get over on the other side of the table and help the entrepreneur find a solution to his concerns and problems—even if I had to call them to his attention. (Kinda like selling insurance: Create a problem so you can offer a solution.)

In the end, the owner of the marketing company retained control of his company and was still the boss (LifeUSA only needed minority interest to accomplish our objective). Plus, he had more cash in his pocket than even he thought was fair and had a guarantee that if he was ever unhappy or wanted to retire, LifeUSA would buy the rest of his company at a guaranteed price.

For LifeUSA, we usually acquired 40 percent of a marketing company for about 20 percent of what it was worth to us, guaranteed that we would have shelf space for our products, and (with a right of first refusal) that no other company could ever buy control of the marketing company and move its agents away from us.

It was a perfect situation. The marketing company owner could sit back and think about how he got the best of Bob MacDonald. And I could go back to the board and tell them what a wonderful negotiator they had as a chairman.

And the Moral of the Story Is . . .

While always testing, negotiation can be a rewarding, enjoyable, and successful endeavor when we are willing to challenge and cheat on traditional rules.

Points to Remember

- Know your minimums and stick to them. You can't lose if you don't make a bad deal.
- Barter for fun and negotiate for real.
- Always give the other party what they want, without giving up anything you need.

The cheat-to-win negotiating program believes that solving problems and reaching agreements ultimately means *building relationships*. There is something both sides have in common—and that is to gain fair value for what they offer. Concentrating on solving these issues to the satisfaction of both parties builds relationships. Good relationships, of course, foster long-term success everywhere you turn.

Constantly remind yourself that when negotiating, be willing to give up anything that you don't want to keep. Let them win on every point except for those things that are inviolate to you. If you don't care about it, then don't argue about it.

Too many times the rule is, don't give *anything*. And that's dead wrong. Instead, get over on their side and help them achieve their objectives without violating the things that you need yourself. If you do that, you can walk out of any negotiation a winner.

Negotiating is neither rocket science nor a mystic art that only the gifted few can successfully handle. The bottom line in effective negotiation is this: Negotiation is a learned skill and must result in a win-win situation. Preparation and planning are vital to a successful result. Know your wants and needs and negotiate the best deal for both parties. Striking a deal will seem much easier when you cheat on the rule that says one should win and one should lose. Instead, make your own rule that says, You win I win!

18

Finding and Financing
The American Dream

*True freedom comes from being willing to risk
all you have to achieve true freedom!*

The Declaration of Independence makes no mention of it. Nor does the U.S. Constitution or the Bill of Rights. I suspect that the framers of those hallowed documents assumed that it was such an inalienable and natural right of Americans that there was no need to spell it out.

I'm referring, of course, to that primordial drive of Americans to "be their own boss." So innate is this inner energy you'd think it was genetically embedded within us. Except for Texas, no other country in the world has a population that exhibits this type of natural entrepreneurial drive that has been (and thankfully continues to be) the foundation and fuel of the American economic miracle.

Like salmon instinctively driven upstream to spawn, at some point in the lives of virtually every man and woman in America (not to mention eight-year-old kids selling lemonade on hot summer days) there arises a dream and desire to start a business and be in control of their fortune. This need for freedom becomes increasingly restive as the W-2s and annual job performance reviews pile up into years. Eventually there comes a pivotal, do-or-die nexus in our lives where we must fish or cut bait. We either forgo the comfort of a steady paycheck for the opportunity to determine our own way, or resign ourselves to being financially imprisoned by others and living under their rules.

At the point when we sufficiently tire of working to make someone else rich and successful; when we have identified a need, nurtured a good idea, and are willing to work as if our lives depended upon it—it's clear what we have to do. We have to start our own business.

Most allow the call of personal freedom to go unanswered by finding a rationale—any reason—for refusing. The rules and peer pressure, not to mention comments from parents ("Johnny, why would you give up your good job with the pension and all to take such a risk?"), convince the fainthearted that it is safer staying put under someone's thumb. Others respond as if it were a siren call of nature. They know it will not be easy, but, despite the odds and rules stacked against them, it is something they must do.

Starting a New Business Life

Is that you? Well, if so, you're not alone. A recent survey conducted by FedEx concluded that 67 percent of Americans dream of owning a business. Fully 55 percent of those surveyed indicated they would quit their job and start their business *today*, if only they had the financial "wherewithal" to do so. Fortunately, despite all the pressures not to, more than 3 million creative (frustrated) souls annually start new businesses.

In doing so they buck up against fearsome odds. Fully 78 percent of all new businesses fail within the first twenty-four months and up to 93 percent fail before five years have elapsed. Of course, these odds are not as bad as they seem. After all, the probability is 100 percent that we will not survive life, and yet we still go on. If you look at the bright side, after all, 7 percent will be successful. And that sounds like pretty good odds to me. (Well, I was a salesman, not an accountant, so humor me!)

If you think about it, the odds dealing with success or failure of a new business are meaningless. The statistics on business failure only report the percentage of people who were not prepared to be successful. They are out there to scare us so that we stay in our place as the *owned* rather than becoming one of the *owners*. The trick is to figure out how to be one of those 7 percent who are prepared for success. You've heard the saying, "Fortune smiles on the prepared!" (Or something like that.) Okay, fine—How do we get a smile from Dame Fortune?

Striking Out on Your Own

There are five essential ingredients required to shift the odds of success in your favor.

- Understand and be willing to accept the risk of being an entrepreneur.
- Identify a need not currently being met in the market.
- Create a solid, workable solution to an identified need.
- Hire employees willing to help achieve the goal.
- Find sufficient capital to survive the harsh early winters.

Success can be achieved without these ingredients in alignment, but when that does happen it falls more into the category of winning a lottery rather than managing a risk. (Might as well keep your job and bet the ponies till you're rolling in oats.) There are certain actions we can take to make starting our business more of a measured risk than wild gamble.

The Risk of Being an Entrepreneur

Nick Saban may have best identified the opportunity when, in a press conference announcing his hiring as head coach of the Miami Dolphins, he said, "I am not here to predict championships. I'm here to formulate a process that helps people be successful. If we can do that, we're going to have an opportunity to win a championship in the future." That is exactly what an entrepreneur does; he takes actions that position the company and its people for the potential to succeed.

As written in the chapter on building an entrepreneurial culture, the entrepreneur is an individual with the experience to recognize an opportunity, the instinct to visualize its fulfillment, and the courage to reach for it. The successful entrepreneur is a risk-taker, not a gambler. A gamble is an event in which there is no control over the outcome. A true gamble cannot be managed or mitigated. Most risk can be managed, and the successful entrepreneur embraces risk, but only risk that can be managed. If the entrepreneur has eliminated much of the gamble and is in a position to manage the risk, then the odds of success begin to shift in his favor.

Defining Need in a Changing Market

Entrepreneurs positioned for success understand that in times of economic stability, the big companies will always win. If the needs of the market—both real and perceived—are being met, there is little opportunity to compete successfully against those currently meeting the market needs. However, during times of change and volatility, it's not the big companies that win, it's the *good* companies.

Of course, big companies can be good, but more often it is the younger, smaller companies that demonstrate the nimbleness to benefit from change. If the needs of a market have changed, or technology has made old solutions obsolete—and the existing companies are not responding—then the opportunity to enter the market opens up to new companies. And make no mistake: change is always more of an opportunity than a threat to entrepreneurs. Change is a virus that threatens institutions as it feeds the opportunists. Without volatility and change, there is little opportunity.

The general rule tells would-be entrepreneurs to be patient and be a small fish in a small pond, a timid feeder in the lagoon. Leave the big fish to themselves. In general. that may be a good rule for a start-up, but there are times when there is a greater reward for cheating on this rule. The successful entrepreneur cheats on the rule and lures the big fish into his pond—where they have little room to maneuver and can become vulnerable to the small fish.

314

Wasn't a small fish called a "Microsoft" told it could not swim with a big fish called IBM? When LifeUSA was founded, the competition seemed to consist primarily of the whales like Prudential, New York Life, and Metropolitan. Under normal conditions, one would not expect that a new company could compete, but in this case (as in the computer industry) there were significant, fundamental changes taking place in the life insurance industry. The "big guys" were not only failing to respond, but were fighting the changes. This left them vulnerable to competition from companies of all sizes.

When the entrepreneur identifies a situation where change is rampant in an industry—and moves in to take advantage by offering new solutions—the odds of success begin to shift in his favor.

Offering a Solid, Workable Solution to an Identified Need

You can't resolve new needs with old solutions. If, Steve Jobs, when he created his new company, had reacted to changes in the computer industry by offering the same products as IBM, then today an apple would be merely an apple. If Fred Smith had purchased mail trucks instead of jets when he started a new business to compete with the U. S. Postal Service, then today FedEx would be a way to describe a retired government employee. If LifeUSA had been founded to offer the same "death insurance" products as Prudential and Metropolitan, then I would never have been able to write this book. (Maybe you are thinking that would not have been such a bad outcome.)

The point is this: When the entrepreneur forms a new company that does not copy the competition, but offers new ideas for new needs, the odds for success will shift in his favor.

Power of the People

The power of talented, motivated, and involved people has been an important part of this book. Let me assure you that this "people power" will be a defining element in the survival and success of any new business. Whether you have 1 or 1,000 employees, how they react and work to fulfill the vision of your company will have a momentous impact on the odds of your success. It's not the number of people you attract that's important, but the type of people attracted to you.

Talented, dedicated, involved, and participating employees can geometrically multiply the entrepreneur's ability to compete, achieve, and succeed—even against the oldest and largest competitors. New companies that survive can trace their success back to attracting good people and involving them in the success of the organization.

This is not new. The American Revolutionary Army was outnumbered by the British (and their mercenaries) by a ratio of 12:1 and the armor and technology of the day by a ratio of 33:1—yet the Americans won. Why? The needs of the people changed. The Americans had a new idea for government and those in the army were dedicated to the success of the cause, because they would benefit directly from the success. (We won't get into the war 200 years later. where America outgunned the North Vietnamese army by a zillion-to-one in technology, yet still lost.)

One of the first lessons lost on institutions is that they likely became institutions because of the people who worked hard to make the organization successful. Successful organizations often succumb to the belief that the institution is more important than the people. When this happens, the organization becomes weak and susceptible to threats from the outside.

LifeUSA was outmanned and outgunned by the large, successful companies in the life insurance industry, but gained the advantage by attracting talented people who were dedicated to helping the company defeat the larger "enemy."

An entrepreneur may have the best idea in the world to meet market needs; he may have plenty of desire, talent, and even money, but only when his efforts attract the right people do the odds of success shift in his favor.

Financing the Dream—The Hunt to Capture Capital

Okay. You have identified the difference between a gamble and a risk; you have experience in an industry that is undergoing fundamental change; the leaders in the industry are ignoring the changes (or fighting them), and you have a great idea that meets the new needs of the customer. And you have some great people who want to help you—even if it is your wife! You have shifted—as much as possible—the odds of success to your side, but now you face the real problem. How do you finance your great idea?

MONEY—The Milk of Human Success!

Whenever I appear at business conference, or deliver a speech, would-be entrepreneurs approach me with wonderful plans for their new businesses and ask one question more frequently than any other: "How do I get the money to finance my idea for a new business?" My answer, of course, is to take the same action advised all through this book—and that is to cheat on the rules. Except in this case, cheating could, perhaps, be more important than at any other time in your business career. And here's why.

Sufficient capital is everything to a new business. A good idea will remain just a dream until money brings it to life. What might have been a first-rate idea becomes a reckless gamble if a business starts with insufficient capital. A business cannot survive, let alone grow, without continuing access to capital. Most businesses fail not for a lack of effort or good ideas, but because they run out of money. And thus the ultimate question for any entrepreneur: "How do I finance my idea?" Right on the heels of that question comes, "If I do find financing, how can I secure it without giving my company away?"

With capital such a crucial element to the success of a venture, it is no wonder that budding entrepreneurs are awash in seminars, articles, and books dealing with raising capital for a new business. You may already be familiar with the established rules for writing business plans, building a business model matrix, and techniques for securing capital. But beware! The players in the financial markets are a mercenary lot, far more determined to make a buck off you than help you achieve your business dream. This is not to be critical of the "money lenders," because that is their business. They accommodate a critical need to finance our economy and are entitled

317

to make a profit for their effort. It is just that the more you are in business to make money for yourself—not for the lenders—the better off you will be.

With the promise of "help," the financiers lay out all the rules for raising cash for your business. There's just one huge problem—these rules are made for their benefit, not yours. And those are the rules you must break if you want to move the odds of success to your side.

What Is the Rule and Why Should You Cheat to Win?

If you need money to fund your business, the rules instruct you to go to people who are in the *business* of providing money. You know who they are—the banks, venture capitalists, factors, leverage buyout experts, angels, equity investment firms (the mob), and so on. That's the rule, and it works well—for them, not you. I'll show you why in a minute.

If you want to cheat to win when financing you new business then understand this: The best way to successfully raise money is to find those who will *benefit* from your success more than they have an interest in financing your success.

Recognize that the most expensive source of capital comes from those who are in the business of providing capital. The least expensive source of capital comes from those who are not in the business of providing capital, but will benefit from your success. This is true for any business, but especially for new and growing businesses.

If you want to have a better chance to be among the 7 percent who succeed, then pay particular attention to the overall *concept* of cheating to win in financing so you can apply it to your own situation. This is such an important point that I have to say it again: *The best way to finance your business is to find the people or other businesses that have an interest in seeing your business succeed.* And believe me, that's NOT those routinely associated with providing start-up capital.

Learning the Ropes

You get your first hint that this is true if you've ever attended one of those "Getting Your Business Funded" seminars. Have you ever noticed the type of organizations that sponsor these meetings? Most often they are companies in the business of providing financing. Is it any wonder they want you to learn the rules—their rules? Thinly disguised as "tips to finance your business," these rules are in place to benefit the people with the money. (So what else is new?) These people understand risk far better than any of us will. They want the odds of success shifted to their side of the table—any way they can. As a result, the capital financing rules are designed to make you even more of a captive then you were as an employee.

One thing you will quickly learn from this exercise is that when you finance your new business – loan value and personal control are inversely related. Here's the rule: *For every dollar you borrow to finance your business, you will give up an incrementally larger degree of control over your company and your freedom to run it.* The only way you can come out ahead in this stupid game is to cheat on all rules—again and again.

The Bitter Lesson Learned Starting LifeUSA

At the birth of LifeUSA, I was just like you: imbued with a rich vein of entrepreneurial spirit. There was no question in my mind that I had a great idea for a new company. Consumer wants and needs were changing rapidly in my industry, and a number of very talented people were primed to follow. But with barely two dimes to rub together, options were limited.

Our challenge was even more daunting than the usual business start-up, because an insurance company is a different breed of animal when it comes to need for capital. The typical company manufactures and sells a *tangible* product, such as a "widget," if you will. Financing for such a company is relatively simple: An initial infusion of capital is obtained to form the company, develop manufacturing capabilities and distribute the widget. After a business is up and running, increasing product sales generate revenues (capital) to cover the cost of continuing operations, fund future growth and spawn profits for the company. But an insurance company is different: By its very nature, the company consumes, rather than creates, capital.

In the beginning, virtually all life insurance policies written by a company are losers; they cost more to issue than they reap in immediate corporate income. It's only after several years of being in force that the average policy turns the financial corner and starts earning a return to the company. During the formative years, a new life insurance company burns through a huge amount of money before it becomes profitable.

As the plans evolved for founding LifeUSA, I was stunned to discover that a minimum of $10 million would be needed just to open the doors. And that was frightening because it was about $10 million more than we had. (We will debate later how stupid it was for me to leave a good job without understanding this little issue of financing.) But the opening gambit of financing was dwarfed by the discovery that, if the company were to be successful, it would need *oceans* of capital—literally *hundreds of millions* of dollars to keep going.

Our challenge, then, was twofold: to find the initial capital necessary to support our business and to then figure out a way to access the ongoing need for cash, all without losing control of our company.

As mentioned, the traditional rules taught in the books and seminars on corporate financing suggested the best way to raise this capital was to go through the "accepted channels." But I am here to tell you that these recommended sources should be your last resort for financing, not the first. First, I'm going to tell you why this is true. And then I'm going to show you how to cheat on the rules and get the money you need to make your American dream come true.

Banks Are from Hell

All of us have been conditioned to think of banks as a good place to get money when we need it; that banks are in the business of loaning money and can't wait to give it to us. But maybe we should take a clue from the fact that all that money is kept locked in a humongous vault. Getting money from a bank to finance the start of a new business is about as easy as guessing the combination to those big safes.

Please understand the simplicity of the banker's role. Banks will lend you a specific sum of money and charge you only simple interest on the loan. At first blush—compared to the requirements of other sources such as venture capitalists, public financing or factoring—a bank loan may seem the least expensive way to finance your business. Don't believe it!

The catch is that bankers expect to get the money back, and (as good as they are at it) they hate to lose money. That's why their deals are structured in such a way as to reduce financial exposure to laughably low levels (in fact, risk-free if they can get it).

Accordingly, banks don't ask for a large piece of your company, control of your board, or your first-born child—those things don't provide enough security for them! What they do want is collateral of all kinds (most of which you don't have). They want a lien on your accounts receivables, your inventory, the dies and tools you use to make your widgets, your house, your car, your mother-in-law's car, your mother-in-law. Makes no difference how good your idea or business plan may be, by its very nature a new business carries a significant element of risk. As a result, your needs are in direct conflict with the dim-witted mentality and objectives of bankers.

Don't even think about bankers being creative, imaginative, or flexible. They have no sense of marketing, creativity, or innovative thinking. (The truth be told, bankers are the reason why there's a law that says first cousins shouldn't marry.) And the banker who shows signs of such traits is quickly weeded out of the system. Bankers will never understand your business, nor do they care. Banking is the catch basin for those who have a good education, but have about as much common sense as owl-poop. They may be intelligent, but the truth of the matter is that I have had goldfish smarter than most bankers. Think I am being too harsh on bankers? Think again!

Transamerica to the Rescue

Do you remember that $10 million needed to finance the start-up of LifeUSA? Well, stupid me, I followed the rules about financing and started searching for it at banks. But at least give me credit for one thing: I was smart enough not to call on the bankers alone. To be sure that the financing deal was a no-brainer for the banks, we secured the financial backing of Transamerica Life Insurance Company. While Transamerica agreed to back our efforts (for their own benefit, as discussed in chapter 16), the company was not in the business of actually providing business financing. Instead, Transamerica agreed to "co-sign" a loan at a bank.

Keep in mind that this was not a simple loan guarantee or letter of credit. No, it was much more than that. Transamerica offered to put their financial statement on the line and would *sign the loan documents as a borrower.* Short of putting up the cash, such action is as strong a commitment as the company could make.

And Transamerica was not any fly-by-night company. They were one of the largest financial companies in America, publicly traded, highly rated, and respected. At first, Transamerica offered to refer us to Bank of America, their lead bank in San Francisco. However, as a company domiciled in Minnesota, our desire was to build a long-term relationship with a local bank, so we passed on the offer. After all, this was a well-secured, simple deal. It was a "done deal," I naively thought. Or was it?

Armed with the heavy artillery of Transamerica support and the bag to carry the money, I began to call on banks in Minneapolis. Even though LifeUSA was a start-up company, I was confident that the banks would fall all over themselves—like greedy lawyers fighting over an asbestos claim—to decide which one would make the loan. Little did I know! After weeks and weeks of jumping through hoops and lifting weights, each and every major bank in Minnesota refused to make the loan. Still not dissuaded, we took our show on the road to major banks in Chicago and New York. Guess what? Same results.

In fairness, most of the lower-level bank employees were supportive and encouraging, (maybe that's why they were lower level), but each time the decision reached the senior executives on the loan committee the financing was rejected. Finally, after a frustrating string of rejections, I invited one of the bankers to lunch and asked him to be honest regarding the real problem with our loan application. After all, I pointed out, the bank was not really making the loan to LifeUSA but rather to Transamerica. The response was as maddening as it was candidly revealing. He said, "We just don't think your business will be successful, and we don't want the hassle of collecting the loan from Transamerica."

With months wasted and ego deflated like the Goodyear blimp in a thunderstorm, I contritely called Transamerica and asked if the offer to call Bank of America was still open. The next morning I was on a plane to San Francisco; by that afternoon I had signed the papers and we had our money.

The Lesson to Be Learned

It's simple, really. If you need financing for your business, don't play by the rules, particularly if they happen to be banker's rules. Not that I am so shallow as to carry a grudge or anything, but following this experience, I swore to never again do business with banks in Minnesota. And we didn't for ten years!

I am willing to acknowledge a good deal of satisfaction when, just a few years later, all the banks that had rejected the initial loan request came back looking for our business. Can you imagine how good I felt (okay, smug) when one of the bankers invited me to a golf outing on his private jet, just so he could solicit our business? (I'm not that easy. They never did get our business.)

OK. What about Other Money-Lenders?

Another time-honored source of financing for a new business is the venture capitalist. Many people like to refer to these individuals as "vulture capitalists," but that is an unfair characterization. The high-rollers involved in the venture capital business are, for the most part, intelligent, creative, flexible, and understanding of risk. Very often, venture capitalists are the only ones in the lineup of established financing alternatives who are willing to step up to the plate.

The trade-off, however, is that venture financing is probably the most expensive financing available. The high cost of venture capital has been attributed to the insatiable greed of these individuals, and has spawned the term "vulture capitalists." While greed may play a part, the real reason for the almost usury expense of venture financing is quite simple.

The venture capitalist is more like a weatherman than a soothsayer when it comes to predicting the success of start-up ventures. They are going to get some of the forecasts right, but it is far from a precise science. Even the best venture capitalist knows that the odds may require an investment in ten ventures to find one real winner. To continue in business, simple math adds up to the conclusion that the venture capitalist needs a return from the one winner that is sufficient to cover the losses from the nine failed investments. That's sound business for the venture capitalist, but not for you.

In order to protect their investment and enhance potential return, transactions structured by venture capitalists always give them significant control over your company and excessive claims on your success. However, you can't build your business without capital, so if the only capital you can raise comes from venture capitalists, you take it and run. (For details on obtaining financing from venture capitalists, see chapter 17—Negotiate to Procreate!)

LBOs Offer the Same Sword of Damocles

Leveraged buy-out firms (LBOs) operate much the same as venture capitalists, with two significant differences. LBOs tend to provide financing to purchase an existing business and add debt to the equation. When your dream is financed by an LBO, you have to earn exceptional returns to cover their failures and to repay much of the financing. In addition, the LBO firm will exert even more control over your business than the venture capitalists.

Another complication is that LBOs do not usually help with the financing of a new business. The LBO expertise is in the buy-out and management of an existing enterprise. Even if you are looking to buy an existing business, working with an LBO firm should be the last resort, not the first.

The problem is threefold. First, since the "L" in LBO stands for leverage (loan), you take on a huge amount of debt relative to the size of the company—and that will create an enormous amount of pressure for performance, right from the start. Second, securing the participation of an LBO firm usually—no, always—requires handing over the business, even though they may know little or nothing about it. And that's a poor formula for success. Third, the demand for the level of return on their investment—to make up for the failures, return the principal, and make a usury-like return—becomes at best unreasonable and often virtually impossible.

What to Do?

If adhering to the traditional rules for financing a new business is not the way to go, what should you do? Easy—cheat on those rules. As mentioned earlier in the chapter, at LifeUSA we discovered that the most reliable and least expensive capital comes not from those in the business of providing financing, but from those who gain the most by benefiting from our success.

That could mean obtaining money from your parents, who will benefit from you getting a job and finally moving out of the house (or who hope you'll support them in their old age). Of course, if you don't have those rich parents, you have to look elsewhere. But there are other options. And here's where you can put on your thinking cap and identify some creative—or back-channel—financing strategies and make them work for you. Nothing (short of illegal activities) should be considered too wild to contemplate. (Did you know that doing away with a mother-in-law to get the insurance proceeds is a legal activity in twenty-six states? So you might consider that option.)

Landlords as Lenders

Let me illustrate just what I mean by considering wild ideas. If the concept of "starting on a shoestring" had not already been invented, it would have been used to describe the extent of the resources available to finance the start of LifeUSA. The need for financing permeated our every thought and everything we did. Little did we know that financing could come from multiple sources—even from a lease of office space—but it did.

Of course, in order to properly open a business we needed a "corporate headquarters." Fortunately for us, there was a glut of office space available in Minneapolis at the time we started LifeUSA, making it easy for us to find suitable accommodations in a good building. That was not the problem, however, The problem was that we didn't have much money for something called "rent." The building identified (happily owned by another insurance company) was virtually empty at the time, and those charged with renting out the building were willing to rent space under almost any condition. It was as much to their benefit to obtain a signed lease as it was for us to find a home for our future empire.

Sauntering in as though seeking to occupy the entire eight-story building, we asked for a proposal for a five-year lease. Of course such a lease had huge benefits to the building managers, who had not seen a prospective tenant in months. Our appearance ignited the imagination of the building managers like prey walking into the den of a hungry but injured rattlesnake. You could tell by the look on their faces that they were ravenous for business—even from a new company. Accordingly, they offered to give us a twenty-four-month rent abatement if we'd go on the hook for five years. Hey! Where's the pen? Let's sign before they change their mind.

This was a terrific win-win deal for both parties. We got two years of free rent—at exactly the time when we most needed to conserve scarce resources, like cash. The building owner was a winner, too. The deal allowed the rental agent to go back to the owners and show them a *signed, five-year lease.* Not only did this start to put people in the building as long-term tenants, but it preserved their balance sheet and the building's evaluation since the lease could be booked as if full rents were to be paid for all five years.

This was great financing. And it gets even better. A few months later our space needs doubled, and we bargained for another 6,000 square feet. The agent tore up the original five-year lease, and we signed a new five-year lease for 12,000 square feet—and we got another two years of free rent.

This went on for about two and a half years. Every time we needed new space they would tear up the lease and write a new one, which, of course, extended our stay but gave us additional rent abatements. We literally went almost three years without paying a dime in rent. And by then, we had a whole floor in the building. (This arrangement worked out well for both parties. LifeUSA grew to occupy virtually the entire building—paying full rent—and today has over 500 employees in the building.)

We were able to obtain this free-rent "financing" that amounted to hundreds of thousands of dollars of capital at zero percent interest and no payback simply because the landlord was desperate. Of course, this specific example may not work for you, but that is not the point. The message here is that when you are starting a new venture and need financing—be creative and look in places that most people don't normally look. The point of these examples is to remind you that when seeking to cheat on traditional financing rules often the easiest to obtain and the least expensive financing comes not from those who offer financing, but from those who benefit when you benefit.

Raising Money from Suppliers

Believe it or not, even suppliers can become a good source of cheap financing. Many are anxious to sell their goods and win-win situations are often available—if you cheat to win. Case in point: What good is an insurance company without computers to process the claim denials? No good at all! What good is a software company that has no one to buy their software? No good at all! Put them together and maybe you can find a good deal for both of them.

Early in the life of LifeUSA, we came across a potential software supplier who was eager to sell programs that were ideal for processing insurance transactions. It was a good product, but he was having trouble convincing established insurance companies to use it and needed a test case to show the value of the product. We loved the software, but had neither the money nor the credit to finance purchasing the hardware to run the guy's software. We needed a deal—and got one.

This software supplier agreed to buy the computers for us if we agreed to buy his software. And in effect, he financed our entire IT operation, not because he was in the business of financing, but because he benefited from our company using his software. And to his business, that was a big deal. He could publicize the effective use of the software and, like dominos in a row, our sale could engender two others, and those two could create four more, and so on. It was just good marketing.

The bottom line? We were able to get financing from an unlikely source that renders obsolete the thinking about professional money-lenders as the best source of start-up capital. In this case the financing was virtually cost free (we were required to use software we would have used anyway) and amounted to several million dollars, when we didn't have several million dollars. Because the "lender" benefited from the deal, low-cost financing was made available to us at precisely the time we needed it most.

Revisiting Transamerica

Early in this chapter I told the story of Transamerica providing $10 million of low-cost "venture" capital to LifeUSA. Why would they do that? It was simple. One of Transamerica's main business segments was reinsurance. This is insurance provided by insurance companies to other insurance companies. LifeUSA needed both capital to finance the company and reinsurance to support new business; Transamerica had boodles of both.

Transamerica agreed to finance LifeUSA if, in return, the company would agree to give Transamerica all of the reinsurance business. A very nice circle! LifeUSA received inexpensive start-up financing, and Transamerica obtained reinsurance business from a new client. This was a win-win deal for both companies. Without this arrangement, LifeUSA would never have existed, so that says a lot. For Transamerica, LifeUSA soon became their largest and most profitable reinsurance client. Not only was the loan to LifeUSA repaid in less than three years, but Transamerica made millions on LifeUSA stock purchased at the time the loan was made.

I repeat: the least expensive and easiest financing to obtain comes not from those in business to finance you, but from those who will gain business by financing you.

Raising Capital from Employees

Probably the most effective use of the concept that calls for financing from those who will benefit from your success was the LifeUSA plan that called for employees to "finance" their own jobs.

But before I tell you about that, let me once again reiterate the overriding principle of this chapter and this book, the bedrock philosophy. And it is this: If you cheat to win the right way, everyone will benefit. If our philosophy was based on anything but this guiding principle, these suggestions would topple like a house of cards. For example, you can't strike a deal with your suppliers if your hidden agenda is to rip them off or otherwise take undue advantage of a generous situation. It just doesn't work. You have to be truly sincere in your dealings. And that's particularly true when raising capital from employees.

Starting LifeUSA allowed me to implement a long-held theory. That theory was: *If people have the ability to add value to an organization, they would be encouraged to do so if they were allowed to share in the value they added.* Simple, easy, almost trite, but I believed it strongly.

For me, the way you allow individuals to share in the value they add to an organization is to allow them to be owners of the organization. As a result, all employees of LifeUSA became entrepreneur-partners in the success of the company. This was accomplished by *requiring* that all employees contribute 10 percent of their pretax pay toward the purchase of LifeUSA stock.

The simple act if requiring all employees to "buy their own job" and become owners of LifeUSA just might have been the critical element to our success. First, it raised capital for our growing company from those who would stand to gain the most by our success—the employees—and, even more important, it built real company camaraderie. Our employees had a concrete and *personal* stake in providing top performance. Why? It's as simple as the nose on Ben Franklin's avuncular kisser on the $100 bill: Their performance had a direct effect on the company's bottom line, and that performance had a direct and meaningful effect on the worth of the company they were financing.

Eventually, the stock became publicly traded and in so doing, *dozens of employees* become instant millionaires and thousands more created family nest eggs they never thought possible before joining LifeUSA. In my way of thinking, offering employees, landlords, suppliers, and kindred associates of your company a stake in your ultimate success is the right way to go—and the best way to cheat on traditional rules of financing.

And the Moral of the Story Is . . .

Go ahead. Follow your heart and chase that dream. You won't be happy till you do. Just make sure you are taking a risk and not a gamble. A risk gives you a measure of control over the outcome; a gamble does not. To give your dream a chance to become reality work hard, but be realistic regarding the odds of success. Before you take the leap, do all you can to shift the odds of success to your side. To do this:

- Understand the risks you are taking.
- Identify a need that is not being met in the market.
- Have a concrete, realistic, workable solution to meet the need.
- Attract people (even if it is only you and your spouse) who make your dream their dream.
- Be realistic about the capital needed and be creative in finding it.

Putting these points in place will not guarantee your success—but going off on your own without them will preordain your failure. People like to say, "Don't worry if you fail, you'll never be happy unless you try!" That's a nice thought. But if you want to try to fly, why try it without wings? Don't be crazy! Yes, go for it, be aggressive, but cheat on the rule that says go for it at any price and against any odds. You have a better chance of being one of the 7 percent of successful business ventures if you do the things successful ventures do—and that is doing all you can to shift the odds of success to your side.

19

Living with the Agony of Success

If you are not making history—you are history!

This chapter is for those who have already broken a ton of rules and have either achieved personal success or have led your organization to eminence. However, if you are not yet in that class, but want to sneak a peek at what is in store for you when you achieve success, then read on.

Let me start by offering my congratulations! When you attain success, you join a very select group of achievers. You are special. It's perfectly OK for you to take a bow, and I salute anyone who has achieved real success. To have realized success means you have outflanked the competition, challenged the established order, confounded skeptics (not to mention your teachers and parents), and proven all of them wrong. You and your company have the right to bask in the limelight as *leaders*, innovators, and the stuff-of-success stories that few accomplish. But I also caution you to realize that scaling to the pinnacle of success is the easy part.

If you thought it took a yeoman effort to get to the top, this is nothing compared to how difficult it is to stay there. If you need any evidence, just compile a list of the top twenty-five market-cap companies of today with the same list ten, fifteen, and twenty-five years ago. Do so and you will discover a very high rate of mortality for companies from one period to another. Excluding the anomaly of the "dot-com" bubble of the late 1990s, the companies that have disappeared from the list were not fly-by-night organizations. Oddly enough, the fallen companies were large, successful, profitable, well known and (for the most part) respected.

Few are surprised by the high failure rate of small, undercapitalized firms led by inexperienced management. But who would have thought that the same percentage of established, highly capitalized, and respected companies also have fallen by the wayside?

The trouble is success creates its own set of distinctive problems and new realities. Most people in this world are forever obsessed with the quest to achieve success, but when you go beyond the quest and actually achieve it, you will face a different problem.

It's a fact that more people rise from failure than survive success, because it is more difficult to survive success than failure. Fail and it is over—no one expects anything more of you! You've followed the rules, crashed, and burned. Big deal. Happens all the time. All of us grow up being conditioned for rejection and learning to cope with failure. (I think that's why God invented singles' bars!)

On the other hand, when you're *different,* when you cheat on the rules to succeed and do so, you have to *live* with that success. The challenge then becomes to *stay on top.* And that causes what I call the "agony of success." And this chapter teaches you what it is and how to avoid it.

Success is a rare commodity that few are prepared to deal with. There are bushel baskets full of books offering advice for getting to the top, but nary a one offers guidance for staying on top. Opportunity is promiscuous and flirts with many, but nearly everyone fails to convert chance into success because they are unwilling to pay the price demanded. Even fewer are comfortable living with success and end up giving it back or losing it, because they become intimidated by the obligation of success—and that's the responsibility to continue to be successful. When you are successful, you step out from the crowd, cheat on some bad rules, and accomplish what many talk about but few do. That is all well and good, but when you do succeed—you have to deal with the consequences of success.

It's Lonely at the Top

Unfortunately, your effort to survive success is not going to get much help from others, because most people don't want you to succeed. They want to revel in your failure. They want to see you get knocked off the perch of power because it offers them an excuse, a justification for their failure. The world is full of those who speak of success, but for most, success is only a dream—it is failure that is the reality. But just because others want you to fail success should not be reason to do so.

The question you ought to be asking yourself is this: Why is it that so many successful companies manage to fail the test of success so consistently? It seems every self-anointed "management expert" is willing to offer a reason why successful companies fall sick and die. Some say changed markets are to blame. Others point to increased competition, technology advances, reduced productivity, product obsolescence, or even government interference as the source of the corporate tailspin. But these are superficial excuses offered by professional rule-followers, and they highlight only the symptoms of the real illness.

After eliminating the suicidal acts of greed, blatant fraud, and inbred incompetence from the list of culprits, there is a simple explanation for the failure of successful companies. Successful companies often become encased in the very rules the company cheated on to become successful. Successful companies start to die when they stop doing the things that made them successful companies in the first place. Successful businesses and the executives who run them become comfortable, lazy, complacent, and less tolerant of risk and innovation. Many fall prey to the illness of entitlement. They lose the very culture that produced their initial success: doing the right thing at the right time, and doing it first, fast, and often.

Building on a Culture of Success

Chances are good that when a company achieves remarkable levels of success it did so as the result of a unique "spirit and culture of success" that developed within the company. It is this distinctive spirit and culture that drives, fosters, and feeds achievement. However, this "spirit of success" is fragile and will exist only so long as it is allowed to exist. To thrive, the very élan for success must be nurtured and protected. If you fail to do that, not only will the spirit that drives your success break down, but you will also lose the soul of what you and your company are all about.

Your culture of success is actually more important today than it was in the past, because once an organization attains a critical size and mass, it is more important to constantly improve the level of performance than to get bigger. The company culture is the key to continued achievement because, as the culture developed, it created the environment that allowed and stimulated constant innovation. Success is the child of audacity. The decline of a successful organization is the offspring of a failure to innovate. Remember, without constant renewal, the ideals of the past fade, only to be buried by the present and forgotten by the future.

Moving Forward to be Better

At the start of any career or enterprise, individuals and organizations are both threatened and motivated by the specter of failure. Fear of failure is a strong motivator. In the beginning, we knew that if we did not conquer failure, we would disappear. There is an even greater challenge to success—yet the consequences are the same. If we do not conquer the challenges of success—we will disappear. To avoid the losing your grip on success, remember two simple rules:

1. You begin to lose when you begin to be afraid to lose.
2. You continue to win when you're never content with what has been won.

Look at it this way. In a competitive environment, if the objective is to avoid failure, as it is with many large organizations, this attitude may actually induce failure since it seeks to maintain only the status quo.

The only realistic option for an organization's victory over the agony of success is a constant, concentrated, and passionate quest to challenge the rules and strive for *more success*. Enterprises are rewarded for creating wealth, not for preserving the status quo—and certainly not for controlling costs. The commitment to win with refreshed innovation, rather than positioning to preserve, becomes an antidote against the malady of organizational obsolescence and corporate decline.

To persist as winners requires us to work harder, to be more focused and constantly vigilant—not so much from the threats of others—but rather, from the threats of our own success. To stay on top is easier said than done because winners constantly come under attack, either from those who want to be where you are or from those who want to bring you down to where they are. Understand that your only protection against these attacks is your unique spirit and culture of success. And, as the driving spirit of an individual or the culture of any successful organization matures, it will be exposed to a creeping corporate virus that manifests itself in the form of complacency and entitlement. And failure is always the curse of complacency.

Remember, the chief reason people stop learning is the assumption that they know all there is to know; the chief deterrent to doing more is the assumption that one has done all that can be done. A high performer can never let up, because you never know where the next competitor will come from; but sometimes the most dangerous enemy is our own success.

Guarding Your Precious Success

Start guarding success by thinking about the rewards for success. As success builds, laurels will follow. But never lose sight of the fact that laurels are what we receive on the way to the future—their only value is to signal that we are on the right path. If we take the laurels as a crown of our achievements, we will get knocked on our asses. If we rest on our laurels, we will get run over.

Surviving success starts by being constantly vigilant to the health and vitality of your spirit and culture of success. This is not always easy, because numbers never tell the real story in real time—numbers are only an echo of reality. Just as the numbers lag in reporting the accomplishments of a growing company, they lag behind as a company falters and begins to coast—not emerging till it may be too late.

If you are relentlessly on guard to look after the health and well-being of your culture of success, it will respond by safeguarding your future. This will come as much from feeling as from knowing. As a passenger on an airliner you can't see the instruments in the cockpit to tell you if the aircraft is turning, ascending, or descending, but you can feel it. It is critical to be sensitive to the same feeling with your culture. Is it straight and level, rising or descending? This sense of cultural feeling is achieved when we are constantly observant and the activities of the culture are kept in perspective.

Feel for Signals—Find Actions

There are questions, feelings, and signals—both good and bad—to help determine the temperature of the culture. Survive success by always being willing to take a fearless and searching review of your business:

- Do we spend more time talking about how good we are today rather than how good we can become tomorrow?
- Is change resisted, tolerated, or welcomed?
- Is experimentation encouraged, important, and constant?
- Is risk regaled or reviled?
- Are we satisfied with what worked yesterday, rather than trying to find new things that will work tomorrow?
- Are we the same "one" that was one group trying to accomplish one goal or are we many "ones" —I, we, they, and them—with sometimes conflicting rather than parallel objectives?

Champion figure skaters know that the key to victory is keeping their skates on what they call "the edge." It is grueling work, but only by keeping on the edge can skaters perform to their full level of potential. The same is true with a business where performing to full potential means keeping its competitive edge. Even the most talented skater can lose the edge if they become a little complacent or lazy. When this happens, skaters lose medals. But remember—in the game you play—the complacent and the lazy lose their future.

Is there a way to recognize if we're sliding off the slope of success into complacency or maybe getting just a little bit lazy, causing the culture to be at risk of losing its edge? Yes! We may be getting lazy and losing our edge when:

- We find we are too busy to take the time to do the little things we took the time to do in the past.
- We find it easier to hire more people from the outside (from cultures that failed) than we grow from the inside.
- We begin to define our success by what we have done, rather than what we could do.
- We begin to feel that getting better is not as important as keeping what we have.
- At first our actions threatened competitors, now the actions of competitors threaten us.
- We become more concerned with what we get for ourselves, rather than what we can give to others.
- We begin to view process and procedure as more important than performance and progress.

These are the telltale signs that your business, management, and employees are more concerned with keeping the status quo than pioneering new pathways to success. The next stop could be the agony of success. If you want to stay on top, preserve, protect, and enhance your success:

- Always act like the leader, but feel like the underdog.
- Always have an enemy to be conquered. (Just make sure it's not you!)
- Don't be satisfied with success—be terrified of its loss.

My bet is that when you started down your path to success, you were out there on the edge, pushing the limit. When others complained that you were too aggressive, it was because you were ahead of the curve. If you now find yourself complaining about others pushing the edge, then maybe you have fallen behind the curve. On the way up we were happy for any little thing we got. If we get to the point where we don't feel we are getting enough for how far up we are, we probably are getting too much. If we feel entitled to more for what we've done, we probably have not done enough.

Never lose sight of this one thought—*If you are not making history, you are history!*

Going There from Here

So, just what can be done to survive the agony of success and create even more of the same? My advice is simple. Don't ever forget that people are the only legitimate drivers of a company's success! Moreover, a company should be led in a single, simple focus to commit, concentrate, and drive passionately to maintain a unique place where success will thrive and survive over time.

In chapter 14 we discussed building an entrepreneurial culture and said that the best way to do so was to create a "Hothouse for Humanity." Remember, this is *a place where people can go to grow to be great.*

If, as you go forward, you remain passionately focused on fostering, building, and maintaining a culture that creates a hothouse for humanity, you will have no problems living with success because continued success will be the natural residue of your efforts.

Remember, the objective is to maintain an environment that encourages people to grow to be great. And how do we do that? When we focus all our strength and effort on maintaining a culture with transparent, free-flowing communication that encourages all members to participate in and benefit from the success achieved; if risk is encouraged and accomplishment rewarded; if ethics are solid, objectives are clear, priorities are maintained, and support is constant—then we will maintain a cultural hothouse for humanity that will encourage people to grow to be great. And, the people will be grateful for your greatness in doing so.

And the Moral of the Story Is ...

As you bask in your own success and the achievements of your company, I encourage you to do something even more difficult. Build on, don't rest on, your success. Do so by maintaining a place where success is respected, fostered, protected, and shared. Do so and the people of your organization will have a place to go to grow to be great—and you will be the greatest of them all!

This chapter can be that nagging voice in the back of your mind that reminds you of your many successes and asks you to remember what you did to come out on top. Then, repeat it again and again in the future.

Use this mind-set to continue to make history. You have a responsibility to build on the success you have achieved. You have done it in the past and you have the opportunity to make history in the future. And you will do so, so long as you measure your decisions and actions against one simple objective: Is what I am doing today building a culture of success—a hothouse for humanity—where people can always go to grow be great tomorrow?

If the answer to the question is always an unequivocal "Yes," then you will accomplish what few before you have done. You will have achieved success, survived the agony of success, and perpetuated it for the generation to follow you. You can leave no more valuable legacy!

20

Now It's Up to You!

If you are going to play the game,
you might as well make the rules work for you!

As you reach the final chapter of this book, my hope (beyond the hope that you have actually read this far) is that you have two thoughts. The first is the feeling, "I could have written this book myself." And second, a reflection that, "There is nothing in the book that I did not already know." If that's the case, then we've both done well. The point I wanted to make by writing this book is that there are no magic bullets or secret formulas when it comes to achieving success. My job, as I see it, has been to reawaken the deep-seated belief that, in your heart, you know the right way to go.

All of us have within us the knowledge, feeling, and ability to define and achieve remarkable levels of success. You know how scientists say that we use only 5 percent of our brain capacity? Their tests (on bankers) have proved that we all have the capacity within ourselves to do so much more. And that is the point I have tried to make in this book. The opportunity and potential to be successful are right in front of us—we know it and feel it—we just have to do it. No excuses, no waiting till tomorrow for something better—now!

I am the perfect poster child for the philosophy espoused in this book. When it was my time to get into the game, it seemed that I had precious little to offer: a spotty academic record, a middle-class family with no built-in connections, no recruiters begging to open doors into the corporate paradise, no fast-track "high potential" designations to clear the path to the top, and no direct access to capital when the time came to start out on my own.

Yet here I am forty years later, with a wonderful wife, great family, scores of friends and followers (at least they tell me they are), a rapid-rise career that put me in my first CEO chair at age thirty-seven, the founder of one of the most successful companies of the 1990s, a sought after candidate to serve on corporate boards and speak at meetings, all the while sitting on the beach in wonderful, warm Key West with beaucoup dollars in the bank. (Well, not in the bank. If you'll recall, I really don't like, nor do I trust, bankers that much!)

Trust me, I bring all this up not to brag about it, but rather to make the point that if someone with my background and seemingly empty briefcase of tools has been able to achieve what I have simply by living by the simple antirules and concepts outlined in this book—then just imagine what you can accomplish!

The philosophy followed all my life boils down to very straightforward concepts and uncomplicated beliefs:

- Learn from where you have been.
- Understand where you are today.
- Know where you want to be tomorrow.

In the process, always seek to do the right thing—even if the right thing may, from time to time, seem like a step or two back. The right thing to do will always be the right thing to do! And if you don't know the right thing to do, do nothing till you do know. When you know an action is the right thing to do, do it right and do it right now.

In the course of reaching for your own personal vision of success, you will encounter innumerable "dos." These are the insipid conventions of action often referred to as can't-dos, must-dos, should-dos, always-dos, and way-we-dos. Presented as a way to "help" you along the way and to "keep you out of trouble," these "rules" have, in many cases, become road blocks rather than roadways to success.

History has proved that those who win big are always those with the ability to identify the rules that have outlived their usefulness, and who have the creativity and courage to cheat on these rules in order to write new ones. The best way to become a part of this select group of successful leaders, like I said, is to seek out the right thing to do and then *always* do it!

During the course of my career, I encountered any number of individuals who seemed to have better opportunities, significantly higher intelligences and deeper talent than I, yet over time my achievements far surpassed what most of these individuals accomplished. Why? Because sometimes the advantages other people seem to have over us turn out to be their own personal curse. Most of these people were so intelligent and talented they seemed to feel "entitled" to find the "secret shortcut to success."

I wasn't smart enough to take a crack at that approach. It was like Hudson trying to find the elusive Northwest Passage, or Ponce de Leon frittering away his life in search of the elusive "Fountain of Youth." Opportunities right in front of them were missed because they were looking for the easy way and "the one big score," like winning the lottery. But basing what you do in life in anticipation of the big hit is more than a bit risky, since in all likelihood you're waiting for a ship that might never come in. Along the way to my success, I discovered no secrets, no shortcuts, and no easy ways. I had no advantage other than the advantage that comes from doing what you know in your heart needs to be done and doing it.

This philosophy is somewhat analogous to the current craze over weight-loss programs. At the time I retired from Allianz Life in 2001 I was a bit like most aging executives—out of shape and overweight. After constant loving-nagging from my wife and death threats from my doctor, I decided to correct the situation. After a few days of reading some basic diet and exercise information, along with the obligatory physical exam (I put this in here because if you try this at home and die, I don't want your spouse to sue me), I set a goal and started on my way.

343

In about fifteen months (and at least three down-sizes in clothing) I had increased my cardiovascular endurance maybe a hundredfold and shed sixty pounds (reducing my weight from 240 pounds to 180; waist size from forty-three to thirty-four inches). People who had not seen me during that period of time were amazed when I would make an appearance. (Talk about an extreme makeover!)

My friends constantly peppered with me with questions about my changed appearance. "You look great, Mac. How did you do it? Did you do Atkins or South Beach?" My response was always the same, "No, none of those diets (I didn't even work out with my Bowflex in Subway restaurants), I went on the PPC diet!" "The PPC diet? What is that?" The PPC diet is the *power of personal control*!

My scientific research on the subject of dieting led me to discover that if each day I would burn more calories then I took in, then I would lose weight. I simply changed my lifestyle to aggressively burn more calories than I had in the past and moderated the type and quantity of caloric intake. The result was a healthier heart, toned body, and shopping for "medium-" instead of "XXL-" sized clothing.

And this is the point. We always want to find the easy, secret, magic formula, the short cut to success—in weight loss, in business, and in life—when there are none (only simple steps to be taken one at a time). We all know them and the only difference between success and failure is *doing* what we know in our heart needs to be done.

All along, my objective (besides making a few bucks) has been that, after reading this book, you will recognize that you do have the talent, opportunity, and ability to be as successful as you desire. The good news, and the exciting part, is that what you have to do is not that difficult. If you always do what has to be done—and do it the right way—you may appear to fall behind the group looking for the shortcut, but you will invariably finish well ahead of those doing the real cheating by cutting the corner and looking for the fast track to success.

My aspiration has been achieved if the ideas, stories, and successes outlined in this book have convinced you of the wisdom buried in the cheat-to-win philosophy. I hope that I have persuaded you that it is worth taking a chance to achieve the success you desire; to get up and make the circumstances of the life you encounter work for you by *using* these principles in your life and profession. That's why I've encouraged you to *think* about the rules that bind us to see how, and to what degree, they impede your career. George Bernard Shaw expressed this sentiment much better when he wrote,

> *"People are always blaming circumstances for what they are. I don't believe in circumstances. The people who get on in this world are the people who get up and look for the circumstances they want, and, if they can't find them, they make them."*

If I've done my job, you can now readily see that many of today's governing rules of businesses have long since lost their relevance, yet continue to be invoked year after bureaucratic year simply because "We've always done it that way."

No Magic Rules from this Side

I have steadfastly resisted the temptation to use this book to hand down a set of specific laws or rules that, if dutifully followed, will lead you through the Golden Door and down the Yellow Brick Road of fame and fortune. I did that for a reason—there are none. And that is the ultimate freedom of opportunity! We are each free to find our own way to do our own thing. When we allow others to lay out the rules and define the path to success that they define, we lose control of our dream. I would be guilty of the same hypocrisy if I were to lay out rules for you to follow. If we follow only the ideas and rules of others, we become controlled, limited, and measured by their standards, not ours. You are better than that!

What is important is the personal philosophy and way of thinking that we apply to the critical issues we face in life and business. Operating from a solid, trusted, and sound philosophy will provide the necessary foundation to analyze, challenge, and cheat on bad rules—while imbuing you with the confidence to write new rules.

As we finish up here, allow me to digress just a bit in order to reiterate a few key principles and morsels of philosophy that I hope you walk away with when you put down this book. They are not intended to be rules, but rather a way of thinking that helps us to see more clearly exactly what the rules should be. Based on what I have learned and experienced during my career, by keeping these thoughts in mind and applying them at all times, you will be well on your way to identifying bad rules, creating new rules, and achieving success as you define it.

A Random Walk through Thoughts on *Cheat to Win*

- Reminisce about the future.
- Know what you want to be and do and why.
- Understand that the future belongs to those who get there first.
- Set high ethical standards—for yourself and others.
- Build parallel interests with all parties.
- Share success and accept responsibility.
- Seek and deliver open, honest, and constant communication.
- Exhibit core beliefs that are not compromised, qualified, or abandoned.
- Never be afraid to do the right thing.
- Have the strength to be consistent.
- Manage like an air traffic controller.
- Revel in change.
- Make things simple, not complicated.
- Do simple things but simply do them till the big things are done.
- Make bunk of bureaucracy.
- Never rush, but always have a sense of urgency to get there.
- Remember that in times of stability the big companies always win, but in times of volatility opportunity emerges,

and it's not the big companies that win—it's the good companies.

- Differentiate, don't copy.
- Never volunteer to play on the competitor's home field. (Unless you can write the rules!)
- Never be too intimidated to intimidate the intimidator.
- Support those who can push you up, rather than rely on others to pull you up.
- Motivate, don't intimidate.
- Take more from negotiations by giving more than you take.
- Do what others won't or can't do.
- Make new rules for the game and force your competitor to follow them.
- Concentrate more on what you are doing than what others are doing (peer group).
- Seek input, help, and participation from others, but never equivocate.
- Cultivate a hothouse for humanity, where you become great by allowing others to grow to be great.
- Set simple, measurable standards of performance for yourself and others—and stick to them.
- Avoid gambles, seek risk, learn from failure, and share rewards.
- Build your power by empowering others.
- Build your wealth by sharing wealth.
- Be surprised if you win the lottery, but not by the results you achieve.
- Always be wary of success and at war with failure.
- Never stop thinking about tomorrow (written by my brother, Fleetwood Mac).

By adopting a way of life inherent in the philosophy of these thoughts, I was able to cheat on what I was "supposed" to do in life and overcome a troublesome start to my career. This attitude enabled me to ignore confining rules and replace them with new, more trustworthy rules of my own.

The first step toward setting yourself free from similar rules is to examine your life, your business, your job to see how, and in what degree, these rules proscribe your life. Once you realize how ruinous some rules can be, you're well on your way to changing them and breaking the control they have over you.

And the Moral of the Story Is ...

Across a broad spectrum of human endeavors, honest cheaters of outmoded rules and traditions routinely come out on top. The individual who breaks free of the mold—that straightjacket of rules that govern our actions—becomes more productive and, ultimately, earns the appreciation and respect of those who lack the right stuff to break free on their own. These winners have an aura about them. They are more mentally alert, more psychologically healthy, more creative, more spontaneous, more *alive,* and more productive in every sense of the word.

Cheat to Win was written to demonstrate that it is not only possible for the individual to survive, but to thrive. I hope it has shown—not the path to success—but how to make your own path and has encouraged you to begin to cut through the outmoded rules learned in college, business school, and management training programs so that you can break out and take personal, individual, and successful control of your future.

I hope this book has helped you develop the critical awareness to begin your program of personal and professional assessment to determine where you are and what you want to accomplish. As noted earlier, the individual who develops an *awareness* of the rules that bind almost subconsciously and irresistibly develops an *interest* in breaking the rules and charting new, more successful, courses of action.

And that's the bottom line for this book: If you've come away from this work with the feeling that many rules of business are simply rules made to be intelligently broken, then you've gained a valuable adjunct to your definition of personal excellence. If you've already started to make changes, terrific! Keep it going. And if you're still standing on the sidelines, get started—right now, *today*—and stick with it! The right kind of cheating to win can make a crucial difference in your life. Implementing the cheat-to-win philosophy means adopting a lifestyle aimed at being the best *you* that you can possibly be. It takes a little daring, a good dose of confidence, guts, and some basic wisdom. Oh yes, and it takes one more thing ... It takes you to decide—right now—to do it.

Now it's up to you!

See you in the future . . .

R.W.M

Epilogue

If you recall, in the early section of the book, called "Thoughts of the Author," I said there was a secret coded message in the book. And the hint to the code were the letters CTW. Have you figured out the code?

Recall the problems I encountered over the title of this book and the concept of actually cheating to win. After reading the book you understand that the philosophy of cheating was not what people naturally assumed. The cheating was, in fact, being totally honest. Understanding subtlety is what separates the winners from the losers: why some were afraid of the title, why others would not read the book, and why others were stimulated by the risk to read.

Now, at the end of the book, I hope you will understand the code of the book—CTW.

While many feared the word "cheat," it is, in fact, only a code word for being "creative." The message is this: CTW—Creative Thinking Wins!

Being creative and winning can only come about after we start to be willing to "cheat" on those rules that inhibit and discourage our creativity.

If you walk away from the book with one memory—make it CTW!